Praise for ABOLITION FEMINISMS

"As inspiring as it is edifying, this phenomenal collection, *Abolition Feminisms, Volume 2: Feminist Ruptures Against the Carceral State,* offers us a broad range of ideas, images, provocations, and organizing approaches enabled by developing theories and practices associated with abolition feminisms. Thanks to the thoroughgoing familiarity of the editors with the grassroots efforts that constitute the groundwork of abolition feminism, we are offered important tools that help us to recognize punitive logics within and beyond conventional carceral contexts and to support us as we struggle for a world of mutual care, transformative justice, and freedom." —**ANGELA Y. DAVIS**, author of *Freedom Is a Constant Struggle*

"This essential two-volume collection maps the shared roots between abolitionist life-making and feminist resistance, showing us how rebellious organizing and radical care are always at the heart of real change. Brimming with dispatches across borders and prison walls, archives of movement building, and striking creative work, *Abolition Feminisms* describes a breathtaking body of freedom practices, galvanizing us to do everything we can to help forge the liberatory future that we urgently need. Anyone who engages this collection is guaranteed to learn something new." —**MARIAME KABA**, author of *We Do This 'Til We Free Us*

"This beautiful two-volume collection of essays, poems, and artwork brings a refreshing vibrancy to the radical work of abolition feminism. Inspiring, accessible, and far-reaching, the books are precisely what is needed right now: clear demands for radical change, reflections on the power of radical organizing, and radical statements of hope. Readers will be lifted up as they turn the pages, where each entry is a reminder of how abolition feminism is critical to freedom struggles, and our movement will therefore be challenged and changed." —**BETH E. RICHIE**, coauthor of *Abolition. Feminism. Now.*

"Contrary to popular belief, revolutions don't come with handbooks or blueprints. They do carry histories, memories, manifestos, maps, moments of clarity and deep contradictions, dreams, principles, and real people who endure the oppressions they are seeking to overturn. This extraordinary collective of activists, artists, and scholars understand that this is what revolutions are made of, and that through study and struggle we see abolition feminism not as a variant or a tendency within some larger liberatory movement but the revolution we need to genuinely overturn things." —**ROBIN D. G. KELLEY**, author of *Freedom Dreams: The Black Radical Imagination*

"*Abolition Feminisms: Organizing, Survival, and Transformative Practice* upends feminism's relegation to an afterthought or appendage of abolition and urges us toward social arrangements defined by caring collectively. One of the most exquisite volumes on abolition feminism to date, this gathering of essays, dispatches, art, and poetry features a constellation of vibrant theorists, including those who have been criminalized and imprisoned. *Abolition Feminisms* offers original insights into the everyday terror and annihilating deprivation facing people inside women's prisons, the work of imprisoned people to challenge gender and sexual oppression, the structuring role of gender violence to the logic and technologies of the carceral state, the nexus of imperial and domestic modes of repression, the carceral production of gender and sexual normativity, settler-colonial and anti-Black carceral violence, and more. Bierria, Caruthers, and Lober effectively establish abolition's feminist provenance in an utterly brilliant account of abolition feminism's decolonial heart, intimate practice, and radical momentum. This collection will be an instant classic in feminist and queer of color critique." —**SARAH HALEY**, author of *No Mercy Here: Gender, Punishment, and the Making of Jim Crow Modernity*

"The creative, political, intellectual interventions in this book, with their deeply intersectional locations of study and methods of analysis, fuel our ongoing work to understand what we are taking apart and to tear it down fully, once and for all. These articles, poems, and images also provide the warm, inviting entry points we need to imagine how bold, risky, ordinary work done by brave, ordinary people is the only path for building a world in which it is impossible for anyone to put anyone in a cage." —**DEAN SPADE**, from the foreword to volume 1

ABOLITION FEMINISMS

FEMINIST RUPTURES AGAINST THE CARCERAL STATE

Volume 2

Edited by
Alisa Bierria, Jakeya Caruthers, and Brooke Lober

Art edited by
Amanda Priebe

Foreword by
Andrea J. Ritchie

Haymarket Books
Chicago, Illinois

Published in 2022 by
Haymarket Books
P.O. Box 180165
Chicago, IL 60618
773-583-7884
www.haymarketbooks.org
info@haymarketbooks.org

ISBN: 978-1-64259-845-2

Distributed to the trade in the US through Consortium Book Sales and Distribution (www.cbsd.com) and internationally through Ingram Publisher Services International (www.ingramcontent.com).

This book was published with the generous support of Lannan Foundation and Wallace Action Fund.

Cover artwork by Eileen Jimenez, www.eileenjimenez.com, @maese.art.by.eileen.jimenez.
Cover design by Amanda Priebe, www.amandapriebe.com.

Printed in the United States.

Library of Congress Cataloging-in-Publication data is available.

10 9 8 7 6 5 4 3 2 1

CONTENTS

FOREWORD

Andrea J. Ritchie

Abolition Feminisms Volume 2: Feminist Ruptures against the Carceral State is the second of two anthologies edited by Alisa Bierria, Jakeya Caruthers, and Brooke Lober offering critical interventions into current conversations about violence, safety, policing, and punishment as wars rage both inside and beyond US borders, and the increasingly deadly consequences of racial capitalism reveal themselves on multiple fronts. *Abolition Feminisms Volume 1: Organizing, Survival, and Transformative Practice* focuses on abolitionist feminist organizing, and volume 2 focuses on abolition feminist theorizing. Together, they weave a rich tapestry of abolition feminist praxis.

Written in the crucible of 2020, the contributions to this volume surface, connect, and add texture to threads of abolition feminist genealogies and futurities that move beyond reactions to carceral feminisms and abolitionist theories that miss the mandate to end gender-based violence. As Whitney Richards-Calathes's powerful epistle to Darnella Frazier (the young Black woman who filmed George Floyd's murder) elaborates, the pieces collected here offer glimpses into both the hidden recesses of worlds built on policing and punishment that were never meant to be seen, and the Black feminist abolitionist practices of survival, rebellion, marronage, and resilience that disrupt and unseat them. These disruptions revolutionize our understanding of what feminism is and means.

As the editors write in their introduction, "abolition feminist theory and practice are strategically positioned to map the sheer breadth and depth of the carceral reach" into every institution, relationship, and even our imagination, thus providing us with the framework to "sense and unsettle systems of confinement, surveillance, and disposability" everywhere they are to be found—including, as multiple contributors point out, in the familial and community institutions and networks we posit as "alternatives" to policing and punishment, exposing the ways in which they engage in "distribution of resources . . . through punitivity."

Currently, "feminism," as consumed and conscripted to the carceral state's ends, is being bandied about as justification for endless and escalating wars everywhere, as it so often has been in the past. The impact of war on Ukrainian women and children, along with the resistance of lionized Ukrainian grandmothers and schoolgirls, are both held up as "feminist" reasons to support *even more* war. Meanwhile, the impacts of ongoing wars against women by police and Border Patrol in the US and by US-backed military forces in Haitï, Palestine, Syria, and Yemen, among countless other global fronts, continue to be endlessly funded and justified as "necessary."

Here in the United States, survivors of violence are once again being held up as the reason we need to continue to pour billions of dollars into policing and militarization by looting our collective resources, including funds intended for pandemic recovery and healing. As the contributions to this anthology clearly illustrate, policing, punishment, and deprivation shape our responses to violence not only through endless investments in police and prisons but also by weaving continuities between prisons, jails, shelters, welfare offices, programs, "treatment," and isolation into what Kayla Marie Martensen describes as a "web of carcerality" that ensnares survivors with devastating and deadly consequences.

Abolition feminisms give us the tools to recognize, analyze, and resist these counterinsurgent deployments of feminism to undermine liberatory struggles, such as the delusion of prison "reform" exposed by Jess Issacharoff through an exploration of Assata Shakur's incarceration on Rikers Island, the lie of police "sanctuary" exposed by Lee Ann S. Wang, and the deceptive terrain of police reform mapped by Ren-yo Hwang. It enables us to pull back the thin veil of "protection" to reveal the viral nature of colonial carcerality elucidated by Rosalie Donaldson-Kronenbuerger and Mark Mullkoff, and the false promises inherent in delivering our loved ones into the policing arms of carceral services highlighted by Martensen.

Like many of the volume's contributors, my abolition feminism grew from experiences of unsafety and longings for safety, of outrage at the violence of policing, of Black feminist theory and practice. Examining policing and criminalization through the lens of the experiences of Black, Indigenous, and Brown women, girls, queer, and trans people more quickly leads to the conclusion that abolition is the only way forward because they expose the reality of policing: it does not and was never intended to protect. Instead policing enforces racially gendered economies, modes of existence, sexualities, and relations of power through surveillance, containment, and control. These insights explain why those movements to end the violence of policing that have explicitly adopted a Black, queer, feminist lens are also explicitly abolitionist, advancing calls to defund and abolish police. As the authors of *Abolition. Feminism. Now.* make clear, "abolition must be feminist and . . . feminism must be abolitionist."[1]

Echoes of the radical feminist abolitionist politic crystallized by INCITE!, a political home for one of the editors and many of the contributors—reverberate through both volumes of *Abolition Feminisms*, not only in the voices represented but also in the visions articulated, sparked by the simple question that guided INCITE!'s analysis and work: What would it take to create safety for racialized, gendered subjects excluded from conventional carceral conceptions of safety? Asking what it would take for women, queer, and trans people of color to be able to experience safety exposes the violence of policing in all its forms—the medicalized punishment of "treatment," policing of service provision, the carcerality of public housing—and points us toward practices of revolutionary mothering and care described by MAMAS and the authors of "ACAB Means Abolishing the Cops in Our Heads, Hearts, and Homes," wielding "connection as contraband," to paraphrase Colby Lenz. This collection not only illuminates the ways in which the logics of carceral control extend beyond social institutions it also highlights how abolition feminist politics of care extend within and throughout our resistance.

Abolition feminisms also point us to the expansiveness of the abolitionist charge to "change everything" in order to uproot all of the interlocking systems of oppression named by the Combahee River Collective, creating infinite points of intervention that enable each of us to start where we are. Whether you are an anti-violence advocate, an anti-war or #DefundThePolice organizer, a healthcare provider, a fighter on the front lines of climate justice, or an educator, there is something here for each of us, some connection to the work we are already doing, some thread we can begin to pull to unravel the criminalizing webs that shape our possibilities and imaginations.

NOTES

1 Angela Y. Davis et al., *Abolition. Feminism. Now.* (Chicago: Haymarket Books, 2022), x.

INTRODUCTION

MAKING A CLEARING

Alisa Bierria, Jakeya Caruthers, and Brooke Lober

We are going to have to learn to think in radical terms. I use the term radical in its original meaning—getting down to and understanding the root cause.

—Ella Baker

How do you abolish something that is so deeply rooted that it disciplines meaning itself?

Angela Y. Davis contends that prisons and policing, *in all their iterations*, proliferate silently because "[they are] there, all around us,"[1] sustaining a network of institutions, ideologies, cultural images, and social arrangements with roots that, like plants, extend several times the width of the shoot we see, feel, and battle above ground. Because feminist critiques of carcerality foreground sites of punishment that are hidden, disguised, or devalued within mainstream, liberal, and even abolitionist analyses of US law-and-order politics, abolition feminist theory and practice are strategically positioned to map the sheer breadth and depth of the carceral reach. If prisons and police, broadly construed, are *all around us*, then abolition feminism provides us with the analytical elasticity needed to sense and unsettle systems of confinement, surveillance, and disposability wherever they take up space, even when they are intentionally obscured, as they often are, in realms of intimacy, kinship, caregiving, and activism.

Abolition Feminisms, Volume 2: Feminist Ruptures against the Carceral State foregrounds a feminist praxis that aims to expose, radically disrupt, and pull from the root "all things punishment," a phrase used by Beth Richie to signal the meaning of "carceral."[2] Prisons and policing operate as both specific criminalizing institutions and resilient paradigms that transform and discipline the meaning and purpose of other ostensibly noncarceral sites, such as domestic violence shelters, the kitchen table, sanctuary cities, or police reform movements. Indeed, works in this volume consistently aim to unravel the epistemic occupation of carceral logics within institutions, policies and practices, and discourses within unspectacular and often unrecognized locales, including and especially locales associated with care, vulnerability, and safety that more readily obscure their punitive and controlling premise. Carceral culture enacts and reinforces a *sensibility* that the distribution of resources ought to be organized through punitivity. This sense is forcibly rendered "common" through violent means: repetition of authoritative discourse, its silencing brutality, and an infrastructure that literally *concretizes* its logics. Cages have become common because common sense has been boiled down to a cage.

The nature and extent of carcerality's long reach in the lives of people rendered inherently criminal via racial, gender, sexual, embodied, and other forms of difference make plain the ways the ideological and structural regimes of carcerality are intimately locked with the logics of debt, reputation, and property;[3] the epistemic violence of criminological bioempiricism and "science";[4] carceral domesticity and policed sexuality;[5] the exclusive white supremacist rights of privacy and surveillance;[6] regimes of respectability and embodied order; and colonial-capitalist notions of democracy, citizenship, borders, and security. Perfected in the "common sense" of slavery, colonization, and US imperialism, these paradigms of carceral regimes create the terms of what counts as "practical," what (and whom) should be discredited, and what is clearly unthinkable.

This volume is a collection of radical reconsiderations and creative critique that aims to help disengage us from the root systems of carcerality and forge a clearing for the emergence of non- and anticarceral modes of living, which 'lend themselves to our needs,' to borrow a phrase from Ella Baker.[7] Through grassroots praxis, critical research, storytelling, diagrams, and striking commentaries via poetry and visual art, the contributors to this collection trouble the ground to reveal oppressive logics buried deep in spaces ripe for rigorous epistemic challenge and material transformation. They build on the legacies of feminist thinkers who formulated abolitionist critiques of policing, surveillance, and control by interrogating the way racist, patriarchal, criminalizing ideological strictures impacted their daily lives. They unsettle the paradigmatic roots of carcerality throughout space, from the rhetoric of sanctuary to rotted shelter food.

This collection's companion volume is titled *Abolition Feminisms, Volume 1: Organizing, Survival, and Transformative Practice* (Haymarket Books, 2022). Where volume 1 offered insight into brilliant and inventive feminist, queer, and trans resistant practices that unmake carceral regimes wherever they exist, the texts in volume 2 take up a race-gender critique of carcerality at the level of meaning itself. Mapping the many roots of rebellion planted throughout radical feminist and abolitionist legacies along the way, contributors in both volumes also pay tribute to remarkable insurgent feminist activist and intellectual genealogies, ensuring that, as Fannie Lou Hamer urges, we never forget where we come from and we always praise the bridges that carried us over.

Diverse in genre and political vision, contributions to this volume are organized across three themes: "Dismantling Carceral Intimacies"; "Refusing Reform, Resisting Captivity"; and "Making a Clearing." In Dismantling Carceral Intimacies, authors and artists explore carceral violence and punitive control within areas of intimacy and vulnerability, including family, friendship, sexual labor, health and well-being, and community care. Beyond the brutal regulation of intimate and relational practice (e.g., "walking while trans" laws, policing of embodied and sexual "disorder," criminalization of survival economies and intimate trade, and the discourse, conditions, and choices around family), the texts in this section lay bare the consequences of intimate state violence in the form of sexual harassment and assault and in forms of terror that operate at the level of spirit and will, including the constant articulation of complete disposability and exile that informs the very project of the large-scale prison regime, even as it exists in institutions associated with "care."

In "ACAB Means Abolishing the Cop in Our Heads, Hearts, and Homes: An Intergenerational Demand for Family Abolition," Tamara Lea Spira, Dayjha McMillan, Madi Stapleton, and Verónica N. Vélez examine the affective and intimate terms of carcerality and its reach into realms of relation. Opening with an activist and intellectual genealogy of the call to abolish the family, the authors go on to share intimate, intergenerational reflections analyzing the carceral logics embedded in the ethics, ideologies, investments, desires, demands, and structures of idealized family and, powerfully, their personal practice in unlearning them. In "State-Sanctioned Suicides and Life-Making Resistance in Carceral Contexts," Colby Lenz uncovers the suicide prevention practices of a California women's prison that Lenz argues constituted, in fact, a relentless system of "mental health punitivity" that enabled and escalated a devastating suicide crisis from 2013 to 2017. This account of anti-carceral resistance inside, outside, and in between prison walls reveals not only how those prison policies coded as "care" can be the most life-threatening forms of carceral violence but also how strategies created by incarcerated people and their loved ones to support each other's lives can radically reshape the terms of intimacy. Edited and with an introduction by Hyejin Shim, "Beyond #StopAsianHate: Criminalization, Gender, and Asian Abolition Feminism" brings together Asian abolition feminists to discuss why they dissented from the widespread call for escalated criminalizing policies as a response to anti-Asian violence throughout the pandemic and the horrific 2021 shooting at an Asian massage business in Atlanta. Rejecting the demand for more hate crime laws and other liberal carceral approaches to violence that invisibilize and endanger those victims of violence who are more vulnerable to being criminalized themselves, these thinkers and organizers connect key points of carceral-patriarchal violence at home, in prison, in media, and at war, tracing a complex map of violence, resistance, and freedom across public and intimate space.

In "'All Canned Foods Are Expired but Still Edible': A Critique of Anti-Violence Advocacy and the Perpetuation of Antiblackness,"

Romina Garcia reflects on the casual punitive disposability directed at Black survivors/victims of domestic violence within a Chicago domestic violence shelter. Building on critiques of the carceral-feminist anti-violence field, Garcia examines how the field transformed into a carceral project through its roots in anti-Black meaning and challenges readers to imagine what victim advocacy can look like outside of the logics of anti-Black punishment and as an abolition feminist speculative project. This section is punctuated by "Stay Connected at All Costs," a revelatory exchange between Alisha Walker and Red Schulte. Completed while Walker was incarcerated in an Illinois prison for defending her life in the context of sex work, her commentary reveals how, in a culture that abandons thousands of survivors in prisons, prison can also be a crucial site of survivor connection, resistance, and collective knowledge production.

The articles in the second section—"Refusing Reform, Resisting Captivity"—explore abolition feminism's critique of carcerality's encroachment into political strategies that are otherwise meant to *suggest* opposition to policing and prisons, such as sanctuary for immigrants, social services, or liberal iterations of #DefundThePolice. While carceral punishment is sustained through "common sense," creeping its way through meaning, and relentlessly warping concepts, relationalities, attempts at social change, and even efforts characterized as "abolitionist," these articles examine modes of radical refusal, including how sites, systems, and discourses that presume a totalized authority over our lives might be upended through philosophical and material rebellions that span the spectacular and the everyday. In "Domestic Terror: Women's Prisons and Assata Shakur's Abolitionist Refusal," Jess Issacharoff closely reads Assata Shakur's "Women in Prison: How We Are" in the context of Shakur's imprisonment at the Rikers Island Correctional Institution for Women. Issacharoff expounds on Shakur's analysis of the domestic terror of the women's prison and contextualizes the multiple ways that Shakur's critical unveiling of domestic carceral logics was joined with her own "domestic" transgressions and led to her being understood as a "domestic terrorist."

In "Bad Apples, Rotted Roots, and the Three Rs of Reformist Reforms," Ren-yo Hwang examines three features and projects of contemporary police reform—rebranding, recruitment, and retraining—and locates in them the residue of carceral feminism. Throughout the text, Hwang describes how these reforms expand and entrench the reach of the police by perversely appropriating and distorting the potential of otherwise transformative language, practices, and principles.

Likewise, Lee Ann S. Wang calls for a more critical review of police-endorsed sanctuary for immigrants in "Refusing the Value of Immigrant Fear: An Abolitionist Feminist Critique of Sanctuary by Police." Contending that anti-ICE/pro-policing liberal formations of sanctuary exploit vulnerability and ultimately entrench violence against immigrants, Wang points us toward abolition feminist of color political critiques as key resources to radically reimagine sanctuary. Composed in the early days of the COVID-19 pandemic, Rosalie Donaldson-Kronenburger and Mark Mullkoff's "Social Work and the Partner Assault Response Program: A Critical Pathology Report" uses experimental prose to reflect on how the structural features and destructive capacity of a virus mirror the criminal justice logics that shape Partner Assault Response (PAR) programs addressing domestic violence. This analysis was produced in the midst of an upsurge of abolitionist activism asserting that "prison is the pandemic" and likewise critiques the colonial violence of PAR programs which have been weaponized against Indigenous communities. Kayla Marie Martensen closes this section with personal testimony of and critical reflection on her time as an "at-risk youth" and a volunteer advocate within a range of youth lockup institutions, a network of social services and carceral spaces she describes as a "web of detainment."

In the final section of the volume, "Making a Clearing," contributors clear ground and make space for abolitionist invention. Where the notion of clearing (as practice and place) gestures toward ripe possibility, the chapters in this section highlight the ethical formations, philosophical reflections, and imaginative structures built on principles as radical as love, mutuality and interdependence, commitment to struggle (indeed, occasional *failure*), and critical self-reflection. While other chapters challenge the carceral corruption of institutions that *should* be built on abolitionist principles like care, the authors in this section point us toward some of the *actual* fertile sites and brilliant methodologies whereby abolitionist futures are being set in motion.

The section opens with Whitney Richards-Calathes's "A Letter for Darnella Frazier: A Black Feminist Abolitionist Map of the Forgotten." In this epistolary reflection addressed to Frazier, the then seventeen-year-old Black girl who captured cell phone footage of the police murder of George Floyd in summer 2020, Richards-Calathes captures the ironies of Frazier's act of witness and argues for a more careful witnessing (and with it, analysis and action) of the forms of state violence experienced by Black women and girls. In "Radical Mothering for the Purposes of Abolition," Nadine Naber, Johnaé Strong, and Souzan Naser discuss the insights uncovered in the work of their collective, Mamas Activating Movements for Abolition and Solidarity (MAMAS). A gathering of mothers impacted by the criminal punishment system (as mothers of the incarcerated or as formerly incarcerated mothers), the organizers in MAMAS point to ways that, conducted against and within the context of captivity and state violence, the collaboration, resource sharing, nuanced analysis, alternate relations, and nonhegemonic, non-bionormative formations of mothering and motherwork demonstrate radical abolitionist potential.

Echoing bell hooks's grounding affirmation that education is about the practice of freedom, this volume closes with two essays reflecting on transformative justice as radical pedagogy. Qui Alexander's essay "Teaching Abolitionist Praxis in the Everyday" engages queer Black feminist theory and other legacies of radical praxis to explore political frameworks that teach us how to learn, imagine, and build a world beyond carceral meaning. Finally, Xhercis Méndez illuminates the nuances of teaching feminist anti-carceral responses to gender-based violence in her review of Mariame Kaba and Shira Hassan's *Fumbling Towards Repair: A Workbook for Community Accountability Facilitators.* This workbook emerged amid a growing landscape of groundbreaking texts about transformative justice, restorative justice, and community accountability, and Méndez's detailed exploration of this workbook and its unique political context teaches us that the art and labor of practical skills-building is essential to making our way toward freedom.

In addition to the experimental diagrams included in two of the essays, this volume integrates striking poetry and visual art in a range of mediums, including graphic art, tapestry, painting, and collage. These creative contributions provoke radical interference and interruptions of carceral meaning, while offering dynamic passageways toward recognizing, describing, and disengaging from carceral violence, wherever it resides. We thank all of the incredible artists who generously contributed their work to this collection, including Tabitha Arnold, kai lumumba barrow, Molly Costello, Yola Gómez, Shana M. griffin, Inés Ixierda, Mon M, Shellyne Rodriguez, Jasmine Tabor, and Summer-Harmony Twenish.

As in volume 1, we deeply appreciate all of the authors and artists whose remarkable contributions expand our organizing toolkits and our ability to create meaning that goes against the carceral grain. They teach us how to disassemble the apparatus of cages, policing, and punitive control that occupies space all around us, showing us how to navigate our way inside its webs and through its interstices and build escape routes beyond its walls—concrete and otherwise. We also extend our sincere appreciation to Amanda Priebe for her consistent and creative leadership as the art editor for this volume; the Abolition Collective for its critical role in activating both volumes; the reviewers for their indispensable comments that strengthened this collection; Interference Archive and Survived & Punished NY for supporting the publication of one of their dispatches across prison walls; and Haymarket's wonderfully supportive editorial team, particularly Alyea Canada and Michael Trudeau for their generous editorial support. Finally, we are so thankful for our friends, family, and collaborators whose support and feedback were essential throughout the development of this project, including Kinneret Azaria Alexander, Wanda Bierria, Shana M. griffin, Xandra Ibarra, Mariame Kaba, Mary Jo Klinker, Colby Lenz, Dean Spade, Emily L. Thuma, Lee Ann S. Wang, Craig Willse, and Satya Zamudio.

May our collective work honor all those rebellious legacies of freedom fighters whose labor, courage, and brilliance cleared a way for its possibility and made a way for its existence.

BIBLIOGRAPHY

Browne, Simone. *Dark Matters: On the Surveillance of Blackness*. Durham, NC: Duke University Press, 2015.

Davis, Angela Y. *Are Prisons Obsolete?* New York: Seven Stories Press, 2003.

Fullwiley, Duana. "Can DNA 'Witness' Race?: Forensic Uses of an Imperfect Ancestry Testing Technology." In *Race and the Genetic Revolution: Science, Myth, and Culture*, edited by Sheldon Krimsky and Kathleen M. Sloan. New York: Columbia University Press, 2011.

Haley, Sarah. *No Mercy Here: Gender, Punishment, and the Making of Jim Crow Modernity*. Chapel Hill: University of North Carolina Press, 2016.

Harris, Cheryl I. "The Afterlife of Slavery: Markets, Property and Race." Presentation at Artist Space, New York, January 19, 2016.

———. "Whiteness as Property." *Harvard Law Review* 106, no. 8 (1993): 1707–91.

hooks, bell. *Teaching to Transgress: Education as the Practice of Freedom*. New York: Routledge, 1994.

Kim, Mimi E. "The Carceral Creep: Gender-Based Violence, Race and the Expansion of the Punitive State, 1973–1983." *Social Problems*, 2019.

Petty, Tawana, et al. *Reclaiming Our Data*. Detroit: Our Data Bodies, interim report, June 15, 2018.

Ransby, Barbara. *Ella Baker and the Black Freedom Movement: A Radical Democratic Vision*. Chapel Hill: University of North Carolina Press, 2003.

Richie, Beth E. "Carcerality." In *Keywords for Gender and Sexuality Studies*, edited by Keywords Feminist Editorial Collective. New York: New York University Press, 2021.

Ritchie, Andrea, J. *Invisible No More: Police Violence against Black Women and Women of Color*. Boston: Beacon Press, 2017.

Roberts, Dorothy. "Abolishing Policing Also Means Abolishing Family Regulation." *Imprint*, June 16, 2020. https://imprintnews.org/child-welfare-2/abolishing-policing-also-means-abolishing-family-regulation/44480.

———. *Fatal Invention: How Science, Politics, and Big Business Re-Create Race in the Twenty-First Century*. New York: New Press, 2011.

NOTES

1 Angela Y. Davis, *Are Prisons Obsolete?* (New York: Seven Stories Press, 2003).

2 Beth E. Richie, "Carcerality," in *Keywords for Gender and Sexuality Studies*, ed. Keywords Feminist Editorial Collective (New York: New York University Press, 2021).

3 Cheryl I. Harris, "Whiteness as Property," *Harvard Law Review* 106, no. 8 (1993): 1707–91; Harris, "The Afterlife of Slavery: Markets, Property and Race," Presentation at Artists Space, New York, January 19, 2016, https://www.youtube.com/watch?v=dQQGndN3BvY&t=2966s.

4 Dorothy Roberts, *Fatal Invention: How Science, Politics, and Big Business Re-Create Race in the Twenty-First Century* (New York: New Press, 2011);

Duana Fullwiley, "Can DNA 'Witness' Race?: Forensic Uses of an Imperfect Ancestry Testing Technology," in *Race and the Genetic Revolution: Science, Myth, and Culture*, eds. Sheldon Krimsky and Kathleen M. Sloan (New York: Columbia University Press, 2011; Tawana Petty et al., *Reclaiming Our Data*, interim report (Detroit: Our Data Bodies), June 15, 2018.

5 Sarah Haley, *No Mercy Here: Gender, Punishment, and the Making of Jim Crow Modernity* (Charlotte: University of North Carolina Press, 2016); Andrea J. Ritchie, *Invisible No More: Police Violence against Black Women and Women of Color* (Boston: Beacon Press, 2017); Dorothy Roberts, "Abolishing Policing Also Means Abolishing Family Regulation," *Imprint*, June 16, 2020, https://imprintnews.org/child-welfare-2/abolishing-policing-also-means-abolishing-family-regulation/44480.

6 Simone Browne, *Dark Matters: On the Surveillance of Blackness* (Durham, NC: Duke University Press, 2015).

7 Barbara Ransby, *Ella Baker and the Black Freedom Movement: A Radical Democratic Vision* (Chapel Hill: University of North Carolina Press, 2003).

PART ONE

DISMANTLING CARCERAL INTIMACIES

ACAB MEANS ABOLISHING THE COP IN OUR HEADS, HEARTS, AND HOMES

AN INTERGENERATIONAL DEMAND FOR FAMILY ABOLITION

Tamara Lea Spira, Dayjha McMillan,
Madi Stapleton, and Verónica N. Vélez

"Our generation must walk the spiritual path that is available to us only in this time, with its own unique combination of wisdom and creation."

—adrienne maree brown, *Emergent Strategy: Shaping Change, Changing Worlds*

We are living in a moment when abolition has come to the fore in public discourse in an unprecedented way. As Karissa Lewis of Movement for Black Lives (M4BL) argues, we find ourselves in "a culmination of multiple storms converging . . . COVID-19, police violence, racial capitalism in crisis, [and] intensified white supremacy," resulting in mass uprisings across the country and the world.[1] Black abolitionists and those involved in M4BL, Dream Defenders, Critical Resistance, and many other collectives are working relentlessly to steer the conversation away from reform and instead "chart a new path forward." This path demands an end to all systems of policing and a redirected focus on community care, accountability, and self-determination. While abolition has recently gained unthinkable mainstream attention, we know that this work has a long lineage emerging directly out of collective freedom struggles.

As renowned abolitionist Angela Davis reminds us, it is important to remember that abolition is a feminist strategy.[2] Abolitionist demands come out of feminist theories, practices, and methodologies that grapple with the interrelatedness of supposedly distinct struggles. This feminist approach allows us to see that "the prison" does not refer to a discrete institution; rather, as Dylan Rodríguez has argued, the "prison regime" always exceeds its own materiality to also include the "fundamental organizing logic of the United States in its local, translocal, and global enactments."[3] That which needs to be abolished is not simply the prison but all that it stands in for. Furthermore, abolition is as much about creatively building up other institutions and social relations as it is about dismantling the obsolete ones.[4]

Toward this end, our collective task is to consider the intimate dimensions of the prison regime, which structures our social relations and imprints our very subjectivities. Abolition feminism reminds us that getting rid of police and prisons means nothing if we do not abolish the ideologies, practices, and affective economies of policing in our interpersonal relationships and communities. We must, in short, transform the "intimate investments" within the prison-industrial complex that come to saturate our very desires, relationships, and modes of relation to one another and ourselves.[5] This requires us to move beyond the desired ideal of the white, nuclear, heteropatriarchal family as well as homonormative desires that are reliant upon "settler sexualities,"[6] bionormative monogamous relations,[7] and anti-Black definitions of normative gender and sexuality.[8]

This essay argues that unlearning the carceral system requires an unlearning of one of our most intimate institutions: "family." By family abolition, we refer to the positive, expansive process of proliferating networks of care, love, and support that crowd out the rigid, hierarchical, privatized nuclear heteropatriarchal family.[9] This challenges negative presumptions of family abolition as the withdrawal of care and nurturing relationships. Rather, we posit that abolition is a practice of the self in relation to community. To fully believe and enact abolition, we must work to abolish the same systems we have internalized as a means of survival. Abolitionist projects cannot be done alone, and it is only when we engage in this work within our communities that the abolition of the family becomes necessary and desirable.

Family abolition is especially important when considering the pursuit of and demand for Black life and liberation, which has more recently propelled the call for abolition of police into public consciousness and political agendas. As communities demand that police budgets be defunded across the country, Dorothy Roberts reminds us that "rather than divesting one oppressive system to invest in another, we should work toward abolishing all carceral institutions and creating radically different ways of meeting families' needs."[10] Following Roberts, we believe that networks of care that are rooted in support and self-determination rather than surveillance/punishment/criminalization are what make revolution sustainable. Family abolition gives us the tools to "break the prison's stranglehold on our imaginations" and build the types of community we actually need.[11]

Before moving forward, we wish to contextualize ourselves and our stakes in this work. We are a collective of two professors and two alumni of Western Washington University.

Dayjha McMillan and Madi Stapleton are (begrudging) Gen Zers who have recently graduated from Fairhaven College at Western Washington University. We are colleagues, roommates, a Gemini/Leo dynamic duo, and most importantly, friends. We hold intimate stakes in this project that are rooted in our specific experiences as Black and white queers who are sometimes women. Both of us came to this work having been failed by the myth of the nuclear family in different ways; we have known in ourselves a yearning for something "different" for a long time. We arrived here grounded in our own queerness(es) and queer politics, which allow us to see that "marriage equality" is far from liberating and that individual formations of "alternative" or "chosen" family will not liberate us all. We came to family abolition already invested in revolution and the abolition of prisons and policing.

Tamara Lea Spira and Verónica N. Vélez are faculty at Western Washington University who began our tenure-track positions within a year of each other. In the fall of 2015, a series of death threats were issued to Black femme students on our campus. As new junior faculty, we understood the very possible punitive consequences of our involvement, yet we insisted that our political practice as faculty must entail a commitment to stand alongside students to name the violence publicly. Going through this together not only prepared us for the ongoing assaults from the administration but also linked our desires to imagine and enact a world otherwise. The intimacy of this shared journey evolved our relationship from close colleagues to friends to family. From here, the four of us came together in 2018 to engage the theory and practice of family abolition intergenerationally.

In what follows, we elaborate upon the concept and practice of family abolition theoretically and in our lives. We first offer a genealogy of differing radical concepts of family abolition. Next, we engage in a dialogue about how we make sense of these questions as we intimately struggle with traditional conceptualizations of "family" and its consequences for radical projects of communal care. We end by raising questions about the imperative of family abolition in our current conjuncture marked by the spread of COVID-19, the continued incarceration of children at the border, and uprisings nationwide to insist upon and center Black life and defund the police state.

LINEAGES OF FAMILY ABOLITION

In 1980, the Black lesbian feminist mother Pat Parker gave a speech titled "Revolution: It's Not Neat or Pretty or Quick,"[12] in which she valiantly traced the connections between feminism, anti-imperialism, and the long and protracted struggle of revolution. Immortalized in the historic anthology *This Bridge Called My Back*, this speech was initially Parker's contribution to the 1980 "BASTA! Women's Conference on Imperialism and Third World War." Parker challenged capitalism and consumerism, linking her support of third world revolutions to the responsibility of US feminists to destroy capitalism from the inside out. She called for a solidarity politics that would unite different oppressed communities to build real political power.[13]

Parker engaged the transnational sphere, linking her call for abolition of the nation-state to the abolition of the private nuclear family.

This was no doubt informed by Parker's multivalent activism that did not separate struggles against racism and imperialism and her work for Black lesbians' health and her leadership as part of the lesbian mothers' custody movement. Importantly, at the heart of all revolutionary struggle, Parker argued, was one central and intimate institution that must be destroyed: the nuclear family. As her speech came to a close, she bluntly asserted that "in order for us to move to revolution, [the nuclear family] has to be destroyed. And I mean destroyed."[14]

Parker's tragic and premature death several years later (at the age of forty-five) did not allow for an elaboration on her call to abolish the nuclear family. However, her work gives us an entry point into a genealogy of Black radical feminist notions of family abolition that, as Tiffany Lethabo King suggests, are necessary for discussion. In King's 2018 article "Black 'Feminisms' and Pessimism: Abolishing Moynihan's Negro Family" she makes a case for family abolition that roots back to Black feminist thought of the seventies and eighties.[15] Through an analysis of Kay Lindsey's "The Black Woman as Woman"[16] and Hortense Spillers's "Mama's Baby, Papa's Maybe,"[17] King argues that their critiques of the family "expose the violence that creates [the family's] conditions of possibility."[18] King harkens back to the words of Lindsey and Spillers in hopes of calling us all to "denaturalize the family as a normative and humanizing institution to which people should aspire to belong."[19] In King's analysis of Lindsey's essay, she argues, "The family as a social formation can be reconceived as an amalgamation of land, slaves, property, conquest and the state. The family could be constructed as a geopolitical unit or assemblage (family-land-slaves-property-state-empire) that creates the American frontier, or the time-space coordinates of the human."[20]

The family can only be understood as something that sustains whiteness through Black death and Native genocide; the private nuclear family tethers whiteness to humanity and produces Blackness as non-human. King casts Lindsey and Spillers as important thinkers within the multigenerational discourse on family abolition, from which they are often seen as separate. She argues that we should continue to listen to Lindsey and Spillers' call for family abolition in the contemporary moment. They show us the "possibility and futurity" for Black subjects who are rendered outside human coordinates, and thus unable to access the humanizing category of family. King argues that the specific position that Black subjects inhabit opens space to find other ways to name and practice modes of relation that reach toward the abolition of the family rather than its reinscription.

Such Black feminist queer interventions lay the groundwork for our understandings of family abolition as an expansive project that links institutions of the family and the state as specific outgrowths of slavery and its afterlives. With this founding in mind, it is important to note that around the same time that Lindsey and Parker were sharing their critiques of the family, the more well-known lineage of arguments for family abolition emerged within socialist feminist circles. In the 1970s, the idea that family is the primary site of women's oppression was a centerpiece of a socialist critique of (one interpretation of) Marx that does not understand reproductive labor to be labor. One of the well-known manifestations of this was the wages for housework movement, wherein demands that women get paid for their reproductive labor brought questions of marriage, motherhood, and patriarchy to the forefront.[21] Feminist Shulamith Firetsone's key text *The Dialectic of Sex* diverged from the focus on housework in its case against sexual reproduction within the patriarchal, nuclear child-rearing family as the key to women's oppression. The only way to end women's oppression, Firestone contended, was by ending the biological family, dreaming of the possibility of a time when reproduction would no longer require patriarchy, or biological men altogether.[22]

Contemporary texts following this feminist lineage of family abolition most directly include *Full Surrogacy Now: Feminism aainst Family* by Sophie Lewis[23] and *Kinderkommunismus: A Feminist Analysis of the 21st-Century Family and a Communist Proposal for its Abolition* by Kade Doyle Griffiths and Jules Gleeson.[24] Both of these texts position the family as irredeemable and instead call for an expansion of relationships of care that would necessitate the undoing of capitalism. Sophie Lewis in particular is "reviving the case for abolishing the family" in public discourse today by sharing her vision of a future where "everyone, regardless of gender, is a surrogate; we mother each other."[25] This joins with the work of M. E. O'Brien, whose powerful piece "To Abolish the Family" argues that love, eroticism, and intimacy must be preserved and that this can only be done once the private bourgeois family is superseded by other forms of collective and communal care.[26]

Beginning in the late seventies and early eighties, radical and lesbian feminists took up a critique of the family through a structuralist analysis of the family as a political institution. This framework put forth the argument that patriarchy and gendered power dynamics render heterosexual marriage an always coercive institution. An early version of this argument about the incompatibility of liberation and the heteronuclear family was made by Ti-Grace Atkinson, whose 1969 pamphlet *Radical Feminism and Love*[27] decried heterosexual love and family as the center of oppression. Adrienne Rich's "Compulsory Heterosexuality and Lesbian Existence" would nuance these politics by naming heterosexuality itself to be an institution that needed to be abolished alongside other oppressive institutions under capitalism.[28] While Rich still held gender to be a universalist category at the root of oppression, she would go on to problematize this in her subsequent work to define a "politics of location," thus allowing a deeper linking of the abolition of heterosexuality, gender, and white supremacy.[29]

Gay liberationists were also invested in critiques of the family, although arguments coming from this branch were more explicitly focused on a critique of capitalism. According to Raewyn Connell, "the most radical departure in the critique of the family was made by theorists of gay liberation . . . they generally saw the family as the factory of heterosexuality, meeting capital's need for a labour supply and the state's need for subordination."[30] According to this analysis, "the repression of homosexual desire, while certainly part of a general authoritarianism . . . had quite specific reasons."[31]

Additionally, it is important to note the articulations of a family abolition politic put forward by the gay liberation movement of the 1970s. While this phase of the gay liberation movement is sometimes critiqued for its underdeveloped understanding of racial capitalism, some branches were putting forth demands that clearly reflected a robust critique of the family beyond the constraints of whitewashed socialism. The Third World Gay Revolution, a collective of Black and Latinx gays and lesbians who broke away from the Gay Liberation Front in New York City, released the 1971 statement "What We Want, What We Believe" modeled on the Black Panther Party's Ten-Point Program.[32] The statement made sixteen demands, including the release of all third world, gay, and political prisoners from jails and mental institutions; an end to "the fascist police force"; the abolition of the existing judicial system and all forms of institutional punishment; and simply "a new society." Nestled among these, the fifth point states, "We want the abolition of the institution of the bourgeois nuclear family." They powerfully argued that "all oppressions originate within the nuclear family structure." Placing family abolition within demands for the abolition of prisons and policing and calls for a society "where the needs of the people come first,"[33] we are reminded that the project of creating systems of relation beyond the nuclear family is integral to all our revolutionary and abolitionist endeavors.

Historian John D'Emilio filled in this critique of the family from a gay liberationist and socialist perspective in his well-known essay "Capitalism and Gay Identity,"[34] where he argued that gay liberation means "creat[ing] structures beyond the nuclear family that provide a sense of belonging," thus allowing the family to "wane in significance."[35] Although he does not use the phrase "family abolition" specifically, this can be understood as an abolitionist approach because it emphasizes building up new systems and crowding out institutions that keep us locked down.

From D'Emilio's perspective, some examples of things to put our energy into that would allow for the dissolution of the family include supporting the autonomy of young people, community- and worker-controlled daycare, and housing/neighborhood institutions that enhance the social unit.[36] He also argues that gay men and lesbians are "well situated to play a special role" in this movement toward family abolition: "Already excluded from families as most of us are, we have had to create, for our survival, networks of support that do not depend on the bonds of blood or the license of the state. . . . The building of an 'affectional community' must be as much a part of our political movement as are campaigns for civil rights."[37]

In essence, queer people have historically lacked access to the normative nuclear family, and this has resulted in the building (or continuance) of different systems of relation for queer people that allow for family abolition to be understood as realizable. This argument is especially relevant within the context of Cathy Cohen's reformulation of queerness and queer politics beyond sexual "identity" so that we may understand how imposed categories of race, class, gender, citizenship, ability, and more also "queer" subjects who sit at the intersections of oppression and resistance.[38]

Finally, the current scholar-activist work on radical mothering, as seen in recent anthologies such as *Revolutionary Mothering: Love on the Frontlines* and *The Chicana M(other)work Anthology* ought to also be seen in relationship to this lineage of family abolition.[39] According to Alexis Pauline Gumbs, Black, poor, Indigenous, and immigrant of color mothers are rarely included in the celebrated categories of mother or family; these communities are queered as parents, irrespective of their sexual and gender identities.[40] This has deep material consequences, most obviously being the historical stealing of and separation from their children through systems of chattel slavery, Native boarding schools, the foster/adoption system, incarceration, and migrant detention centers, all of which have been rationalized through the racialized depiction of the bad/unfit mother or the revocation of the term altogether. Within this scholarly and activist project on radical mothering, the assertion of the right to mother isn't mobilized via an appeal to access the normative (imagined white) privatized nuclear family role in order to right these horrendous wrongs, but rather to transform the category "mother" altogether beyond the coordinates of the nuclear family.

Core to this work is refiguring mothering as a political category that, as a verb, implicates our work in the service of future generations against all odds. As Mai'a Williams argues, "the practice of mothering is fundamental to creating co-liberatory revolutionary movements and societies."[41] From this perspective, mothering ought to be seen not as a gendered, biological category, but rather "a queer practice of transforming the world through our desire for one another and another way to be."[42] This desire and practice of transforming our relations makes revolutionary mothering a project that is in alignment with family abolition.

Furthermore, both revolutionary mothering and family abolition are frameworks/practices that are grounded in the politics of reproductive justice. Here, we follow the reproductive justice movement's call for "the right to maintain personal bodily autonomy, have children, not have children and parent the children we have in safe and sustainable communities."[43] By running with these necessary demands toward a reconfiguration of motherhood, revolutionary mothering allows us to imagine beyond the nuclear family and instead name our relations in a way that is untethered and liberatory.

COMING TOGETHER: AN INTERGENERATIONAL DREAMING

We write as a product of the aforementioned entangled genealogies, and on the heels of their contradictions, submerged insights, inspirations, and ongoing projects. Where do they bring us in the present? In this section, we pursue these questions on a different register through a more intimate lens. Methodologically, this section employs collaborative autoethnography to focus on self-interrogation and analysis.[44]

Concretely, we interviewed one another about our experiences with and dreams of family and family abolition in our lives. Our aims were to reveal how our individual and shared experiences shape and are shaped by specific contexts. We found collaborative autoethnography to most clearly enable us to wrestle with the project of abolition in our "personal" lives (and with each other) in order for our revolutionary dreams to be made more tangible.

Abolishing the Family: Why the Family Failed Us

The first line of questioning we pursued collectively engaged our experiences and memories of the family in our lives. While our different social locations and life experiences created much variation, three core themes kept emerging in each of our stories. The first was a critique of normative family forms that wove through our experiences as children and adults. Secondly, anti-Blackness shaped our familial upbringings, which differentially propelled each our biological families' desires to achieve the illusory norm of the nuclear family, enforced and organized as it is by affective economies of policing in our interpersonal relationships and by the state. The final theme was that out of our experience of the family as failed, there emerged other kinds of practices and visions that propelled us toward more expansive and rich modes of making family.

Two of us were predominantly raised in nuclear families with parents married into heterosexual unions (until death), while two of us were raised by "single" mothers. One of us is a mother, albeit with considerable struggle with the word "mother," due to the exclusive assumptions regarding biology and heterosexuality that often attach to the term. After a long fertility battle another one of us learned to claim motherhood as a verb and political identity outside of the nuclear family, while working to heal from the impact of draconian immigration policies that led to the separation of extended kin. Thus, our relationship to normative family was also greatly informed by race, sexuality, class, and citizenship status.

Despite this variation, family as a failed endeavor rang throughout all our narratives. Naming the violence of the nuclear family form ensconced within white supremacy, patriarchy, and coloniality was essential to building otherwise. This was expressed cogently by Madi and Dayjha, who explicitly articulated the modes of white supremacist heteropatriarchy that rendered the nuclear family to be a failed project. Madi directly named herself to be "failed by the myth of the nuclear family during [her] upbringing." As she elaborated, "This was present not only because of the more blatant effects of patriarchy; the myth of the nuclear family also infiltrated my relationships that were supposed to be a 'haven,' making it quite easy for me to now see that 'alternatives' can only stretch so far when we're not striving for abolition." From Madi's perspective, "our struggles to create different ways of relation can't simply be boiled down to our own family's trauma, but rather the trauma of 'the family' in general."

Racialization added a layer of complexity to Madi's narrative, as the heteropatriarchal family was simultaneously steeped in a whiteness that allowed Madi and her mom to access the narrative of the "sometimes valorized white 'independent' single mother/daughter duo." This differed with Dayjha, who articulated a vexed historical relationship to family informed by histories of slavery and anti-Black racism that have historically rendered the family inaccessible to Black people while also pathologizing them for this so-called lack.[45]

Echoing some of these contradictions, Dayjha named the family as a site of simultaneous yearning, failure, and violence—and profoundly so. As she put it,

> The family, historically and present day, has been a site of failure and violence. . . . This story has plagued many members of my biological family. This story has failed my biological family and in turn, this family has failed me. This idea, or Institution, of the family, has left far too much room for neglect, inside and outside of the "home." What I mean by this, is that the absolute desire of many members of my biological family to access this family structure has left us feeling broken, unworthy, angry, distant, secretive, and obscenely proud. These feelings have manifested under different names like physical, emotional, sexual abuse, drug dependency, homelessness, domestic violence, and "invisible" mental illnesses, to name a few.

Dayjha uses the word "failed" multiple times, emphasizing an idea articulated by Madi above. Dayjha's repetition pushes back on the historic pathologizing of Black families by underscoring the ways in which the people in her family were not failures; rather the "story" of the family has failed them. Dayjha denaturalizes the family and names it for what it is: a mythology, ideology, and political institution. Using the language of the family as an "idea" or "Institution," she deromanticizes the family, instead revealing it to be a disciplinary structure that bolsters white supremacy by forever locking out many and, through pathologizing and criminalizing discourse, enacts profound control over the lives of those thought to transgress it.

Despite this critique, the power of "the family" as a desired yet unattainable object has still left deep scars. Dayjha argues that, by forever denying access to the very privileged family forms that Black people cannot inhabit, the ideology of the family "reinscribes the notion that some are unworthy of humanity, which means they are unworthy of care/community/love." As Dayjha continued,

> Our socialization to build our lives in pursuit of family supposedly signals a happy and successful life. We are taught that to be a valuable and legitimate person in this society, you should have biological families and all that it supposedly comes with. (A monogamous relationship, children, marriage, a house, a college degree, land, etc.) In order to be deemed "valuable" and "legitimate," one must ask whose humanity is stolen and stifled.

Concepts of value, success, and legitimacy punctuate this narrative. Importantly, these social values are linked to material wealth, colonial land acquisition, and bourgeois notions of education; the ideology of the normative nuclear family cannot be read outside of white supremacist capitalist patriarchy and coloniality. Moreover, it is not simply that certain communities are excluded; rather, the entire apparatus of the acceptable family is built upon the labor, lives, and exclusion of those whose humanity—in this case, Black people—has been "stolen" and "stifled" in the construction of the US settler state.

These narratives voice a tension between an ideological critique of family and the affective work that family as a fetishized norm has done. Anti-Blackness was present in Madi's familial arrangements due to her white mother's ability to present herself as a respectable single mother (à la Lorelai Gilmore) while Black single moms are pathologized and have their children stolen from them, a theft made possible through the deputization of child and family services and a perverse but repeated rhetoric of "protection." Gaining this respectability required Madi's mother to distance herself from the racialized stereotype of the "welfare mother" and adopt the bootstraps narrative, thus distancing herself from Blackness and misogynoir.

Tamara and Verónica were both raised in families aspiring toward acceptable heterosexual union, within which contradictions of race, religion, ethnicity, class aspirations, and illness made the family a forever fleeting site to grasp onto. For Verónica, the daughter of parents from México and Panamá, migration is deeply interwoven into how the nuclear family was both disrupted and reconstituted within a climate of fear. Both her parents left home in pursuit of the "American dream," like other migrants who fled largely propelled by the harsh realities of poverty and tumultuous political contexts informed by colonialism and neocolonialism. Verónica's father arrived in the US as an older teenager with the promise to return for his mother and siblings, who had been rejected by his father's family after his fahter's untimely death. Verónica shared:

> Upon my grandfather's death, my father fled Panamá after his father's Ecuadorian family rejected him, his mother, and his siblings as a result of anti-Blackness that targeted his mother's Panamanian identity. A family friend, who had previously migrated to the US and established residency, claimed him as his son and provided "papers" for my father that allowed him to enter the US without much suspicion. My father fought for his family to remain together, immigrating his siblings and mother under the most challenging conditions, not realizing that the patriarchy he was emboldening as the "new" head of the family was the very violence that had contributed to his and his family's departure from Panamá. In other words, he fled patriarchy only to embrace it full force in the US, all in the name of saving his mother, brother, and sisters. He later went on to become a cop, a role that further entrenched the structures of patriarchy and anti-Blackness that were rooted in the rejection he felt as a child from his father's family.

The conditions that led to Verónica's father's migration had everything to do with preserving the nuclear family. His actions were celebrated, as he was essentially viewed as the "hero" who made possible the reunification of his mother and siblings. And because he was the formidable "head of the family," few questioned him, often expressing that they owed him a debt. Verónica often shared the challenges of growing up in a household where daily life was organized around her father's desires, rather than supporting a collective well-being that was deeply impacted by structures of anti-immigrant, sexist, homophobic, and racist violence.

Tamara's mother and father, both survivors of family violence, gave their all to provide a stable home for their children. As Ashkenazi Jews, they also worked exceptionally hard to create a socially accepted family unit, even as they struggled with the contradictions between norms of the private nuclear family and the broader communities that had always been a source of critical intimate bonds for them and their children. This friction between a family unit to aspire to and one that actually provides what children need animated Tamara's childhood, coming to a head when her father died:

> As someone who was raised off and on in an extended community that exceeded blood family, I am a strong adherent in the belief that the privatized family is no way to raise a child. My father died when I was nineteen and were it not for an extended network of "parents" who had held me up my whole life, I do not know how I would have gotten here thus far.

Tamara speaks to the contradictions between the fantasy of the private domestic family that her parents felt the need to emulate and the lived communal realities that were much richer and more supportive. Notably, this idea of assimilation is premised upon anti-Black ideas of the US nation that rest upon a fundamental Black/non-Black and Native/settler rift between those who might aspire toward the norms and privileges of national belonging and those for whom this will never be. Locating a privileged position within this schema, Tamara lived with a sense of needing to hide her (subtly ethnically coded) "excesses" growing up because they signified, she internalized, an inferiority of her nuclear family. This held until the facade of her private family fell apart. Her father's death, itself a consequence of capitalism, rendered the myth of the private family impossible, as she, her mother, and brother needed the emotional, financial, and spiritual support from a broader community who was always a source of support.

This experience rebounded forward into Tamara's process to parenthood that reproduced many of these dynamics within a capitalist context, especially with the 2009 economic collapse and the restructuring of higher education that led most academics privileged enough to get jobs far away from their communities. Reflecting upon this, she stated,

> Even before the pandemic, the geographic exile from much of my community as an academic has made the first few years of

> parenthood rough. When our first child was born in 2017, I grieved the geographical distance from many of my beloved family, blood and chosen. As the reality of the Trump era hit, I could not shake an alarming sense of how unsafe I felt to be two states away from the majority of our safety net and our people. Now, navigating my partner's late pregnancy and the early tender newborn days with our second child in quarantine under COVID only brings a fundamental truth I have learned into sharper relief: living in the isolated unit of the nuclear family is no way to nurture and cherish life in all its stages.

Tamara articulates the ways that the pain of family privatization and isolation reared its head again in this moment of collective crisis. The isolation and privatization she had worked so hard against in her own youth returned full force as something to contend with, the stakes of raising her small children on the forefront.

All our narratives revealed cracks and fissures in the facade of a nuclear family, showing the deeper racial, economic, ethnic, and political histories that cracked the veneer of the family as polished and cohesive. Our discussions also revealed the dangers of the private sphere as a cover for violence and exploitation. Here, Dayjha's narrative was particularly powerful as she worked to tease out the ways that the family fiction had functioned in relationship with generations of internalized oppression manifesting in violence and abuse. As she wrote,

> My very poor and Black family has a lineage of abuse nestled near our hearts. The abuses we have endured, and enacted among each other, is easily traced through the history of slavery. Physical, emotional, sexual abuse is a symptom of white supremacy and settler colonialism. My familial history of abuse and incest has been a multigenerational secret that stays "inside of the home." I have reason to believe this is in connection with our mistrust of police and punitive legal systems. I also would like to believe that my family is full of undisclosed abolitionists, that we hold truths that healing must be done without state intervention. I am not excusing the violence that I, and my biological family, have endured because of the harm that we engage in, but I'm holding compassion and empathy and reiterating the urgency of abolition.

The private/public divide allows cover for family "secret(s)" when no other modes of coping with intergenerational violence are available. Above, Dayjha bravely names the wincing narratives of the violences "nestled" in the "hearts" of her family members, passed down through sexual and physical violence when there is no other outlet. Behind the cover of the "private family," the damages of slavery and colonialism are passed down and perpetuated through generations. The private family thus shrouds these "secrets," mystifying their true source.

As Angela Davis famously argued in her foundational 1972 essay, "Reflections on the Black Woman's Role in the Community of Slaves," there is a contradiction embedded in the figure of the feminized slave, and her dispossession is also her power. Davis writes of "a strange twist of affairs: in the infinite anguish of administering to the needs of men and children around her . . . she was performing the *only* labor of the slave community that could not be directly claimed by the slave master."[46] Dayjha's narrative embeds the contradiction of political power seeded in the experience and positionality of anguish and suffering. A mistrust of the police is borne from an inherently antagonistic relationship to the state.

Dayjha's phrase "undisclosed abolitionists" opens up her lineage of pain and violence to one of transformation. It also reveals the potentialities for resistance, revolution, and worlds lived otherwise that always linger beneath the surface, threatening to bubble up. As we have learned from multiple traditions of abolitionists, our project is as much about generating and investing in different practices and possibilities, and recovering stolen cultural traditions, as it is about simply tearing existing institutions down. It is these alternative imaginaries and lived realities—the spaces of "undisclosed abolitionists"—that we find hope, possibility, and transformation that can help guide collective movements for the forms of freedom that have yet to be achieved.

Imagining Otherwise: Beyond the Nuclear Family Toward Radical Communities of Care

Laying bare our painful relationship to the "family" led us to a second theme: an alternative vision of abolition that comes from building. As we collectively learned from movements of the past, we asked each other, *What makes the current moment different? What are we trying to build in the here and now?* In one of our conversations, Tamara suggested that "the consequences of not centering radical care are so acute . . . in a way that wasn't quite the case in the past." Both Tamara and Verónica reflected on their involvement in movement building and organizing since the nineties, through which they witnessed that unwavering "dedication" to the movement eventually contributed to chronic illness and early death.

In the current moment, this practice of sacrificing one's body for the movement has become so obviously incompatible with what we need in order to reach our revolutionary and abolitionist dreams. We write this as wildfires ravage the West Coast and the government neglect toward the COVID-19 pandemic continues to kill people every day. All four of us are forced to work through this collective tragedy. It is painfully clear that our movements cannot replicate this strain on our bodies. Among all our narratives, we have returned to the necessity of building a movement grounded in care. In grappling with this, Verónica suggested that "maybe it's about reimagining the movement altogether" rather than continuing to propel the same movement and simply tacking "care" onto it. At the same time, the concept of "care" itself is being heavily co-opted under the neoliberal logic of individualized "self-help." In resistance to this, our conversations have aligned with contemporary theorizations of "radical care." Anchored in this ethic, "rather than romanticizing care or ignoring its demons, radical care is built on praxis."[47]

With the understanding that the labor of care is traditionally undervalued, gendered, racialized, and exploitative, we must situate radical care as "a roadmap for an otherwise."[48] This otherwise is what we have been working through together in our writing and conversations. In this process, we have come to realize that radical care must be a practice that strives toward family abolition; this work must be seen and felt as something that contributes and is central to all abolitionist projects. Care without (family) abolition—and, implicitly, the radical reconstruction of deeper networks of care, life, and love—will result in continued exploitation of racialized and feminized labor, and abolition without care will result in an unfinished project that replicates systems of harm.

Based on their yearslong conversations on the politics and intimacies of nurturing of future generations, Verónica and Tamara beautifully articulate their abolitionist dreams of a movement based on care. Verónica described abolition as something that "provides the generative space to dream new ways to care for the next generation." In Verónica's reflections on her grassroots organizing work with migrant mothers, she brings forth her desire for (and witnessing of) mothering as a political practice that is grounded in collective care:

> The necessity to form different family structures led to a desire to expand those structures . . . this fed a feminist collective of women where they could be vulnerable, where they could just be, and restructure how to care and be cared . . . that required a different imagining of collectives that stemmed from a desired and needed rupture with the nuclear family that bred the violence that had hurt them so much and that was keeping them from seeing their children. They linked the need to abolish borders with the need to abolish the nuclear family.

Tamara's dreams, desires, and practices of building a new world also center strongly on restructuring the category mother, dissolving the mythical boundary of movements "in the streets" versus "in the home" and nurturing future generations as a profoundly radical act. As the mother of a newborn and a two-year-old at the time of this writing, she found herself "in the peculiar position of arguing that the family does not work at the same time that [she is] happier than [she has] ever been." Finding herself sitting within this embodied contradiction allowed her to come to this project with many searing questions:

> What is at stake in the bearing of a child, biologically or not, in the cultivation of life, in the ushering in of life forms that overlap with ours, but which neither begin nor end with us? How might our babies be harbingers of the new? How does this connect to the abolitionist work happening out on the streets as we remain locked inside our homes to protect immune systems and build the strength

> of new life? Is not the radical building of life against all odds the foundation of an abolitionist practice? Such are the questions that singe and burn, to which I have no choice but to return at 2:00 a.m., 4:00 a.m., 6:00 a.m. as I rise with our littlest one. These questions lay out the stakes of family abolition for me: the sustenance and continuation of sacred life, itself.

This sustenance and continuation of sacred life requires an ethic and practice of care that can only reach its full potential when we let go of our attachments to structures that harm us, including the nuclear family. In a conversation with Verónica and Tamara, they both reflected on the ways that we fall back on what we know and what we have internalized, including allegiances to abusive family members and patterns of abuse and harm that come out of us. In the midst of a global pandemic where her children have not been able to spend time with anyone other than Tamara and her partner, this "social and physical isolation . . . only highlights the deep need to create a world that can meet them in their love, awe, beauty, and hope."

For Dayjha, her desires are similar in that "the future(s) of kinship and communities that [she] seeks center radical care, love, accountability, mutual aid, and people power." Tamara and Verónica often located a radical reimagining of mothering as their primary entry point into their dreams for family abolition. Dayjha finds herself entering into these conversations through the lens of critical polyamory.[49] She writes,

> When dreaming and thinking about the kinships/connections I envision for my future, I know that it's rooted in practicing polyamory. . . . To me, the lifelong practice of polyamory is a commitment to abolition and anti-coloniality; it is a commitment to abolishing bodies and land as property and investing in nonhierarchical ways of relating and connecting to all sentient life.

Dayjha describes her desires for "autonomy, vulnerable and intimate nonhierarchical connections, and abolition" to be housed within the practice of critical polyamory, and thus she finds it central to her vision of abolishing the nuclear family. The future she desires is "inherently queer, sustained through mutual aid and disability justice, and . . .

forever rooted in caring for life, especially Black trans life, while we are alive."

Similar to Dayjha, Madi's writing and discussions on the future of our world came back to theories and practices of mutual aid:

> When I think about what I'd like to build among the ruins of the systems we are abolishing, I return to mutual aid as a tangible practice that is already being enacted in the here and now. Building that out with love and care is something that I/we need to do in order to make abolition of the family, prisons, policing, etc. a realizable and desirable goal. Something that has become magnified for me during COVID-19 is how much collective capacity we have to show up for each other and crowd out the state systems that are supposedly about "care" but are often instead used to target, criminalize, control, selectively abandon, or kill (social services, healthcare system, police, etc.).

While many may argue that mutual aid is an anarchist-communist theory, Regan de Loggans (Mississippi Choctaw / Ki'Che Maya) reminds us that "Mutual Aid has and always will be a non-western tradition. Mutual Aid is Indigenous lifeways and sovereignty; it is Black thrivance and power, which will outlive anarcho-communist theory."[50] One of its key tenets is "solidarity not charity" (charity includes temporary reallocation), which often occurs during crises such as COVID-19 and then dies out. Mutual aid means long-term commitment to community control; abolition; freedom from capitalism, white supremacy, and settler colonialism; skill and knowledge sharing; and a dedication to seeing communities thrive rather than simply survive through repeated crises.

Ultimately, any serious conversation about abolition of the family returns us here: to the wisdom of communities who have been struggling with these violent institutional forms since their inception. For example, Michi Saagiig Nishnaabeg scholar Leanne Betasamosake Simpson situates Indigenous resistance and survival as something that requires her nation to "join together in a rebellion of love, persistence, commitment, and profound caring and create constellations of co-resistance" and defines Nishnaabeg nationhood as something "based on a series of radiating responsibilities."[51] Here, Simpson exemplifies a practice that sits in opposition to the nuclear family, which is predicated on the logic of (property) ownership, individualization, and a profound lack of care.

Simpson explicitly connects the heteropatriarchal family to the continuance of settler colonialism by arguing that "the more destruction our relationships carry, the more destruction our political systems carry, and the less we are able to defend and protect our lands, and the easier it is to dispossess."[52] Furthermore, she argues that two-spirit and queer (2SQ) Indigenous youth are particularly situated, due to their direct threat to settler notions of gender, sexuality, and heteropatriarchy, to rebuke this form of dispossession that manifests via the nuclear family.[53]

Kim TallBear, a Sisseton Wahpeton Oyate scholar, expands upon these arguments in her critical work on "making love and relations beyond settler sex and family."[54] TallBear argues that white colonizers attempted to eliminate Indigenous peoples via assimilation into whiteness, and that a key part of this elimination/assimilation occurs via the institutional enforcement of marriage, nuclear family, and monogamy.[55] Emerging most powerfully alongside the nineteenth-century General Allotment Act and boarding school system, this imperative to replicate the white nuclear family was "simultaneously lorded over Indigenous peoples as an aspirational model and used to justify curtailing their biological reproduction and steal their children."[56] In response to this continued weaponization of the nuclear family as a tool of settler control, TallBear argues that "we must collectively oppose a system of compulsory settler sexuality and family that continues building a nation upon Indigenous genocide and that marks Indigenous and other marginalized relations as deviant."[57] Ultimately, TallBear issues a demand that decolonial projects must "recogniz[e] possibilities of other kinds of intimacies—not focused on biological reproduction and making population, but caretaking precious kin that come to us in diverse ways."[58]

Both Simpson's and TallBear's work help ground our understanding of family abolition in the necessity of Indigenous resurgence and decolonization; the nuclear family took shape as a tool of the nation-state, and its abolition necessitates the prioritization of Indigenous knowledge, sovereignty, and self-determination. Honoring this call, we have worked from our various vantage points with honesty and vulnerability to do our own work toward these shared ends.

CONCLUSION

My grandparents willed me strength,
My parents willed me pride,
I will to you rage.
I give you a world incomplete,
A world where women still are property and chattel,
Where color still shuts doors,
Where sexual choice still threatens,
But I give you a legacy of doers,
Of people who take risks,
To chisel the crack wider.

—Pat Parker, "Legacy"

Above, we reflect upon the radical practices of creating communal family structures, offering collective care to the young, critical polyamory, and mutual aid. These practices are not meant to be an exhaustive list; rather they help to offer us some glimpses into an alternative praxis of family abolition in the making in our lives.

We close where we began our genealogy: with the words of Pat Parker. Her beautiful poem, "Legacy," above, is dedicated to her then-young daughter Anastasia just years before her own death.[59] Ultimately, we feel that family abolition is oriented around this insistence to honor the legacies of past generations that are always feeding the next, creating a throughline of wisdom and strength. This power, beauty, and strength is often associated with the bonds of bionormative family, but as Parker writes, what sustains it is the intensity of love, rage, and desire for freedom.

As an intergenerational group, our writing process has been the work of grasping at this line, mapping the knowledge and wisdom we have received from past and present struggles to abolish the family. In alignment with the tenants of abolitionist feminism, we moved from our intimate lives to articulate a praxis of family abolition that deconstructs the "out in the streets" versus "in the home" divide when it comes to revolutionary work. By bringing our "private" lives into contemporary theorizations of family abolition through the lenses of radical mothering, critical polyamory, mutual aid, and more, we found just how much we need one another. We need love, accountability, collective care, connection, interdependence, and radical commitment to each other. Moreover, our movements need to be oriented around these actions. This is no easy task, but it is the one to which we must commit. This is the legacy that we must struggle to pass down to all who will continue the weaving of our abolitionist dreams.

In many ways, this process has raised more questions, tensions, and contradictions than it has answered. In particular, we find ourselves grappling with the world in a moment when we are torn between the political mandate to take to the streets in movement and attend to the intense, urgent, and daily care work in the domestic sphere. This emerged as particularly tricky as we all worked to navigate our own relationships toward social relations for which there are no established roadmaps.

We were astounded by the depth and power of issues that rose to the fore when we committed to these conversations, and this essay only scratches the surface. One thing that strikes us as we reread this analysis is the extent to which we are all survivors who carry great resilience and, often, unharnessed strength. What power could be directed toward political transformation if we de-privatized our narratives as energy toward our shared movements? How might we who call ourselves abolitionists collectively prioritize the nurturance and survival of radical/abolitionist healers, who have and will always chart our path toward another world beyond the family?

We also remain convinced that the polar dichotomization of care work and political work causes great harm. With these realizations in mind, we end with more questions, which we hope will invite the reader into further struggle with us: What would a movement look like that did not allow for the false dichotomies of the streets and our homes as sites for revolutionary work? How is the abolition of family a requirement for the dismantling of other borders of nation, citizenship, race, and more fundamentally, a division between those afforded life and those whose lives are constructed to be expendable? And, what does it mean to fully contend with the praxis and totality of family abolition as a mandate in all our movements for social justice?

BIBLIOGRAPHY

Atkinson, Ti-Grace. *Radical Feminism and Love.* (The Feminists, 1969).

Belinsky, Zoe. "Gender and Family Abolition as an Expansive and Not Reductive Process." Medium, September 11, 2019. https://medium.com/@malkekvmachashayfele/gender-and-family-abolition-as-an-expansive-and-not-reductive-process-d933f1f71da2.

brown, adrienne m. *Emergent Strategy: Shaping Change, Changing Worlds.* Chico, CA: AK Press, 2017.

Caballero, Cecilia, et al., eds. *The Chicana M(other)work Anthology: Porque Sin Madres No Hay Revolución.* Tucson: University of Arizona Press and Feminist Wire Books, 2019.

Capper, Beth, and Arlen Austin. "'Wages for Housework Means Wages against Heterosexuality': On the Archives of Black Women for Wages for Housework and Wages Due Lesbians." *GLQ: A Journal of Lesbian and Gay Studies* 24, no. 4 (2018): 445–66.

Connell, Raewyn. *Gender and Power: Society, the Person, and Sexual Politics.* Stanford, CA: Stanford University Press, 1987.

Critical Resistance Publications Collective, "Critical Resistance to the Prison-Industrial Complex," *Social Justice* 27, 3 (Fall 2000): 1–5.

Davis, Angela Y. *Are Prisons Obsolete?* New York: Seven Stories Press, 2003.

———. "Uprising and Abolition: Angela Davis on Movement Building, 'Defund the Police' and Where We Go from Here," June 12, 2020, *Democracy Now!* https://www.democracynow.org/2020/6/12/angela_davis_historic_moment.

Davis, Angela Y., et al. "Sunday School: Unlock Us, Abolition in Our Lifetime." Dream Defenders, June 14, 2020. https://www.facebook.com/watch/live/?v=615123319385564&ref=watch_permalink.

Davis, Mike. "Hell Factories in the Field: A Prison-Industrial Complex," *Nation* 260, no. 7 (1995): 229–34.

D'Emilio, John. "Capitalism and Gay Identity." In *Powers of Desire: The Politics of Sexuality*, edited by Ann Snitow, Christine Stansell, and Sharon Thompson, 100–13. New Feminist Library Series. New York: Monthly Review Press and NYU Press, 1983.

Firestone, Shulamith. *The Dialectic of Sex: The Case for Feminist Revolution.* New York: Farrar, Straus, and Giroux, 1970.

Franklin, Sarah. "Revisiting Reprotech: Firestone and the Question of Technology." In *Further Adventures in the Dialectic of Sex: Critical Essays on Shulamith Firestone*, edited by Mandy Merck and Stella Sandford, 29–60. London: Palgrave, 2010.

"Gay Liberation in New York City." OutHistory. Accessed June 21, 2020. http://outhistory.org/exhibits/show/gay-liberation-in-new-york-cit/3rd-world/pg-1.

Griffiths, Kate, and Jules Gleeson. *Kinderkommunismus: A Feminist Analysis of the 21st-Century Family and a Communist Proposal for Its Abolition*. Subversion Press, 2015. https://subversionpress.wordpress.com/2015/06/30/kinderkommunismus.

Guinier, Lani, and Gerald Torres. *The Miner's Canary: Enlisting Race, Resisting Power, Transforming Democracy.* Cambridge, MA: Harvard University Press, 2002.

Gumbs, Alexis Pauline, China Martens, and Mai'a Williams. *Revolutionary Mothering: Love on the Front Lines.* Oakland, CA: PM Press, 2016.

Gumbs, Alexis Pauline. "'We Can Learn to Mother Ourselves': A Dialogically Produced Audience and Black Feminist Publishing 1979 to 'Present.'" *Gender Forum: An Internet Journal for Gender Studies* 22 (2008): 39–55. http://genderforum.org/wp-content/uploads/2017/04/0822_BlackWomensWritingRevisited.pdf.

Gutierrez, Aleyda Marisol Cervantes, et al. "The Demand: Pasts, Presents and Futures of Black, Indigenous, and Queer of Colour Feminisms." In *Gendering Globalization, Globalizing Gender Postcolonial Perspectives*, edited by Gul Caliskan, 305–24. London: Oxford University Press, 2020.

Hansberry, Lorraine. "The Negro Writer and His Roots: Toward a New Romanticism." *Black Scholar* 12, no. 2 (1981): 2–12.

Hobart, Hi'ilei Julia Kawehipuaakahaopulani, and Tamara Kneese, "Radical Care: Survival Strategies for Uncertain Times." *Social Text* 38, no. 1 (2020): 1–16.

HoSang, Daniel, and Joseph E. Lowndes. "State Abandonment and Militia Revolt: White Occupation, Native Land, and Black Lives." In *Producers, Parasites, Patriots: Race and the New Right-Wing Politics of Precarity*, 129–52. Minneapolis: University of Minnesota Press, 2019.

King, Tiffany Lethabo. "Black 'Feminisms' and Pessimism: Abolishing Moynihan's Negro Family." *Theory & Event* 21, no. 1 (January 2018): 68–87.

Levy, Terry. "Four Styles of Adult Attachment." Evergreen Psychotherapy Center, May 26, 2017. https://www.evergreenpsychotherapycenter.com/styles-adult-attachment/.

Lewis, Sophie. *Full Surrogacy Now: Feminism against Family.* London: Verso, 2019.

Lindsey, Kay. "The Black Woman as Woman." In *The Black Woman: An Anthology*, edited by Toni Cade Bambara, 103–108. New York: Signet, 1970.

Mogul, Joey L., Andrea J. Ritchie, and Kay Whitlock, "Setting the Historical Stage: Colonial Legacies." In *Queer (In)justice: The Criminalization of LGBT People in the United States*, 1–19. Boston: Beacon Press, 2011.

———. *Love without Emergency: I Want This but I Feel Like I'm Going to Die / Writing on Trauma, Attachment, and Polyamory.* Montreal: Clementine Morrigan, 2019.

O'Brien, M. E., "To Abolish the Family: The Working-Class Family and Gender Liberation in Capitalist Development." *Endnotes* 5 (October 2019): 360–417.

Parker, Pat "Revolution: It's Not Neat or Pretty or Quick." In *This Bridge Called My Back: Writings by Radical Women of Color*, 3rd ed. Edited by Cherríe Moraga and Gloria Anzaldúa, 267–72. Berkeley, CA: Third Woman Press, 2002.

Rainier, Dachine, and Holley Cantine. "Prison Etiquette 1950." In *The New Abolitionists: (Neo)Slave Narratives and Contemporary Prison Writings*, edited by Joy James, 5–12. Albany: SUNY Press, 2005.

Rich, Adrienne. "Compulsory Heterosexuality and Lesbian Existence." In *Blood, Bread and Poetry: Selected Prose, 1979–1985*, 23–75. New York: Norton, 1986.

———. "Notes toward a Politics of Location." In *Blood, Bread, and Poetry: Selected Prose, 1979–1985*, 210–31. New York: Norton, 1986.

Roberts, Dorothy. "Abolishing Policing Also Means Abolishing Family Regulation." *Chronicle of Social Change*, June 16, 2020. https://chronicleofsocialchange.org/child-welfare-2/abolishing-policing-also-means-abolishing-family-regulation/44480.

Rodríguez, Dylan. *Forced Passages: Imprisoned Radical Intellectuals and the US Prison Regime*. Minneapolis: University of Minnesota Press, 2006.

Solis, Marie. "We Can't Have a Feminist Future without Abolishing the Family." *Vice*, February 21, 2020. https://www.vice.com/en_us/article/qjdzwb/sophie-lewis-feminist-abolishing-the-family-full-surrogacy-now.

Spillers, Hortense J. "Mama's Baby, Papa's Maybe: An American Grammar Book." *Diacritics* 17, no. 2 (Summer 1987) 64–81.

TallBear, Kim. The Critical Polyamorist: Polyamory, Indigeneity, and Cultural Politics in the US and Canada. http://www.criticalpolyamorist.com/.

———. "Identity Is a Poor Substitute for Relating: Genetic Ancestry, Critical Polyamory, Property, and Relations," April 13, 2020. http://www.criticalpolyamorist.com/homeblog/identity-is-a-poor-substitute-for-relating-genetic-ancestry-critical-polyamory-property-and-relations.

———. "Making Love and Relations beyond Settler Sex and Family." In *Making Kin, Not Population*, edited by Adele Clarke and Donna Haraway, 145–64. Chicago: Prickly Paradigm, 2018.

———. "Yes, Your Pleasure! Yes, Self-Love! And Don't Forget That Settler Sex Is a Structure." *Critical Polyamorist*, April 22, 2018. http://www.criticalpolyamorist.com/homeblog/yes-your-pleasure-yes-self-love-and-dont-forget-settler-sex-is-a-structure.

Third World Gay Revolution. "What We Want, What We Believe." In *Out of the Closets: Voices of Gay Liberation*, edited by Karla Jay and Allen Young. New York: Douglas Book Corporation, 1972.

Tuck, Eve, and K. Wayne Yang. "Decolonization Is Not a Metaphor." *Decolonization: Indigeneity, Education & Society* 1, no. 1 (2012): 1–40.

Vélez, Verónica, "Madres en Lucha: Forging Motherhood as Political Movement Building across Borders." In *The Chicana M(other)work Anthology: Porque Sin Madres No Hay Revolución*, edited by Cecilia Caballero et al. Tucson: University of Arizona Press and Feminist Wire Books, 2019.

Wang, Jackie. *Carceral Capitalism*. Semiotext(e) Intervention Series 21. South Pasadena, CA: Semiotext(e), 2018.

Williams, Mai'a. "Radical Mothering as a Pathway to Liberation," *Millenium: Journal of International Studies* 47, no. 3 (2019): 498–512.

Wyland, Francie. *Motherhood, Lesbianism and Child Custody*. 1st ed. Toronto: Wages Due Lesbians, 1977.

NOTES

1 Angela Y. Davis et al., "Sunday School: Unlock Us, Abolition in Our Lifetime," June 14, 2020, Dream Defenders, https://www.facebook.com/watch/live/?v=615123319385564&ref=watch_permalink.

2 Davis et al., "Sunday School."

3 Angela Y. Davis, "Uprising and Abolition: Angela Davis on Movement Building, 'Defund the Police' and Where We Go from Here," June 12, 2020, *Democracy Now!*, https://www.democracynow.org/2020/6/12/angela_davis_historic_moment.

4 Dylan Rodríguez, *Forced Passages: Imprisoned Radical Intellectuals and the US Prison Regime* (Minneapolis: University of Minnesota Press, 2006), 7.

5 Angela Y. Davis. *Are Prisons Obsolete?* (New York: Seven Stories Press, 2003).

6 Anna M. Agathangelou et al., "Intimate Investments: Homonormativity, Global Lockdown, and the Seductions of Empire," *Radical History Review*, no. 100 (2008): 120–43.

7 Kim Tallbear, "Making Love and Relations Beyond Settler Sex and Family," in *Making Kin Not Population*, ed. Adele E. Clarke and Donna Haraway (Chicago: Prickly Paradigm, 2018), 145–64.

8 Angela Willey, *Undoing Monogamy: The Politics of Science and the Possibilities of Biology* (Durham: Duke University Press, 2016).

9 Cathy J. Cohen, "Punks, Bulldaggers, and Welfare Queens: The Radical Potential of Queer Politics?" *GLQ: A Journal of Lesbian and Gay Studies* 3, no. 4 (1997): 437–65; Roderick A. Ferguson, *Aberrations in Black: Toward a Queer of Color Critique* (Minneapolis: University of Minnesota Press, 2004); Aliyyah I. Abdur-Rahman, *Against the Closet: Identity, Political Longing, and Black Figuration* (Durham: Duke University Press, 2012).

10 Tiffany Lethabo King, "Black 'Feminisms' and Pessimism: Abolishing Moynihan's Negro Family," *Theory & Event* 21, no. 1 (2018): 68–87; Sophie Lewis, *Full Surrogacy Now: Feminism against Family* (London: Verso, 2019); Zoe Belinsky, "Gender and Family Abolition as an Expansive and Not Reductive Process," Medium, September 11, 2019, https://medium.com/@malkekvmachashayfele/gender-and-family-abolition-as-an-expansive-and-not-reductive-process-d933f1f71da2.

11 Dorothy Roberts, "Abolishing Policing Also Means Abolishing Family Regulation," *Chronicle of Social Change*, June 16, 2020, https://chronicleofsocialchange.org/child-welfare-2/abolishing-policing-also-means-abolishing-family-regulation/44480.

12 Jackie Wang, *Carceral Capitalism* (South Pasadena, CA: Semiotext(e), 2018), 316.

13 Pat Parker, "Revolution: It's Not Neat or Pretty or Quick," in *This Bridge Called My Back: Writings by Radical Women of Color*, 3rd ed., eds. Cherríe Moraga and Gloria Anzaldúa (Berkeley, CA: Third Woman Press), 267–72.

14 Tamara Lea Spira, "'I Give You a World Incomplete': Pat Parker's Revolution and the Unfinished Legacy of 1970s Feminist Radicalisms," *Feminist Studies* 48, no. 1 (2022, forthcoming).

15 King, "Black 'Feminisms' and Pessimism," 68–87.

16 Kay Lindsey, "The Black Woman as Woman," in *The Black Woman: An Anthology*, ed. Toni Cade Bambara (New York: Signet, 1970), 103–08.

17 Hortense Spillers, "Mama's Baby, Papa's Maybe: An American Grammar Book," *Diacritics* 17, no. 2 (Summer 1987): 64–81.

18 King, "Black 'Feminisms' and Pessimism," 68.

19 King, 70.

20 King, 74.

21 Francie Wyland, *Motherhood, Lesbianism and Child Custody*, 1st ed. (Toronto: Wages Due Lesbians, 1977); Beth Capper and Arlen Austin, "'Wages for Housework Means Wages against Heterosexuality': On the Archives of Black Women for Wages for Housework and Wages Due Lesbians," *GLQ: A Journal of Lesbian and Gay Studies* 24, no. 4 (2018): 445–66.

22 It is important to contextualize Firestone's understanding of gender as part and parcel of the discourse of her contemporaries, which has since been critiqued for essentialist understandings of gender. For an important contemporary rereading of Firestone, please see Sarah Franklin, "Revisiting Reprotech: Firestone and the Question of Technology," in *Further Adventures in the Dialectic of Sex: Critical Essays on Shulamith Firestone*, eds. Mandy Merck and Stella Sandford (London: Palgrave, 2010), 29–60.

23 Sophie Lewis, *Full Surrogacy Now: Feminism against Family* (London: Verso, 2019).

24 Kate Griffiths and Jules Gleeson, *Kinderkommunismus: A Feminist Analysis of the 21st-Century Family and a Communist Proposal for Its Abolition* (Subversion Press, 2015), https://subversionpress.wordpress.com/2015/06/30/kinderkommunismus/.

25 Marie Solis, "We Can't Have a Feminist Future without Abolishing the Family," *Vice*, February 21, 2020, https://www.vice.com/en_us/article/qjdzwb/sophie-lewis-feminist-abolishing-the-family-full-surrogacy-now.

26 M. E. O'Brien, "To Abolish the Family: The Working-Class Family and Gender Liberation in Capitalist Development," *Endnotes* 5 (October 2019): 86–137. We are thankful for the anonymous reviewer who brought this text to our attention.

27 Ti-Grace Atkinson, *Radical Feminism and Love* (The Feminists, 1969).

28 Adrienne Rich, "Compulsory Heterosexuality and Lesbian Existence," *Blood, Bread, and Poetry: Selected Prose, 1979–1985* (New York: Norton, 1986).

29 Adrienne Rich, "Notes Toward a Politics of Location." *Blood, Bread, and Poetry: Selected Prose, 1979–1985* (New York: Norton, 1986), 210–31.

30 Raewyn Connell, *Gender and Power: Society, the Person, and Sexual Politics* (Stanford, CA: Stanford University Press, 1987), 37.

31 Connell, *Gender and Power*, 37.

32 Third World Gay Revolution, "What We Want, What We Believe," in *Out of the Closets: Voices of Gay Liberation*, eds. Karla Jay and Allen Young (New York: Douglas Book Corporation, 1972).

33 "Gay Liberation in New York City." OutHistory. Accessed June 21, 2020, http://outhistory.org/exhibits/show/gay-liberation-in-new-york-cit/3rd-world/pg-1.

34 John D'Emilio, "Capitalism and Gay Identity" in *The Lesbian and Gay Studies Reader*, eds. Henry Abelove, Michèle Aina Barale, and David M. Halperin, (New York: Routledge, 1993), 467–76.

35 D'Emilio, 475.

36 D'Emilio, 475.

37 D'Emilio, 475.

38 Cohen, "Punks, Bulldaggers, and Welfare Queens."

39 Alexis Pauline Gumbs, China Martens, and Mai'a Williams, *Revolutionary Mothering: Love on the Front Lines* (Oakland, CA: PM Press, 2016); Cecilia Caballero, ed., *The Chicana M(other)work Anthology: Porque Sin Madres No Hay Revolución*. (Tucson: University of Arizona Press and Feminist Wire Books, 2019).

40 Gumbs, Martens, and Williams, *Revolutionary Mothering.*

41 Mai'a Williams, "Radical Mothering as a Pathway to Liberation," *Millennium: Journal of International Studies* 47, no. 3 (June 2019): 497–512.

42 Gumbs, Martens, and Williams, *Revolutionary Mothering: Love on the Front Lines*, 116.

43 "What Is Reproductive Justice?" SisterSong. Accessed June 21, 2020, https://www.sistersong.net/reproductive-justice.

44 Heewon Chang, Faith Wambura Ngunjiri, and Kathy-Ann C. Hernandez, *Collaborative Autoethnography*, Developing Qualitative Inquiry, vol .8 (Walnut Creek, CA: Left Coast Press, 2012).

45 Cohen, "Punks, Bulldaggers, and Welfare Queens"; Ferguson, *Aberrations in Black*; Abdur-Rahman, *Against the Closet.*

46 Angela Y. Davis, "Reflections on the Black Woman's Role in the Community of Slaves," in *The Angela Y. Davis Reader*, ed. Joy James (Boston: Blackwell, 1998), 111–29.

47 Hi'ilei Julia Kawehipuaakahaopulani Hobart and Tamara Kneese, "Radical Care: Survival Strategies for Uncertain Times," *Social Text* 38, no. 1 (2020): 1–16.

48 Hobart and Kneese, 1–16.

49 Here we learn from the work of Kim TallBear. Please see Kim TallBear, "Making Love and Relations beyond Settler Sex and Family," in *Making Kin, Not Population*, eds. Adele Clarke and Donna Haraway (Chicago: Prickly Paradigm), 145–64.

50 Regan de Loggans, "Let's Talk Mutual Aid," n.d., https://dochub.com/rloggans/jo3xELpR3ZO8yz8wJBa7nr/loggans-mutual-aid-zine-pdf?dt=Ls_myQXhz6RrrzS59DVW.

51 Leanne Betasamosake Simpson. *As We Have Always Done: Indigenous Freedom through Radical Resistance*. (Minneapolis: University of Minnesota Press, 2017), 9.

52 Simpson, 123.

53 Simpson, 127, 144.

54 TallBear, "Making Love and Relations."

55 TallBear, 147.

56 TallBear, 147.

57 TallBear, 152.

58 TallBear, 154.

59 Pat Parker, "Legacy," in *Jonestown and Other Madness* (Ithaca, NY: Firebrand Books, 1985), 67–75; Spira, "'I Give You a World Incomplete': Pat Parker's Revolution."

Shellyne Rodriguez, "Purgatorio (Shelter System after Displacement)," 2015

STATE-SANCTIONED SUICIDES AND LIFE-MAKING RESISTANCE IN CARCERAL CONTEXTS

Colby Lenz

I went to borrow scissors from the guards last week, and I was told that they don't hand out scissors anymore because they have special industrial scissors now for cutting down bodies. He showed them to me. That's how normal it is.

—April Harris, California Institution for Women, April 2015

SUICIDE CRISIS: CALIFORNIA INSTITUTION FOR WOMEN

Between 2013 and 2017, the California Institution for Women (CIW)—one of two California state women's prisons—sustained a suicide rate far worse than the average rate for imprisoned women across the US.* The suicide rate at CIW was eight times the national average and five times the average for all California prisons.[1] Since 2013 there have been at least seventeen preventable deaths at this prison and, until recently, no state investigation or intervention. The majority of the women who died by suicide were low-income women of color who, at the time of their deaths, were isolated in segregated mental health units. Most were in their twenties and thirties. The suicide attempt rate also increased dramatically through these years—even when accounting

* The Bureau of Justice Statistics, the primary statistical agency of the Department of Justice, produces statistics on suicide rates of imprisoned people in federal, state, local, and tribal jurisdictions. They assign gender by gender-segregated correctional institution, which is not reflective of the populations in these institutions. In particular, this practice excludes transgender and gender nonconforming people from data collection, analysis, and dissemination.

for the well-known prison practice of under-reporting suicide attempts.[2] While the suicide rates have been the highest at CIW, the death and suicide attempt rates at the other California state women's prison, the Central California Women's Facility (CCWF), have also been alarming.

In California, there is no institution with the authority to both monitor and intervene in state prison conditions.* Without an oversight body with the authority to investigate, report on, and enact accountability for wrongdoing in California prisons, aggrieved people and communities are left to plead their cases to the media or to elected officials. Most elected officials have very little access to information about prison conditions, very little commitment to constituents behind bars, and very little experience exercising power over law enforcement by demanding investigation and proactive disciplinary action. In the case of CIW, without grassroots organizing within and across prison walls, the crisis would have accelerated and the women who died in custody would have been further disappeared by the active concealing of the conditions that led to their deaths.

The statewide organization California Coalition for Women Prisoners (CCWP) organizes with incarcerated people and impacted family and friends to track and report negligent and deadly prison conditions and demand answers and accountability. Since 1995 CCWP has been advocating across prison walls for the survival and release of imprisoned people. A volunteer-based grassroots social justice organization with members inside and outside prison, CCWP challenges the institutional violence imposed on women, transgender people, and communities of color by the prison-industrial complex (PIC).† CCWP sees the struggle for racial and gender justice as central to dismantling the PIC and prioritizes the leadership of the people, families, and communities most impacted in building this movement. Since the suicide crisis escalated at CIW, CCWP worked to expose the crisis and demand its end. We learned about the

---

* In California, several ongoing, decades-long class action lawsuits (e.g. Plata/Coleman v. Newsom) have instituted monitoring agencies for prison healthcare and mental healthcare. While these agencies provide some types of monitoring, their oversight is limited by the terms of the lawsuits and does not qualify as independent, comprehensive oversight of healthcare in California prisons.

† I have been working as a volunteer legal advocate and organizer with CCWP since 2003.

crisis through working closely with incarcerated people at CIW and by connecting with family members who reached out for support after learning of the deaths or suicide attempts of their loved ones in custody.

The following account analyzes how prisons construct and institutionalize "mental illness" and suicide through a death-making culture and multiple practices of permanent and deadly confinement. Examining specific examples of *mental health punitivity* at CIW reveals how prisons interpret, manage, and punish human connection as threat and contraband. Critically, this analysis also explores life-making insights and disruptions of prison practices born out of a community organizing campaign to address state-sanctioned deaths at CIW. In this campaign, imprisoned people, their families, and other advocates developed resistant strategies that challenged and sometimes subverted death-making practice and culture through sustaining human connection and organizing for the survival and release of imprisoned people.

PRISON SUICIDE WATCH: MENTAL HEALTH AS PUNITIVITY

The multiple convergences between criminalization and mental health tell a story about incarceration's core destructive purpose: to stigmatize, control, punish, and isolate. For example, people labeled with mental illness are disproportionately vulnerable to policing and incarceration because mental illness is constructed as a crime.[3] The lack of community-based mental healthcare drives the criminalization of people with mental health needs that exceed the resources available to them, creating a crisis in which local jails and state prisons are used to warehouse thousands of people with acute mental health needs.[4] Prison officials and parole boards also use junk science to characterize "criminal behavior" in terms of pathology, such as sociopathy, not to enable mental health services, but to justify prolonged incarceration and escalated punishment.*

* For example, to justify preventing media from speaking with incarcerated people, J. P. Tremblay, assistant secretary of the Youth and Adult Corrections Agency, remarked that media interviews would give "inmates" an "opportunity for a public forum in which they can espouse their often sociopathic philosophies," Wisely, 1997.

Further, mental health institutions themselves are often carceral institutions. While some psychiatric treatment centers are formally integrated into state and federal prison systems, disability activists have argued that even those psychiatric lockup institutions that are not officially structured within a prison system are still part of the prison nation as punitive systems of forced confinement.[5] Finally, the experience of incarceration itself—the ongoing traumatic violence of constant surveillance, forced caging, physical and sexual violence, lack of control over one's future, and forced separation from loved ones and other forms of social isolation—creates profound mental health consequences and intensifies existing mental health struggles.[6] This interlocked relationship between carceral violence and criminalized mental health set the stage for how the CIW suicide crisis unfolded. The CIW suicide crisis demonstrates how prisons actively merge mental healthcare with punitivity, distorting the terms through which to understand the practice of care, and ultimately constructing new forms of "mental illness" and "treatment" through violent and punitive terms. For example, in carceral contexts, suicide prevention *is equated with* punitive isolation. The isolating, punishing practice of "suicide watch," as I explore below, is a clear example of this punitive merge. Prisons create new terms to label the ways that imprisoned people adapt and manage punitive isolation, constructing adaptive mental illness to justify increasing punishment, including extended incarceration. Therefore, in prison, death-making conditions are asserted as conditions that are *required* to support mental health. Within this carceral logic, various forms and levels of isolation and torture are refigured as mental healthcare.

Prison mental healthcare relies on multiple structures and techniques of isolation and deprivation, both by isolating people in sustained, violent ways and by isolating *itself* from the public. Isolation structures prison practice from the scale of the individual to the relational to the systemic. For example, prisons produce biochemical and psychological isolation of incarcerated people by forcibly medicating them, denying them useful medical and mental healthcare, or punishing them for actions interpreted or labeled as symptoms of psychological disturbance.

Prison mental health crisis policies deny people access to any available human connection and support—both inside and outside of the prison—by caging people in various forms of isolated housing (segregation, suicide watch, psychiatric inpatient, and more). Studies increasingly show the destructive power of isolating individuals within prisons, including its particular impacts on people already traumatized or mentally vulnerable, as well as its power to undermine and destroy human sociality.[7] Indeed, researchers repeatedly assert that prison isolation policies are a form of psychological violence that both compounds existing mental health crises and *creates* new ones. Further, denying incarcerated people human contact limits opportunities for people to report the existence and impact of the violence they experience in the name of mental healthcare. The prison, therefore, isolates to punish as well as to conceal punishment.

Structurally, prisons produce organized systems of isolation to streamline the management-punishment of people with mental health needs, including those labeled as mentally ill before and during incarceration. For example, the California Department of Corrections and Rehabilitation (CDCR) uses a multitiered pyramid system to sort and organize the containment of people labeled with differing degrees of mental illness (see "Levels of Care" and "Levels of Punishment" diagrams below as a reference). Described in an audit report as "escalating levels of mental health care to inmates,"[8] the pyramid reflects a taxonomy of increasingly intensified forms of punitive isolation that correlates with assigned levels of mental health needs.[9] The Correctional Clinical Case Management System (Triple CMS) classification is at the bottom level and is applied to anybody who accesses any kind of mental healthcare, including onetime requests for counseling. Many people avoid accessing basic Triple CMS services because the classification officially flags a mental health issue in their record and can stigmatize those who seek support. This can become a disadvantage when seeking prison release because the parole board and other prison officials routinely use Triple CMS status as evidence of mental health instability to justify denying parole and prolonging punishment.

The next three ascending levels on the pyramid—Enhanced Outpatient Program (EOP), Crisis Beds (or suicide watch), and Inpatient Care (called Psychiatric Inpatient Program or PIP at CIW)—all include explicit pro-isolation policies and treatment protocols. The EOP, called the Special Care Unit (SCU) at CIW, houses people classified as needing more mental healthcare than those labeled Triple CMS. While the unit is structured by shared cells, its standard practice includes isolating people in standing cages within the unit's program office when they "misbehave," a category that can include anything from attempting suicide to threatening to submit a complaint against a guard. People who cut or show other known signs of mental health vulnerabilities are routinely subjected to increased isolation as treatment-punishment. People in the EOP are also repeatedly threatened with and sent to the next level on the pyramid: isolated crisis bed cells. In this level, people in acute mental health crisis are held captive in solitary cells, a practice commonly referred to as "suicide watch."

At the top of the pyramid is Inpatient Care, or the PIP, which contains people classified as requiring the highest level of control-care. Touted by the CDCR as one of their best mental health inpatient programs, PIP "provides care for inmates whose conditions cannot be successfully treated in the outpatient setting or in short-term mental health crisis bed stays."[10] According to reports of people who have been imprisoned in PIP, the "highest level of care" can include twenty-three hours per day in a solitary cell, no access to phone calls, extremely limited access to mail and property (such as books), and zero to limited access to programming.[11] If allowed access to programming, people who have been in PIP report that it typically amounts to forty-five minutes of watching a movie or coloring while shackled to a wheelchair.

Table below from the report, *California Department of Corrections and Rehabilitation: It Must Increase Its Efforts to Prevent and Respond to Inmate Suicides* (California State Auditor, 2017). Sources: Corrections' 2009 *Mental Health Program Guide* and 2014 *Annual Accomplishments* report.

Levels of Care in Corrections' Mental Health System

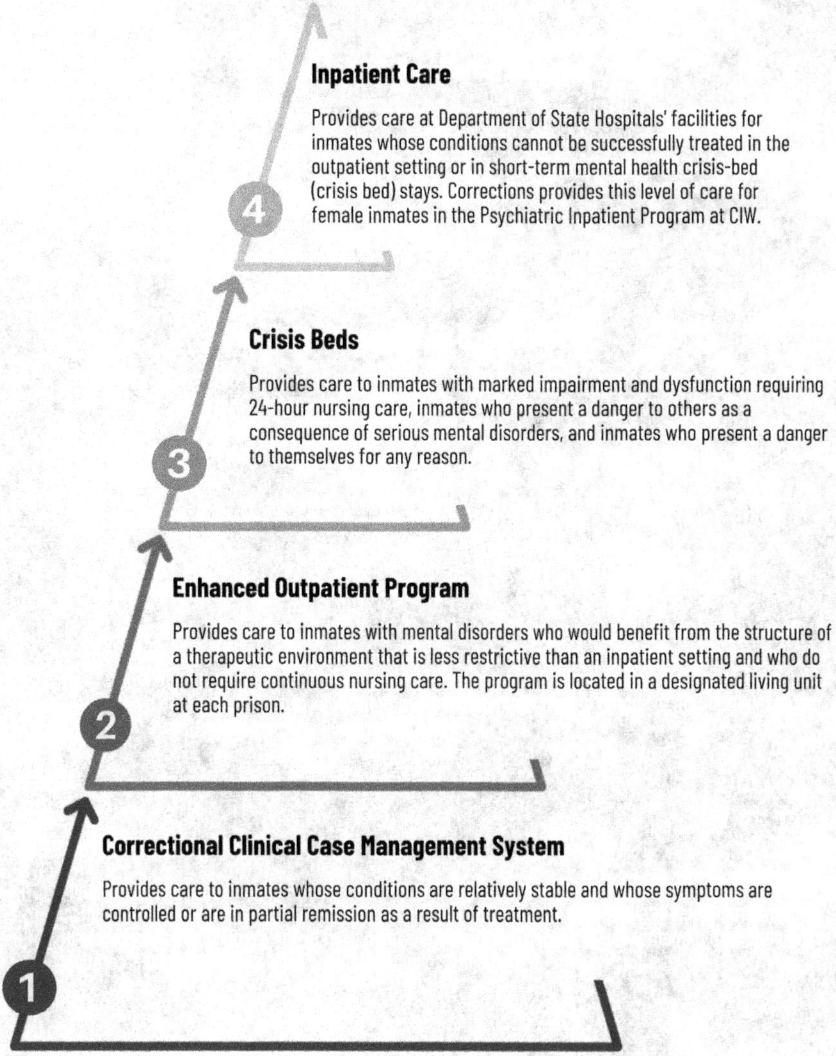

4

Inpatient Care

Provides care at Department of State Hospitals' facilities for inmates whose conditions cannot be successfully treated in the outpatient setting or in short-term mental health crisis-bed (crisis bed) stays. Corrections provides this level of care for female inmates in the Psychiatric Inpatient Program at CIW.

3

Crisis Beds

Provides care to inmates with marked impairment and dysfunction requiring 24-hour nursing care, inmates who present a danger to others as a consequence of serious mental disorders, and inmates who present a danger to themselves for any reason.

2

Enhanced Outpatient Program

Provides care to inmates with mental disorders who would benefit from the structure of a therapeutic environment that is less restrictive than an inpatient setting and who do not require continuous nursing care. The program is located in a designated living unit at each prison.

1

Correctional Clinical Case Management System

Provides care to inmates whose conditions are relatively stable and whose symptoms are controlled or are in partial remission as a result of treatment.

Table below provided by author to mirror the "levels of care" as described by the California Department of Corrections' "mental health system" pyramid, shown on the left. The corresponding "levels of punishment" reflect prison policies and practices, as well as reports from incarcerated people.

Levels of Punishment in Corrections' Mental Health System

OFF THE MAP: "Psychiatric Segregation Unit (PSU)"

PSU isn't included on the CDCR pyramid, but is operated by the California Institution for Women. Like level 4, it removes all contact from others inside and outside of prison, except here there are no opportunities to "earn" less isolation.

4 Extreme Isolation & Social Exile

Up to 23 hours per day isolation in a solitary cell, no access to phone calls, extremely limited access to mail and property, and zero to limited access to programming. Some report being denied any level of outside engagement if seen having friendly connection with other incarcerated people.

3 Suicide Watch as Solitary Confinement

Crisis Beds, commonly referred to as Suicide Watch, cage people who are in acute mental health crisis in often freezing cold solitary cells – empty except for a thin mattress on the floor – where they are stripped down and clothed in a sleeveless nylon vest, denied undergarments, and watched under bright light 24 hours a day.

2 Caging as Treatment-Punishment

People who show any signs of mental health vulnerabilities can be sent to the Enhanced Outpatient Program (EOP) unit. Standard practice includes isolating people in standing cages when they "misbehave," which can include anything from attempting suicide to stating an intention to submit a complaint against a guard. Includes repeated threats to be sent to higher levels of "mental health care."

1 Institutional Stigma

Entry level into the prison mental health system. Anyone who accesses mental healthcare, including one-time requests for counseling, is flagged in the Correctional Clinical Case Management System as someone with a "mental health" issue. This stigma has been used by the parole board as evidence of "instability" to justify denying parole, prolonging incarceration.

Furthermore, if those imprisoned in PIP attempt to have positive connection with others (such as interacting with friends), they are punished with further isolation and denied any level of outside engagement. CIW operates an additional mental health unit called the Psychiatric Segregation Unit (PSU) not mentioned in their multitiered care program. Though people in the PIP may be able to "earn" less isolation, people in the PSU are held in isolated cells for at least twenty-three hours a day and are not afforded similar opportunities. The PSU is off the map of both the CDCR mental healthcare pyramid and the rest of the prison population. It is the mental health counterpart of Secure Housing Units (SHU) in that people in PSU are removed from all contact with others inside and outside of prison.

Many of the people who lost their lives to suicide in the CIW crisis had been imprisoned in various mental health units, including at the level of suicide watch, the central location of prison "suicide prevention." In the wake of ongoing deaths in 2016, CCWP gathered information from people imprisoned at CIW about their understanding of the conditions leading to the rise in suicide attempts and suicides. We engaged with people in the mental health units, where the majority of the deaths and suicide attempts continued to take place. We gathered information about prison suicide prevention policies and practices, including the practice of isolating suicidal people. In suicide watch cells, incarcerated people are stripped down and clothed in a wraparound sleeveless nylon vest loosely held together by Velcro. People are confined to a solitary cell—empty except for a thin mattress on the floor—where they are watched under bright light twenty-four hours a day. The prison "healthcare aide" who sits outside their cell in a roving nursing station cannot provide them with any needed supplies, so people in crisis rely on correctional officers who regularly make them wait for hours for basic needs supplies, like toilet paper or sanitary pads. If a person eventually acquires a sanitary pad, they are forced to stand with it between their legs, since they are denied undergarments. People regularly report being freezing cold in their cells, as well as being denied water, adequate food, toilet paper, toothbrush and powdered toothpaste, and sanitary pads.[12]

Notably, people under these conditions rarely complained about trouble accessing mental healthcare, including emergency mental health counseling, since they already assumed that mental healthcare was not available to anybody at CIW, including people in crisis and isolated for suicidal ideation and attempts. Suicide watch is understood by imprisoned people as a punitive, isolating practice with no suicide prevention purpose. In fact, people disclose being *more* suicidal upon release from suicide watch, and refuse to reveal suicidal thoughts or plans for fear of being forced to return isolation.

While under suicide watch, people are prevented from seeing family or friends on weekend visiting, routinely and unlawfully denied access to visits from legal representatives, blocked from receiving peer-based mental health support, and denied access to mail and phone calls. One day before her parole hearing, thirty-five-year-old Erika Rocha lost her life to state-sanctioned suicide in CIW. Before she died, she made it clear in her letters that her attempts to access the mental healthcare system in CIW ultimately led to the deterioration of her well-being and capacity to survive.[13]

Suicide watch is one of many examples of how criminalized and ableist mental health constructions contort the philosophy of healthcare into systematized psychological torture. Denying parole to incarcerated people classified as mentally ill is another example of mental health punitivity. Since the suicide crisis at CIW, CCWP learned that, in over twenty years, not a single person had been granted parole while housed in CIW's largest mental health unit, the EOP. This barrier to release experienced by people imprisoned at EOP is severe, consistent, and targeted. People who have been imprisoned at EOP report that they are told by parole commissioners that as long as they are "unstable" enough to require mental health services in an EOP unit, they are a threat to public safety and thus ineligible for prison release.

The EOP is the step-down mental health unit, a unit offering less "care" than the PIP. CDCR has not provided public data on parole grants for people housed in the inpatient program or temporarily in suicide watch, but since they are in higher mental health "care" units, their parole grant rates are likely worse. We do know that prison and parole officials consider Crisis Bed placement as an indicator of psychological instability, which negatively affects one's parole chances. Accessing services therefore becomes conflated with being a public safety risk, which, in effect, automatically makes one ineligible for prison release. Many imprisoned people therefore avoid being classified as having a mental health issue—by avoiding taking psychiatric medication or not asking to speak to a clinician when in need—since accessing mental health services, especially "higher levels of care," means one is likely to be denied release. Through this form of mass disability discrimination, imprisoned people classified as mentally ill thereby face de facto permanent incarceration as another form of mental health punitivity. This drives and shapes prison staff's "suicide prevention" efforts into active death-making practices, or practices that facilitate, trigger, or pressure imprisoned people toward suicide.

When critiqued at all, the failure to prevent suicides in prison custody is usually constructed as a problem of passivity (for example, guards neglecting to take action, such as failing to follow their own suicide prevention policies).[14] However, while passive failure to save people's lives is a crucial problem and a standard practice of imprisonment, prison staff regularly use their power to *enact* pro-suicide violence, including psychological violence, on imprisoned people in crisis. In the majority of recent deaths by suicide and suicide attempts at CIW, the women and trans men faced neglect by guards as well as active and ongoing death-making practices. In one case, guards cut a woman down from hanging without supporting her body, causing a head injury that may have contributed to her death.[15] Prison staff regularly provoke or worsen mental health crises by humiliating and harassing imprisoned people, while also neglecting to provide access to emergency healthcare or other urgent needs. For example, guards harassed one of the women when her previous suicide attempts were not successful, taunting her that she was so incapable she could not even kill herself.[16]

These normalized death-making practices also incorporate gendered forms of humiliation and psychological violence, building on systems of carceral gender violence and vulnerability. The vast majority of people in women's prisons are survivors of domestic or sexual violence or both, 70 percent are mothers, and most are primary caregivers; and people in women's prisons are less likely than most people in men's prisons to have family support and visits, because these care practices are a gendered labor that is disproportionately done by women who visit cis men.[17] This context reflects how incarceration creates specific forms of gendered vulnerability, which prison staff can exploit for punitive purposes. For example, guards have weaponized discourses of family connection and care as tools to demean and dehumanize people in women's prisons. Before she died by suicide while imprisoned at the EOP mental health unit at CIW, one woman disclosed that guards told her that her family did not care about her and would not notice her death. Others have reported that guards have used their experiences with domestic and sexual violence, their gender identity, and scarce visits from children and other family members as psychological ammunition to intentionally undermine their ability to survive in mental healthcare units, including isolated cells.

Gendered death-making practices must be considered when examining the ongoing trend of "gender-responsive" prison policies, or policies that purport to provide gender-specific carceral care to women in prison.* When CCWP brought concerns about endemic violence within suicide watch at CIW to California state officials, we were met with rhetoric about making suicide watch more gender-responsive as a strategy to repair this violence. For example, in a 2016 meeting with state representatives, activists conveyed reports from those imprisoned in suicide watch, revealing a profoundly humiliating and deadly system that contributes to, rather than prevents, suicide.

---

* Gender-responsive prisons is a carceral strategy to create more prisons for women in order to establish "parity" between incarcerated women and incarcerated men, and to make those new women's prisons more "family friendly," more caring, and more relevant to the assumed conditions of women's lives (Braz, 2006; Heiner and Tyson, 2017). Because this approach to prisons ignores, and therefore further legitimizes, prison's implicit structural violence, and it reinforces a patriarchal and anti-trans social structure by only imagining "women" as cisgender while reducing them to stereotypes, critics have argued that this "equal treatment" approach is little more than a pinkwashed prison expansion agenda (Braz, 2006).

One issue discussed included the practice of forcing people in suicide watch to strip down and put on a suicide vest. The vests were modeled to fit what was imagined as a standard cisgender "male prisoner body," and consequently they did not fit to cover the bodies of many people, including in women's prisons. This was particularly disturbing to CCWP members in the context of the rampant sexual violence and harassment by guards in California prisons, violence that disproportionately impacts trans and cis women and gender nonconforming people.

Though seemingly engaged in the broader discussion about isolation and torture in suicide watch, the representatives circumvented these systemic issues by suggesting a "gender-responsive approach" that recognized that people of "all genders" are incarcerated, so a more universal restrictive suicide watch vest should be developed. Constructing gender responsiveness within pro-carceral terms enables a disregard of the structural gendered violence of prisons, actively limiting what can be imagined to address gender violence in suicide watch, as well as how prison itself is gender violence. In other words, the same absurd contradiction that lives in "health-punitivity" manifests in efforts to make prisons "friendlier" toward women, making mental healthcare gender-responsive violence.

However absurd and contradictory, mental health punitivity is part of a carceral logic that aggressively refuses reform by using a self-perpetuated cycle that both *produces* isolation and is *enabled by* isolation. The prison functions by isolating both criminalized people and itself from the public. This isolation, in turn, causes suicide and protects the causes of suicide. The structuring principle of isolation severs prison and its employees from the usual conditions that enable public accountability, such as transparency, oversight, the acknowledgment of even the possibility of institutional fallibility, and any sense of civic responsibility for the lives of people behind bars. Operating as isolated systems with no independent route to reporting or accountability allows gross negligence and abuse behind prison walls to continue unchecked until it becomes naturalized as part of the prison ecosystem.

Furthermore, criminalization and imprisonment radically limit who can be seen as a legitimate source of information such that only some people get to be understood as credible witnesses. So even when incarcerated people and their families organize to create routes to report and expose neglect and abuse, they are considered untrustworthy and their claims are discredited. People who reveal wrongdoing are also at great risk for retaliation, especially imprisoned people but also their family, friends, advocates, and on rare occasion whistleblower staff. The threat—and experience—of mental and physical retaliation for advocating for one's rights adds to the experience of isolation and the force of its cycle.[18] Retaliation for reporting prison violence is a systemic example of how carceral systems refuse reform.

"Bad apple" explanations for violent prison guards and staff obscure the structural enabling of guards' individual acts of violence. Prisons instill an extraordinary amount of institutional and individual power over the lives of imprisoned people within an almost completely concealed system. The concealment is fortified by treating criminalized people as disposable, which creates an ever-expanding acceptance of the level of punitivity and violence that is considered acceptable (or even desirable) for others. As a result, people who staff prisons work in a context in which they are rarely held accountable for anything, including violent attacks on incarcerated people, such as sexual assault, psychological torture, physical assault, or facilitating someone else's death.

Prisons reproduce carceral constructions of mental health and mental illness. With this carceral logic, all meaning is manipulated back to punishment and control. The result is that prison mental healthcare is not incidentally traumatizing as if it is an unintentional side effect that could be reformed, but purposively traumatizing. Prisons enact traumatizing mental healthcare at three levels: individual, systemic, and structural. At the individual level, guards and clinicians make their own choices to brutalize imprisoned patients psychologically and physically. Systemically, prisons mobilize this brutality through institutional policies and the active protection of guards and clinicians who punish and torment imprisoned people. Structurally, the core framework of carceral mental health treatment conceptualizes health through punitive terms, including emergency suicide prevention protocols in the form of suicide watch isolation.

Mental health policies within a system designed for punitivity, control, and violence are thereby organized primarily, and often exclusively, for those purposes. In this cycle of individual, systemic, and structural domination, violence leads to trauma, which leads to imprisoned people's consequential actions becoming interpreted or designated as "noncompliance," which leads to more punishment through control and violence, which leads to more trauma, which leads to more punishment, and so on, thus endorsing, legitimizing, and denying the violence. In the CDCR care pyramid, every level of mental healthcare response amounts to increased isolation and control, therefore escalating torture and decreased expectations of survival.

SURVIVAL AS THREAT TO CARCERAL POWER

Mental health punitivity is in functional opposition to the survival of imprisoned people who have been profiled as requiring mental health services. Therefore, the survival of imprisoned people poses a critical threat to carceral power in multiple ways. First, people who survive are a living witness to the abuse. As the most extreme form of carceral disappearance, suicide erases the possibility of testimony about prison violence from the person most directly affected by that violence, further obscuring the prison's role in actuating the suicide. Survival, however, potentially makes it harder for the prison to disappear its abuse and render its violence unknowable, and therefore nonexistent or inconsequential, to the outside public. That is, the survival of people imprisoned in suicide watch means the potential survival of their testimonies about their experience of mental health punitivity, which creates the possibility of breaking the rote normalization of carceral violence. Second, imprisoned people's psychic and physical survival resists the core destructive purpose of prisons, shaking the foundations of carceral state power. Collective survival, witness, and resistance, within and across prison walls, destabilize the constructed legitimacy backing up structures of carceral power and the efforts of carceral institutions to uphold this power.

It is not only individual survival, but collective and relational survival that are fundamental threats to carceral power. Care and connection between imprisoned people are often crucial resources that help people manage the desperation that can precede and motivate suicide attempts. The institutional response to this challenge to carceral power is the active destruction of human care networks between imprisoned people. For example, when imprisoned people take action to save lives in the case of attempted suicide or overdose, they often face arrest, punitive isolation in segregation, and criminal charges for tampering with "state property," which, according to prison guards, is how the bodies of imprisoned people are officially designated.*

One vivid example is the 2016 case of Mara Plascencia and Kathy Auclair,[19] two women imprisoned at CIW who experienced direct consequences of the criminalization of care in the context of prison suicide and shared their experiences with CCWP. Mara found Kathy in the showers with a noose around her neck and having seizures. Mara called the guards, but given her experience with the guards' slow response time in a crisis, she and another incarcerated woman took quick action to save Kathy's life by holding her body and trying to loosen the noose. The guard who was there froze, leaving Mara to work harder despite knowing that she would likely be punished for her life-saving actions. She continued to loosen the noose enough that Kathy could breathe again, and she held Kathy carefully as she came

---

* For example, when researcher Ryan Watson interviewed Jane Dorotik, who was formerly incarcerated at CIW, she remarked that "because the body is state property, women who have been severely sunburned during outdoor activities in the prison have been given '115s,' a penal code term for disciplinary action that results from defacing state property" (Watson, 2021). Though I have not located a formal policy that defines imprisoned people as state property, perhaps because internal prison policies are intentionally made inaccessible, as I've argued here, Dorotik's recollection is not uncommon. Similar testimonies by people incarcerated in other states also recount guards punishing them for reasons related to their status as state property. See, for example, McKeithen, 2020.

back to consciousness. More guards arrived, and one remarked, "All this for a bed move?"

Kathy had requested a bed move because she was very ill and in unsafe cell conditions that guards refused to remedy. She had recently been held in solitary confinement because a guard found a pair of scissors in her cell; Kathy's children could not reach her there and were not told why. By the time Kathy was returned to general population,* her children had become upset about her absence, blaming her and interpreting it as a lack of care for them, leading them to stop communicating with her at all. Before her suicide attempt, Kathy had begged the guards for mental health services, medical services to treat her worsening physical illness, and a bed move. The guards ignored all of her efforts to seek care for herself. After her suicide attempt, Kathy learned that she had contracted valley fever while in a women's prison in Chowchilla, California, a deadly infectious disease that, left untreated, can induce emergency physical and mental health symptoms.†

A few hours after saving Kathy's life, Mara was interviewed by prison staff about the incident, and the next day she was handcuffed on the prison yard, arrested, and read her Miranda rights. She was sent to the SHU and ultimately threatened with an attempted murder charge. Mara herself was traumatized as a consequence of intervening in an alarming suicide attempt, being forcibly isolated from her support network, and facing the terrifying possibility that her incarceration could be extended after she had already been in prison for twenty years. When others imprisoned at CIW learned that she was being isolated and potentially prosecuted for saving a woman's life, they organized a campaign to free her from the SHU, reaching out to advocates outside of prison to help. These incarcerated activists wrote a petition and gathered hundreds of signatures across CIW demanding Mara's release and the end of punitive action against incarcerated people who act to save each other's lives.[20] Advocates outside prison collaborated with Mara's family to plan a call-in action to the prison

* "General population" is a term used to refer to incarcerated people who have not been segregated or isolated into separate housing as a form of discipline.

† Valley fever is under-researched and disproportionately affects people in prisons located in California and the Southwest.

warden, demanding that she release Mara immediately and drop the charges.

This series of events starkly reveals the criminalization of care in carceral contexts, including the commitment to withhold care from people in crisis, deprive people of access to caring connection through isolation, and punish people for demonstrating care for others. Prisons transform care into an illegal practice so that connection is rendered into a form of contraband, or an illegal resource traded to and among incarcerated people. Connection as contraband is a foundational principle of carceral control. Within a structure that relies on isolation as a central operating principle, supportive connection among incarcerated people is an act of insurgency. Connection between incarcerated people is criminalized because it demonstrates the capacity for people to survive and reach life beyond the death-making prison agenda. Further, connection subverts the legal assertion that people are property of the state because connection is a relational practice that opens up the possibility for incarcerated people's mutual recognition as persons. Dehumanizing carceral logics are displaced by humanizing relationships. The punitive social control of prisons aims to break caring connections between incarcerated people as well as caring connection across prison walls.

In the case of Mara and Kathy, prison staff were incentivized to disrupt and punish caring connection because connection facilitates communication and information, which can potentially be used against staff. Eight days before Kathy's suicide attempt, Erika Rocha ended her life at CIW, both events becoming a part of a devastating, emerging pattern of suicides and suicide attempts at CIW. Due to organizing pressure inside and outside of the prison, this pattern attracted rare public scrutiny of the prison,[21] and staff likely felt pressured to hide Kathy's suicide attempt from the public by isolating both the person who attempted suicide and the person who intervened as key witnesses to the series of prison failures to rescue Kathy's life.

The connection-as-contraband logic evident in this episode reflects strategic choices by prison staff to avoid public scrutiny of their failure to act. However, the logic to punish lifesaving connection between incarcerated people also defines the very purpose of prisons. Prisons routinely criminalize demonstrations of care and connection through punitive policies and everyday practices of guards meting out discretionary discipline. For example, transferring people to different prisons to intentionally separate friends or couples; punishing people for expressions of care or friendship, such as gesturing a heart symbol, toward people in isolation; and punishing people for "homosecting," any actual or imagined physical affection interpreted as queer sexuality or sociality, are all common retaliatory moves or simply mundane acts of cruelty.

Prison staff often target care acts across prison walls, including mistreating and humiliating friends and family members who visit, arbitrarily denying visits from family or legal representatives, or lying to visitors about their loved ones as a punitive tactic. Any human care exchange can be subject to punishment. Even prison staff who incarcerated people experience as helpful are often fired for "overfamiliarity."

Outlawing care transforms connection into contraband, forcing incarcerated people to navigate illegalized intimacies by essentially smuggling care as a crucial resource for survival. Mara understood that intervening to save Kathy's life would likely subject her to severe punishment, situating her rescue as an embodied care trade in which she exchanged her own physical and psychic safety for the life of another. Illegal care exchanges like Mara's reflect insurgent relationalities that disrupt the "business as usual" death-making of incarceration.

Finally, connection as contraband highlights additional contradictions in gender-responsive approaches to prisons, particularly rhetoric advocating for more "women-friendly" prisons that encourage more social-emotional connection. The argument that women need more "caring" prisons than people in men's prisons further institutionalizes sexist tropes, the premise of a gender binary, and carceral patriarchy, while also failing to recognize that holding people in captivity countermands claims of caring for them. Further, because prison staff particularly target and punish women, trans, and gender nonconforming people for their attempts to care for one another, which is a form of gendered violence, advocating for more carceral "care" effectively makes people in women's prisons more vulnerable to gendered punishment.

ORGANIZING AS LIFE-MAKING PRACTICE

Galvanized by the courage and resolve of grieving friends and family members, CCWP increased its efforts to expose the state-sanctioned deaths at CIW and force action to end the crisis. We worked to expand our survival support network and organizing base across prison walls to advocate systems change at the intersections of gender (responsive) violence, racism, ableism, and criminalization. We organized media attention to expose the prison conditions that caused each preventable death at CIW. We demanded that prison officials and the CDCR answer questions from family members and friends about the direct forms of neglect and active death-making that led to the deaths of their loved ones. We organized vigils and protests outside of the prison. We achieved the forced resignation of the CIW warden who oversaw the prison through the first three horrible years of the crisis and took no action to stem the crisis, including failing to hold a single correctional officer accountable for neglecting to save people's lives. We demanded specific changes to deadly conditions in the isolated mental health units at CIW and called for a prison investigation by the inspector general. We learned that the Office of the Inspector General no longer had the independent authority to investigate prisons but could do so if ordered by the governor, the Senate Rules Committee, or the California State Assembly speaker.

However, none of these authorized representatives would speak to us or pursue the process of ordering an investigation. In fact, they were not even aware the policy had changed and that they now had the authority to order investigations in the prisons; neither did they appear to care. We learned that no California state body has independent authority to investigate any state prison. We lobbied for the attention of state legislators and were ignored. We pleaded that the crisis of deaths at CIW would continue and escalate if no serious action was taken. Eventually, we were told by one legislative committee that they would not take action because they were worried any action might cause "suicide contagion." We argued that if suicide contagion is a real concern, years of state institutions ignoring the suicide crisis at CIW was likely now a causative factor in the crisis.

Throughout our organizing and advocacy, we sought strategies to tackle an isolation that is both structural as a driving logic embedded within prison policies and practices, and structuring as a force that produces, enforces, and normalizes death-based social systems. Our interventions focused on supporting imprisoned people's survival through connection and collective care and advocacy, as well as demanding system oversight and accountability, while we work to de-carcerate and dismantle prisons. Our organizing with grieving families and friends included working to make sure that their loved ones are recognized and valued, sharing information about the conditions that led to their loved ones' deaths, and offering families and friends ways to connect and platforms to speak. This kind of organizing requires deconstructing the isolating, bond-breaking design of the system itself, including the ways the system isolates itself from view, accountability, and change.

As a consequence of our organizing, the California State Auditor completed a suicide audit of CIW, CCWF, and two additional prisons.[22] The audit was a major organizing win, a modest chip at the wall of carceral concealment by the only independent government office empowered to investigate CDCR's institutional practices, though it is powerless to enforce any consequences based on its findings. While the audit was damning in its account of the many systemic failures of prison staff to follow even the most basic suicide prevention policies and practices, it assessed the problem as mainly one of passivity, or a failure to act according to policy. The report did not account for the more central problem of how prison, prison staff, and prison policies actively created and promoted deadly conditions that were a direct cause of the increasing suicide rate. We learned that a reform-focused report like this audit can be helpful and strategic for organizers, even though the scope of its critique would never address the heart of the issue: the destructiveness of the institution itself.

These organizing efforts and accomplishments were facilitated by the resistant life-making practices among imprisoned people, across prison walls, and with family, friends, and advocates outside of prison. Incarcerated people identified acts of care, connection, and intimacy among them as essential experiences for survival, particularly for those who have experienced suicidality. These contraband connections also create a relational context for community organizing. For example, incarcerated people's organizing inside CIW demanding Mara's release reflects both a collective act of care for Mara and a defense of care acts for the community.

This crucial inside effort then incited and fueled outside advocacy efforts that also called for Mara's release and the end of punitive responses to lifesaving acts. Once extended to the outside through a network of formerly incarcerated CCWP members, this collective care was also carried forward by advocates as mediums of information and advocacy. Mara was isolated in the SHU and did not know if Kathy ultimately survived her suicide attempt, or even if she wanted to survive. If Kathy had survived, Mara was worried about how she was managing. Through CCWP's broad inside/outside network, organizers were able to report back to Mara that, not only had Kathy survived, but she was beyond thankful to Mara for saving her life, particularly because she understood that, in doing so, Mara risked her own freedom.

The critical resource of information, and the care behind intentional sharing of information, are important aspects of connections across prison walls that are often constructed as contraband. As another example, family members of those who have died at CIW are given virtually no information about what happened to their loved ones. Sheri Graves, whose daughter Shaylene also died from state-sanctioned neglect at CIW during this period, learned details about her daughter's death only through Shaylene's currently and formerly incarcerated friends.*

When Bong Sook Chavez died at CIW, she had no nearby family to even advocate for information about what happened. CCWP advocates learned about the details of her death through their connections with people incarcerated in the mental health unit where she was confined before she died. Some of the women who lost their lives to

* Shaylene "Light Blue" Graves died at CIW in June 2016 after prison staff neglected to save her life. She made multiple attempts to seek safety through a bed move, which guards ignored. In an attempt to cover up its active role in Shaylene's death, CIW claimed she died by suicide. See Sheri Graves v. California Department of Corrections and Rehabilitation, case no. 5:17-cv-01086-JGB-SP (C.D. Cal 2019).

state-sanctioned suicides also shared critical information about deadly prison conditions before they died, strengthening activists' capacity to organize on both sides of the bars. For example, Erika Rocha spoke out through letters and during visits, describing the isolated torture of suicide watch and the cruelty of guards who mocked suicidal people, making her a key contributor to the fight for the survival of others. Media representatives are not allowed in prisons in California because of a prison media ban,[23] so the only way that any information can get outside prison—independent from those who have an active liability investment to suppress the information—is through these connections across prison walls.

Connections within, across, and outside prison walls also instigate powerful coalitions. For example, families of those who died at CIW built a context of organizing together through first mutually recognizing each other's loss in the midst of total erasure by the prisons. Family members compared stories about their experiences interfacing with the prisons, shared vital information with each other about how to engage often hostile prison and sheriff/coroner staff in the wake of their loved one's death, and developed organizing visions and strategies in collaboration with each other. At a 2016 direct action protest at CIW, Graves reflected on her relationships with other family members who have lost loved ones at CIW stating, "Alone, I felt lost, but together, we were strong. Being connected to these families and all of the allies at California Coalition for Women Prisoners has been a life-giving experience."

Advocates and activists both inside and outside of CIW have also found ways to connect and care across prison walls that transcend the reach of barbed wire and isolated "mental health" units. For example, CCWP activists organized broad coalitions to lead direct actions outside CIW to protest the death-making conditions inside.[24] Though some incarcerated people could not see the action from their cells, they could hear the drumming from the protests, creating a powerful sonic connection—care contraband exchanged via airwaves. As Shana Redmond writes, music can be a method of rebellion that "[takes] flight" (2013). Incarcerated people and outside advocates have also exchanged chants to affirm their mutual recognition and bond from across the barbed wire, including the following examples:

We want dignity, we want it now!
No more isolation, shut it down!
We want freedom, we want it now!
No more overcrowding, shut it down!
We want respect, we want it now!
No more abuse, shut it down!

If it's on the INSIDE,
It's NOT SUICIDE!

ONE! We are the people!
TWO! A little bit louder!
THREE! We want freedom for our people!

Even though prison administrators typically responded to these various forms of care insurgencies by locking down the prison, shutting down the yard as well as any possibility of across-the-wall communication, our shared resistance resonated beyond their attempts to stifle, punish, and control. Against persistent efforts by prison staff to undermine and interrupt life-making connection, communication, and information sharing, activists inside and out forge an alternative plane where incarcerated people's lives are valued, the loss of those lives are collectively mourned and resisted, and relationship-based advocacy and organizing create possibility for life-making, survival, and the fight for freedom.

BIBLIOGRAPHY

ACLU. *Still Worse Than Second-Class: Solitary Confinement of Women in the United States*. New York: ACLU, 2019. https://www.aclu.org/sites/default/files/field_document/062419-sj-solitaryreportcover.pdf.

Aron, Hillel. "Why Are So Many Inmates Attempting Suicide at the California Institution for Women?" *LA Weekly*, July 20, 2016. https://www.laweekly.com/why-are-so-many-inmates-attempting-suicide-at-the-california-institution-for-women/.

Ben-Moshe, Liat. *Decarcerating Disability: Deinstitutionalization and Prison Abolition*. Minneapolis: University of Minnesota Press, 2020.

Blodgett, John M. "Protesters Critical of High Suicide Rate at California Institution for Women in Chino." *Daily Bulletin*, October 1, 2016. https://www.dailybulletin.com/general-news/20161001/protesters-critical-of-high-suicide-rate-at-california-institution-for-women-in-chino.

Braz, Rose. "Kinder, Gentler, Gender Responsive Cages: Prison Expansion Is Not Prison Reform." *Women, Girls & Criminal Justice*, November 2006, 87–91. Available at https://criticalresistance.org/wp-content/uploads/2022/07/WG-CJ-Kinder-Gentler-Gender-Responsive-Cages.pdf.

California State Auditor. *California Department of Corrections and Rehabilitation: It Must Increase Its Efforts to Prevent and Respond to Inmate Suicides*. Sacramento: California State Auditor, August 2017. https://www.bsa.ca.gov/reports/2016-131/index.html.

Clayton, Gina, et al. "Because She's Powerful: The Political Isolation and Resistance of Women with Incarcerated Loved Ones." Los Angeles and Oakland, CA: Essie Justice Group, 2018.

DeVeaux, Mika'il. "The Trauma of the Incarceration Experience." *Harvard Civil Rights–Civil Liberties Law Review* 48, no. 1 (2013): 257–77.

Harris, April. "The Coronavirus Chronicles." Edited and introduction by Colby Lenz and Alisa Bierria. In *Abolition Feminisms: Organizing, Survival and Transformative Practice*, edited by Alisa Bierria, Jakeya Caruthers, and Brooke Lober. Chicago: Haymarket Books, 2022.

Heiner, Brady T., and Sarah K. Tyson. "Feminism and the Carceral State: Gender-Responsive Justice, Community Accountability, and the Epistemology of Antiviolence." *Feminist Philosophy Quarterly* 3, no. 1 (March 23, 2017). https://doi.org/10.5206/fpq/2016.3.3.

Henderson, Marcus. "Protesters' Vigil at CIW for Women Who Took Their Own Lives." *San Quentin News*, January 31, 2017. https://sanquentinnews.com/protesters-vigil-at-ciw-for-women-who-took-their-own-lives/.

Kazem, Halima. "I Was 'Sent to the Hole' for Trying to Stop a Suicide." *Women's eNews*, September 9, 2016. https://womensenews.org/2016/09/i-was-sent-to-the-hole-for-trying-to-stop-a-suicide/.

Law, Victoria. "Erika Rocha's Suicide Brings Attention to the Dire Need for Mental Health Care in Prison." Rewire News Group, May 20, 2016. https://rewirenewsgroup.com/article/2016/05/20/erika-rochas-suicide-brings-attention-dire-need-mental-health-care-prison/.

Levin, Sam. "'PTSD Is Real, I Wake Up Crying': The Activist Who Stood Up to Prison Guard Abuse." *Guardian*, October 8, 2020. https://www.theguardian.com/us-news/2020/oct/08/prison-guards-abuse-california.

Lithwick, Dahlia. "Prisons Have Become America's New Asylums." *Slate*, January 5, 2016. https://slate.com/news-and-politics/2016/01/prisons-have-become-warehouses-for-the-mentally-ill.html.

McKeithen, Will. "Life in Prison: Biopolitics, Ill-Being, and the Neoliberal Penitentiary." Dissertation, University of Washington, 2020, 155n101.

Pell v. Procunier, 417 U.S. 817, 817, 94 S. Ct. 2800, 2802, 41 L. Ed. 2d 495 (1974).

Redmond, Shana L. *Anthem: Social Movements and the Sound of Solidarity in the African Diaspora*. New York: NYU Press, 2013.

Richie, Beth E. *Arrested Justice: Black Women, Violence, and America's Prison Nation*. New York: New York University Press, 2012.

Shirk, Adrian. "Why Don't You Ever See TV Interviews with Inmates?" *Atlantic*, July 15, 2014. https://www.theatlantic.com/politics/archive/2014/07/why-dont-you-ever-see-tv-interviews-with-inmates/374447/.

Sims, Georgia. "The Criminalization of Mental Illness: How Theoretical Failures Create Real Problems in the Criminal Justice System." *Vanderbilt Law Review* 62, no. 3 (2009): 1053–83.

Travis, Jeremy, Amy L. Solomon, and Michelle Waul. *From Prison to Home: The Dimensions and Consequences of Prisoner Reentry*. Washington, DC: Urban Institute Justice Policy Center, June 2001.

Watson, Ryan. *Radical Documentary and Global Crises: Militant Evidence in the Digital Age*. Bloomington: Indiana University Press, 2021.

Wisely, Willie. "California Bans Media Interviews with Prisoners." *Prison Legal News*, March 15, 1997. https://www.prisonlegalnews.org/news/1997/mar/15/california-bans-media-interviews-with-prisoners/.

NOTES

1 California State Auditor, *California Department of Corrections and Rehabilitation: It Must Increase Its Efforts to Prevent and Respond to Inmate Suicides* (Sacramento: California State Auditor, August 2017), https://www.bsa.ca.gov/reports/2016-131/index.html; Hillel Aron, "Why Are So Many Inmates Attempting Suicide at the California Institution for Women?" *LA Weekly*, July 20, 2016, https://www.laweekly.com/why-are-so-many-inmates-attempting-suicide-at-the-california-institution-for-women/; Victoria Law, "Erika Rocha's Suicide Brings Attention to the Dire Need for Mental Health Care in Prison." Rewire News Group, May 20, 2016, https://rewirenewsgroup.com/article/2016/05/20/erika-rochas-suicide-brings-attention-dire-need-mental-health-care-prison/.

2 In 2015, California's Office of the Inspector General began requiring the California Department of Corrections and Rehabilitation to report suicide attempts at prisons designed for women. See Office of the Inspector General, *Semi-Annual Report*, vol. 2 (Sacramento, CA: January–June 2016), 5, https://www.oig.ca.gov/wp-content/uploads/2019/05/OIG_Semi-Annual_Report_Volume_II_January-June_2016.pdf.

3 Georgia Sims, "The Criminalization of Mental Illness: How Theoretical Failures Create Real Problems in the Criminal Justice System," *Vanderbilt Law Review* 62, no. 3 (2009): 1053–83.

4 Dahlia Lithwick, "Prisons Have Become America's New Asylums," *Slate*, January 5, 2016, https://slate.com/news-and-politics/2016/01/prisons-have-become-warehouses-for-the-mentally-ill.html.

5 See Liat Ben-Moshe, *Decarcerating Disability: Deinstitutionalization and Prison Abolition* (Minneapolis: University of Minnesota Press, 2020). The analytical concept "prison nation" was coined and developed by Beth E. Richie (2012).

6 Mika'il DeVeaux, "The Trauma of the Incarceration Experience," *Harvard Civil Rights–Civil Liberties Law Review* 48, no. 1 (2013): 257–77.

7 ACLU, *Still Worse Than Second-Class: Solitary Confinement of Women in the United States* (New York: ACLU, 2019), https://www.aclu.org/sites/default/files/field_document/062419-sj-solitaryreportcover.pdf.

8 California State Auditor.

9 California State Auditor.

10 California State Auditor.

11 Correspondence between incarcerated people at CIW and the author. Some sources' identities must remain anonymous for safety reasons.

12 Many of these punitive healthcare conditions were replicated at CIW and other prisons across the US during the COVID-19 pandemic. See, for example, April Harris's firsthand account in her journal, titled "The Coronavirus Chronicles," in *Abolition Feminisms, Volume 1: Organizing, Survival, and Transformative Practice* (Haymarket Books, 2022).

13 Correspondence between Erika Rocha and the author, February 2016. See Rocha v. State of California Department of Corrections and Rehabilitation, case no. 1:14-cv-00842-BAM (E.D. Cal., 2015).

14 California State Auditor.

15 Personal conversation with warden of CIW, December 2016.

16 Anonymous source no. 1, reported to the author, May 2016.

17 Gina Clayton et al. "Because She's Powerful: The Political Isolation and Resistance of Women with Incarcerated Loved Ones" (Los Angeles and Oakland, CA: Essie Justice Group, 2018); Jeremy Travis, Amy L. Solomon, and Michelle Waul, *From Prison to Home: The Dimensions and Consequences of Prisoner Reentry* (Washington, DC: Urban Institute Justice Policy Center, June 2001).

18 For instance, see Rojas v. Brown, 1:17-cv-01514 (E.D. Cal., 2017); Sam Levin, "'PTSD Is Real, I Wake Up Crying': The Activist Who Stood Up to Prison Guard Abuse." *Guardian*, October 8, 2020, https://www.theguardian.com/us-news/2020/oct/08/prison-guards-abuse-california.

19 Both women have shared information about this incident publicly. See Aron, "Why Are So Many Inmates Attempting Suicide," and Halima Kazem, "I Was 'Sent to the Hole' for Trying to Stop a Suicide." *Women's eNews*, September 9, 2016, https://womensenews.org/2016/09/i-was-sent-to-the-hole-for-trying-to-stop-a-suicide/.

20 For more details about these activist efforts, see Marcus Henderson, "Protesters' Vigil at CIW for Women Who Took Their Own Lives," *San Quentin News*, January 31, 2017, https://sanquentinnews.com/protesters-vigil-at-ciw-for-women-who-took-their-own-lives/, and John M. Blodgett, "Protesters Critical of High Suicide Rate at California Institution for Women in Chino," *Daily Bulletin*, October 1, 2016, https://www.dailybulletin.com/general-news/20161001/protesters-critical-of-high-suicide-rate-at-california-institution-for-women-in-chino.

21 Hillel Aron, "Why Are So Many Inmates Attempting Suicide at the California Institution for Women?" *LA Weekly*, July 20, 2016, https://www.laweekly.com/why-are-so-many-inmates-attempting-suicide-at-the-california-institution-for-women/.

22 California State Auditor, 2017.

23 Pell v. Procunier, 417 U.S. 817, 817, 94 S. Ct. 2800, 2802, 41 L. Ed. 2d 495 (1974); Adrian Shirk, "Why Don't You Ever See TV Interviews with Inmates?" *Atlantic*, July 15, 2014, https://www.theatlantic.com/politics/archive/2014/07/why-dont-you-ever-see-tv-interviews-with-inmates/374447/.

24 Henderson, "Protesters' Vigil at CIW."

BEYOND #STOPASIANHATE

CRIMINALIZATION, GENDER, AND ASIAN ABOLITION FEMINISM

Edited and introduced by Hyejin Shim

Over the course of the United States' rising antagonism toward China and the emergence of the COVID-19 pandemic, violence against Asian Americans has steadily increased. Public discourse on the coronavirus and its apparent Chinese origins, fueled in large part by Trumpian remarks about the "China virus" and "holding China accountable" for the pandemic, gave rise to a national scapegoating of Asian immigrants as vectors for the virus. Amid increasing fears and tensions, attacks on elderly Asian immigrants and women were filmed and disseminated online with increasing virality. Then on March 16, 2021, a young white man embarked on a multistop shooting spree with the intent of murdering the women who staffed local Asian massage businesses—places where he himself had procured various sexual services from these workers on numerous occasions. It was a horrific massacre that claimed the lives of eight people, and captured the anguish, rage, and fear of Asian Americans across the nation. For many, it stood as a grim and bloody confirmation of escalating violence against Asians in response to COVID-19, as well as an undeniable reminder of the persistent dehumanization embedded into Asian American experiences.

It is here that #StopAsianHate materialized as a clarion call for Asian Americans to unite under a common cause. Thousands of people across the country rallied to Stop Asian Hate. Overnight, all manner of Asian American talking heads—ranging from politicians and celebrities to activists, academics, and influencers—came forward into a morbid limelight to offer commentary on the tragedy. As they did so, many put themselves in the shoes of the women who had been targeted for murder. At protests, speakers shouted, impassioned, that they could have been those women. Yet these speakers, largely nonprofit executives and other American-born, middle-class, and college-educated professionals, could not have been those women: immigrant, undocumented, poor, surviving capitalism by trading low-wage physical labor and in some cases, sexual services, to survive.

Though these expressions of empathy gestured toward solidarity in a common struggle, they did so while masking significant economic inequality, political divergence, uneven levels of exposure to violence, and the widely different orientations of the state toward women like those targeted by the shooter as opposed to the Asian Americans speaking on their behalf. They also did so by doggedly scrubbing any mention of sex work from their talking points. Asian women face enduring hypersexualization from white men, they said, and to discuss the victims as potential participants in the sex trade was not only to miss the point, but to give credence to the shooter's disgusting self-justifications. To discuss the victims in the context of immigrant women workers potentially trading sex to survive became taboo, shameful; disrespectful of the dead. But to not name this reality—that many immigrant women will exchange sexual labor for cash and other necessities, whether or not they ever conceive of themselves of sex workers—is to not only ignore the dynamics of what transpired but also to further marginalize the experiences of countless women whose lives run parallel to those of the victims. Reminiscent of the troubling, incomplete analyses of white feminism, the politics of Stop Asian Hate were predicated on these critical erasures—erasures made possible only by viewing the erased as too victimized to have their own voices, let alone able to speak for themselves.

It is doubtless that the Atlanta shooting intensified the fear of racialized violence among Asian Americans across many different experiences.

Yet, how this fear rippled out across gender, class, and immigration status reveals more than just the hidden experiences of hate violence. The proposed solutions—increased policing, harsher hate crime legislation—also reveals the utter disavowal of the experiences of working-class and poor Asian migrant women who face regular threats of racialized gender violence and criminalization from police.

The following excerpt is from a transcript of "Beyond #StopAsianHate: Criminalization, Gender, and Asian Abolition Feminism," a roundtable discussion between Asian abolition feminists, hosted on June 16, 2021, by Haymarket Books. This conversation was meant as an intervention into the deadly limitations of a pan–Asian Americanist discourse that protects little more than a bourgeoisie faith in the police as an arbiter of justice. We wanted to invite more humanity, more complexity, and more solidarity into conversations that simply begin and end with a legible body of "Asian Americans" and their uniform persecution, and uplift not only those who passed on March 16, but also all who continue to live, work, and love at these precarious intersections.

Stephanie Cho (SC): For sex workers, criminalized and incarcerated people, survivors of domestic violence and sexual violence, the fight to end anti-Asian violence cannot be in conversations of racism alone. How did you really start organizing against violence in your communities? How did you come to the intersections of anti-violence and abolitionist work?

Yves Tong Nguyen (YTN): I started organizing after the death of Trayvon Martin in 2012. Over time I grew into the type of organizing that I do now. I organize with Survived & Punished New York, which supports criminalized survivors of gender-based violence because I myself am a survivor. Often, as survivors of interpersonal violence, you see the ways in which the system fails you. And I'm also a sex worker, so I'm criminalized for the way that I choose to survive.

Ny Nourn (NN): I started my roots in organizing when I was incarcerated at the Central California Women's Facility, the largest women's prison in the world. Here, I realized that being a survivor is not isolated;

it's very common, especially for myself, coming from my background. My family is from genocide. We are refugees, Southeast Asians. I was born into violence and witnessed domestic violence from the young age of six. I even learned that my mom herself survived sexual violence before she had me. For me and for others that are incarcerated, we have so much of that compounded trauma. Again, it's not unique. So many other survivors are like me. When I was criminalized for my abuse, I was sentenced to life without parole, a young woman. I was barely eighteen years old when I met my abuser. And I thought that the US was there to protect me, especially being a survivor. But instead, I experienced courtroom violence during my trial, and I learned others experienced that as well. From there, the trajectory of my life, I started organizing not only for my own freedom, but others' freedom as well. To think about how can I—when I get out—help free people, help free survivors, with a critical lens to dismantle these systems that are really out to target immigrants, refugees, people of color, Black folks, our communities. And to say that, You know what? My story is not unique. There are other criminalized survivors too. And we need to work together and protect each other.

Connie Wun (CW): I was the first-born here in Oakland to a family who were war refugees, similar to Ny. We were survivors of war in Vietnam and across Southeast Asia. And that meant that . . . when my family got here to this country, we were poor. And didn't speak much English. And I knew growing up that I had to figure things out for my family. I think my journey toward becoming an organizer in part was because I was learning a racial literacy of what it means to be Asian in America. . . . That curiosity bred through my own struggles with racial violence; and gender violence, I started doing a lot of work on gender-based violence because of my own experiences as a first responder at home and then in my own life. It became a way of figuring out my life and then making sure that others weren't experiencing violence similarly.

Hyejin Shim (HS): My roots in organizing, like everyone else, start at home with my own family and the multiple generations of violence. Intergenerational legacies of not only war and colonization but also domestic violence, sexual assault, and child sexual abuse have animated my family's trajectory in the United States and in my own life today. My entry into organizing was really informed by those experiences and wanting to make sense of them.

SC: I want to go back on the sort of stigma and narrative against sex workers within the Asian American community and also how it's perceived externally. And how it can produce situations like the shooting.

HS: Asian people in the sex trade, whether they're full-service sex workers, online workers, or workers in nonsexual professions that may occasionally provide sexual services to customers, or even survivors of trafficking, occupy this strange place in our communities and beyond in the public space. There's a really deep disgust that's leveled at them, while there's also the deeply paternalistic impulse to rescue them. The disgust and the "rescue" impulses are two sides of the same coin, driven by the mission to remove the threat of perversion. Meanwhile, this is all very woven through with misogyny, Orientalism, and desire. And it's linked to how Asian sex workers, trafficking survivors, and generally, how Asian people in the sex trades are talked about, treated, dissected.

To me, the way that Asian women, in particular, have been racialized is shaped by wartime sexual violence and postwar economies of sex and exploitation, which continue today in occupied Asia, from Korea to the Philippines. I see that as a key part of racial violence that Asian women face; that the way we are racialized and gendered has not only to do with our perceived proximity to sex work, but to the normalization and justification of violence against people in the sex trade. The normalized violence that people in the sex trade have to navigate daily. If you engage in sexual labor—for any number of reasons that are often far more complex than the dichotomies of "choice" or "coercion"—violence against you is just expected and accepted as an inevitability. How does this perceived inevitability actually normalize, or even justify violence against people in the sex trade? Violence from police or clients or loved ones.

In my time working at a domestic shelter for Asian immigrants and refugees, and in my time organizing to free gender violence survivors from prison, I've had to think a lot about how organized abandonment happens in our communities along the lines of gender and class. And it's hard for me to think of a group of people within our communities that's more projected on to, that's more disposed of, that's more erased and made invisible than sex workers, people in the sex trade. In political spaces, organizing spaces, either they're thought of as being too privileged to be listened to, or too exotic and abject to have voices of their own. And in communities and families, they're made into shameful secrets to not be talked about. So, there's rejection and abuse from both inside and outside of the community on so many levels. Meanwhile, the reality is that most people start sex working out of economic need, which can look like needing to support children or other loved ones. But also, this need is often shaped so deeply by the need to escape or survive other forms of violence and abuse that are often happening at home. Whether it's child sexual abuse, domestic violence, or sexual assault. The family is a primary site of gender-based violence, which has been both researched and proven time and time again.

When I was attending vigils for victims of the Atlanta shooting, it felt really heartbreaking and infuriating to me when the organizers and speakers could not and would not even name that the shooting was an attack intended for Asian women who were perceived as sex workers, because it was perceived as bringing shame on the victims. The question of shame and bringing shame into the conversation when we lift up that element of the story, I really want to ask like, Whose shame is it? And who does that shame belong to? I don't think it's the shame of the victims and survivors ultimately. I remember reading this interview with one of the victim's sons who gracefully answered this invasive question about if he knew what his mother did for work. He answered that he knew what she did, and that it included some sex work. That he had often worried for her. And that he had been so proud of her, loved her, adored her. So again, whose shame is it, and whose shame shapes the boundaries of the conversations we can have publicly?

I was talking to a coworker yesterday about what happened in Atlanta. I asked her, you know, if any of the massage workers in Atlanta that day had been armed and had successfully defended themselves, how would this have been perceived, by both the media and our communities? Those we lost are seen as these legible, mournful victims in death. Yet in life, how is their self-defense, their self-preservation understood? Is it? Could you imagine what those headlines would have been if those victims had defended themselves and survived? "Asian massage prostitutes gun down man of faith" with a photo of him holding a puppy, going to church, or something. It's not hard to imagine. This is how violence against sex workers is constantly framed.

It's just really saddening to me that the struggles of sex workers can represent us when we want our community's victimization to be validated. But only in death, and only on very specific terms. And not in life when they're speaking out. Not in life when they're organizing. Not in life when they're working to care for each other and their loved ones. And why that is, is a question that we all need to be asking and answering and organizing in our personal lives. Because even in the most radical of organizations, sex workers are pushed out, harassed, even in friendships, partnerships, they are surveilled, distrusted, abused. If you don't think you know any sex workers or Asian sex workers personally, chances are they think you're not a safe person to share with. This is all connected. And we cannot address the issues like what happened in Atlanta, or the legacy of racialized sexual violence that Asian women inherited for many years now, without answering to this.

YTN: As I think about Atlanta and the shooting, I think that in the aftermath, and Hyejin mentioned this, a lot of people made an effort to sanitize and also to distance the massage workers who were killed from sex work. I will not say whether or not they did sex work or whether they ever engaged in anything that we might consider sex work and if they identified with that. Because these are really political terms, and the idea of being in the sex trade is not what a lot of people identify with because of shame, because of stigma, and for a lot of reasons. But in the aftermath, because this became a national issue, it became something that became a really large issue for a lot of people. And then people feel the need to distance the victims and survivors from the sex trade. Whether or not they engaged in it. I've gotten a lot of hate for even mentioning that massage workers are often thought about as being in the sex trade and are harmed by whorephobia, that they are harmed by anti-sex-work narratives. And partially what I want to address is there's an idea of perfect survivors. There's an idea of perfect victimhood. And the truth is, one, Asian women are never going to fit under that idea anyways, no matter who they are, but especially not those who are migrant women. They're never going to be considered perfect survivors or perfect victims. So, in order for this story to have been lifted up the way that it has, to demonstrate anti-Asian violence, in order for mainstream organizations and Asian men and other entities to benefit from this, it had to be sanitized. And to sanitize it, they couldn't be sex workers. Then they would have been deserving of violence. They're not the perfect idea of what a victim is meant to be. And I think that's really important for us to think about in terms of criminalization, in terms of stigma. And when you talk about this, the exact distancing that people try to do when they're like, oh no, no, they're not sex workers, we don't want to victim blame them by saying they were sex workers—it's exactly the type of logic that led to them being killed in the first place. It leads sex workers, massage workers, or anybody attached to the sex trades or to trafficking, to face violence on a daily basis. And a lot of the low-wage work that Asian women engage in are those types of labor.

People don't want to talk about it. But the person who killed them clearly viewed them as being sex workers, right? Whether or not they were. And that is at the root of this. People feeling like they would be deserving of violence if they were sex workers. And that leads to sex workers facing violence every day. Anybody thought of as a sex worker faces violence every day. We know in history many Black, Indigenous, people of color women are viewed as sex workers whether or not they actually are. And they wouldn't have been deserving of violence whether or not they were. But because of those narratives and people's unwillingness to rip it apart, instead of saying sex workers, people in the sex trades, all of these different people don't deserve violence, never did, and that this violence is rooted in white supremacy, rooted in imperial wars, all of these things; instead, they'd rather say, "No, no, no they're not sex workers. No, they would never sell sex. They're not whores." Right? And I think that is at the root of the issue.

CW: It's important to note that if they weren't sex workers, or weren't perceived to be sex workers, that would not make Asian communities the perfect victims either. There's this idea of distancing ourselves from the underground economy, from anything that is potentially a poor mark on our Asian communities because then that would render us not the good immigrant, or, you know, not the good victim. That, to me, was probably one of the most painful parts of having witnessed mainstream America hijack and kind of marginalize the narratives and the stories of the victims and survivors in Atlanta. So that was one of the reasons why we wanted to make sure that that was amplified, to address the nuances and to not try to reinforce the violence against our criminalized communities, our sex workers, or migrant workers, we don't want you to further harm our communities by distancing or erasing reality.

I've only recently disclosed that I have been a part of the trade. And in fact, there are people in my family who have long been a part of the trade in ways that are not for me to disclose. What is important is the amount of shame that our communities, myself included, have felt throughout the process, the fears that we felt because we had to live very hidden lives, right? That is what renders us vulnerable to even more violence, because there are men like the twenty-one-year-old white man [shooter] who feels as though he can do harm against us, because no one will fight for us. There's also the legacy of seeing Asian women, in particular, as expendable. The day he shot and killed these people, it was also the anniversary of the My Lai Massacre in Vietnam, whereby women and children were killed, hundreds of us were killed, because we are seen as disposable. So when folks are thinking about violence against our communities, we have to think about the people who have survived multiple forms of violence against them, that are still actually hiding from the violence that we may be committing against each other.

SC: Thank you. This is such an important conversation. And again, the reason why we wanted to have this conversation was because so much of the coverage, and in Atlanta too, how it got put out there in this particular kind of way. But anti-Asian violence is not simply an issue of individuals. The media was painting it only as these individual acts, but it is the structures as well. What does anti-Asian violence look like in the system, prisons, et cetera, and how is this affected by gender and queerness?

NN: First, who is running these systems? Because we know that they have been created throughout history by white patriarchy, misogyny. These are carceral systems. What does it look like? It can be hard to imagine unless you're actually experiencing it, you're a family member, or you're someone that's working with people inside. It can be hard to imagine it because Asian people are considered the model minority, so when we are in these systems, we are often—myself, survivors, immigrants, refugees—we are all erased. And then we're funneled into these immigration systems. There are Southeast Asian refugees, about sixteen thousand total, who are in limbo now facing deportations. Over two thousand Southeast Asian refugees have been deported. These are things we don't hear enough of in terms of anti-Asian violence. We're abandoned and again, overlooked. In the early nineties, young refugees like us were resettled in impoverished places, and along with our Black and Latinx communities, they were policed. They were harassed and arrested as youth, at a young age. No adequate resources, and no mental health resources and support for refugees who carry traumas from the war, which builds into intergenerational trauma.

School for myself, and I think for other Asian refugees, was hard to navigate. Especially day to day, just trying to figure out how to survive. Though I was sheltered in a home with my mom and my stepdad, the majority of Southeast Asian refugees, that was not always common for them. And I'd hear from my family about their friends' children being arrested and incarcerated. And then when I was incarcerated that people were being deported as immigrants and refugees. There is a lot of anti-Asian violence that's happening within systems that are overlooked. We also really need to think about how many people who are criminalized and in detention are survivors, as this is how many Asian women come to be criminalized. Policies created to protect domestic violence survivors like the Violence against Women Act don't always apply, even to refugees or legal permanent residents, if they are immigrant or refugee women with convictions like myself. We're just looked at as our conviction.

Fortunately, I was able to garner support from organizations that realized the impacts of being a woman, a refugee. That my story is really not unique. That there are other immigrants and refugees that have been funneled into prison and into ICE [Immigration and Customs Enforcement] and deported. More so now. Currently in California, we're working to build protections for those like myself that have served time in state prisons. Decades, fifteen, twenty years. But for immigrants, it's hard for us to be given an equal chance, of being able to be released on parole to rebuild our lives. Especially because we didn't have the chance to build our lives up in the first place.

But Asian Americans are a growing population in the US. We need to have data that helps us to see what resources we really need, because we can't rely on these criminal legal systems for protection, not even from hate crimes. And these hate crime laws, the way they are applied end up ultimately harming Black and brown communities most. We have to think about the root causes of mass incarceration, the growing violence against Asians, and so on. We need to have these serious discussions instead of working against each other, instead of saying it's not my problem, not my issue, let the advocates and people impacted deal with it. There's still that divide and tension within AAPI [Asian American and Pacific Islander] communities. If it's not happening to them or their family members, they don't want to be a part of it, sometimes due to shame. But we can't fight against white supremacy, against these laws and policies unless we, you know, get it together. And for LGBTQ people, gender and queerness also has impacts when it comes to incarceration. With white supremacy, it's either you get with this, our rules, our laws, or get out. That's what they're doing. People like migrant workers and in the sex industries are criminalized within these systems that are not built to support or protect them—instead, they're diminished, distorted, and disappeared. They're deporting our friends, our family members, our community members.

But I have to think about how we got here in the first place. Southeast Asian refugees, we have been here a little bit over forty-five years because of US involvement in the war. Now, with this wave of more anti-Asian violence, it's clear they want to get rid of us because they say we are the problem, but we're not. Yeah, I have a murder conviction and what? I was once at a city council meeting where they said, we need to deport the ones with the murder convictions and the rapists. I stood up and said, "So, you want to deport me. Let's talk about it and the reasons why, and why I was never offered resources." Get to know me and how I was failed by the systems. So many young people get sentenced to this egregious sentence, life without parole, but yet they heal and grow, and become leaders and mentors while incarcerated. And now we're out here joining together working again to disrupt these systems. To expose for what it is: white supremacy and patriarchy. That's what we need to think about in these discussions.

Inés Ixierda, "Protect Celeste Guap"

The newspaper published the name and social media photos of a female minor and called her a teen prostitute after it was revealed almost a dozen police officers were involved in her sexual exploitation and trafficking. Every detail that comes out was worse than the one before. So many looked away.

I condemn the paper. I curse the police. I spit on the misogynist media. I light candles contra la ley and I hex the patriarchy. I make offerings for our protection and tributes to our intentions.

This altar calls for the protection of Celeste Guap.

Celeste, may you be surrounded with safety in all that you do. May the strength of your spirit and heart be steady and strong as you move forward and leave all that you don't need behind you. May you find healing and ease in this life. May you win all the lawsuits. May you have justice in all the ways you need and deserve.

"ALL CANNED FOODS ARE EXPIRED BUT STILL EDIBLE"

A CRITIQUE OF ANTI-VIOLENCE ADVOCACY AND THE PERPETUATION OF ANTIBLACKNESS

Romina Garcia

All canned foods are expired but still edible. . . . This is a sign that was posted in the kitchen of a Chicago domestic violence (DV) shelter in 2016. I was told that these types of practices are normal and that families are just happy to be eating. This horrifying display of advocacy exemplifies the abuse some Black women experience within anti-violence advocacy services. If this is care work and advocacy, when did advocacy become a process of dehumanization and violence? In this paper, I argue that the expiration of food in this context is more than the date on a gallon of milk; it signifies the systemic gratuitous violence targeted against Black women that they are expected to endure and accept with gratitude. The production of meaning within this sign speaks to the current state of anti-violence advocacy. Reviewing the neoliberal impact on anti-violence services and the illegibility of "Black DV victim" in the discourse of anti-violence advocacy, I contend that some forms of anti-violence advocacy not only support antiblack carceral logics but are also themselves antiblack carceral projects.

Beth Richie has argued that the early anti-rape and battered women's movement in the 1960s and 1970s homogenized victims of gender-based violence by asserting that "all women" were vulnerable to these forms of violence, disappearing the specific vulnerabilities experienced by victims on the margins, especially Black women.[1] While the early national discourse on violence often trivialized race and racism, women-of-color-led organizations recognized the racialized and racist gaps and understood the intersectional capacity needed to end violence against women. By the mid-1970s, these organizations established a range of services specifically for women of color DV victims where previously there existed none.[2]

At the same time as the disappearing of Black women and their experiences from the social and political language of DV victimization, laws were also being introduced to more firmly establish domestic violence as a crime. Anti-violence organizations called for a carceral reconceptualization of rape, anti-rape laws, and violence against women in general. As anti-violence advocacy attempted to become more visible and accessible for "all" DV victims, advocacy's dependency on the law as a form of redress and safety was becoming increasingly evident.[3]

By 1976 the law and the anti-violence movement culminated with the passing of the Domestic Violence Act, which allowed DV victims to have their abusive partners removed from their shared home using a civil injunction while also leaving open the possibility of attaching powers of arrest for the abusive partners' subsequent violation, although this "possibility" is an illusion created by the state in this carceral context. The "power of arrest"—the concept that positions the state as benevolent protector while normalizing the act of arresting individuals—and anti-violence advocacy were now functioning on the same side of the equation; both strategies were interchangeable and implemented to remedy the violence women were experiencing. The anti-violence movement's reconceptualization of violence against women tethered criminality and carcerality to safety from gender-based violence, and the occupation of the law within anti-violence advocacy was guided by the dominant construction of domestic violence and sexual assault (SA) as social-problem crimes. Via law, anti-violence advocacy groups were now complicit participants with the state.

Advocacy groups were directly calling for state responsibility for preventing and treating victims of DV and SA. Ronald Reagan's first term as president signified the "incorporation of the feminist anti-violence movement into the apparatus of the regulatory state."[4] The focus for anti-violence leaders in the eighties was almost exclusively on legal and legislative strategies[5]—gender anti-violence advocates pushed for the criminalization of the violence being experienced by women. The national discourse on domestic violence turned toward criminality and carcerality. The issue of domestic violence began to be framed as a social problem based on "personal choices and immoral behavior [rather] than persistent lack of resources and structural arrangements."[6] The shift in the national understanding of what DV is and what DV does opened the door for the carceral treatment of women of color, specifically Black women, in these contexts.

Domestic violence was now a consequence of "personal choices and immoral behavior" that could only be remedied through criminalization and carceral logics. The demand for redress marked bodies involved in domestic violence, both victim and abuser, with a need for surveillance, containment, and regulation. The modification of DV narratives altered which bodies signified the DV problem.[7] By the early 1980s, a number of texts were published that specifically identified DV as an issue for Black women.[8] The positionality of Black women within the emerging liberal narratives that situated domestic violence as a consequence of "personal choices and immoral behavior" highlights the antiblack carceral logics that underpin current anti-violence advocacy.[9] The initial demand for responsibility, prevention, and treatment of victims by the state and the ways the anti-violence field was subsequently shaped by that demand created an intimately violent relationship between Black women survivors/victims and the state, a relationship that constructed Black women who identified as DV survivors/victims as always needing state intervention and "protection."

In this political context, protection for Black women meant surveillance, containment, and regulation. The imposition of surveillance, containment, and regulation became naturalized in the state's shifting narratives on DV. The effects of neoliberalism and its push on the "individual" shifted the discourse about domestic violence from being a consequence of structural racism and deteriorating communities to a by-product of poor personal choices.

CARCERAL ADVOCACY AS PRACTICE

As an illustration of how these dynamics unfold in the context of anti-violence services, I turn to a case study based on my own experience as an anti-violence advocate. In 2016 I worked at a DV crisis center located in the predominantly Latinx neighborhood of Pilsen, Chicago, that mostly served Latinas regardless of their citizenship status, as well as a DV shelter that is located on the West Side of Chicago in the Garfield Park neighborhood that mainly served Black women and their families. The DV crisis center in Pilsen portrayed itself as a very inclusive space, but it aimed only to serve Latinas—specifically Spanish-speaking Latinas with precarious citizenship statuses. While this particular demographic is a highly vulnerable group of people, it is this rigid definition of a deserving identity that I came to experience as problematic and violent. During my time at the crisis center I witnessed non-Latinx, non-Spanish-speaking, or Black clients come in seeking support be turned away by the agency. The staff believed that serving a non-Latinx demographic was a "difficult" undertaking that they were neither prepared for nor adequately versed in.

By refusing to service and support non-Latinx people, the crisis center purposely created a dichotomy for who they considered worthy and unworthy, deserving and undeserving, non-Black and Black. Situating the refusal of services under the umbrella of their own "inadequacy" obscures the logics of antiblackness driving the organization and the advocacy they offered. It was not a question of being too unskilled to serve Black clients but more a question about how the concept of Black victims of DV are rendered impossible in these spaces because Black victims cannot exist: they have been intentionally structured as illegible since slavery.

Government funding, particularly the passing of the Violence against Women Act (VAWA) in 1994, saturated anti-violence services and created an advocacy that only continued domestic violence and sexual assault, while also and continuing the violence of antiblackness and carcerality.[10] Because of the organization's limited budget, my time at the Pilsen crisis center was solely on a volunteer basis. I volunteered for seven to eight hours daily for six months, working the twenty-four-hour hotline, doing walk-in intakes, and helping out at the daycare while clients attended support groups or individual counseling. The crisis center's budget was saturated with federal, state, and city funding, meaning its reliance on funding from the nation-state ultimately dictated their approach to advocating against and understanding violence against women, making advocacy and the carceral neoliberal state virtually inseparable.[11]

As Mimi Kim argues in her analysis of the carceralization of antiviolence services, the advocates eventually became the cops.[12] For example, the crisis center serving Latinas required an intake specialist to offer and encourage women to sign up for group counseling. That group counseling had a two-year waitlist. Despite the additional services or alternative forms of support at the crisis center, it adamantly informed its volunteers that alternative and additional services can be given to clients only if specifically asked for by the client. After some quick research, it was discovered that surrounding agencies had readily available services with no waitlist. Supervisors continued to promote the idea that these victims/survivors were our clients and that services should be kept within the agency because numbers were needed in order to demonstrate to funders that DV services were greatly needed in the area. By definition a client receives services, but within this capitalist formula, clients were denied services because they were no longer victim/survivors but placeholders for the purpose of justifying the organization's need for funding. If waitlists were empty, programs were at risk of being cut or defunded entirely. Therefore, full waiting lists were left as is to the detriment of our clients.

Additionally, the women seeking support at the crisis center were routinely encouraged by the boundaries and limitations of VAWA and, by extension, the court system and the police to remedy the violence they were experiencing. VAWA came with a cost. As Richie writes,

VAWA represents "a set of harsh laws that disadvantaged some of the same communities that the population of women who are most vulnerable to male violence come from."[13] Noncarceral support was not available in these spaces. The law was and is the remedy because the remedy is only ever imagined as law. Carcerality / carceral logics and advocacy worked together in this Latinx-serving space.

Domestic violence and other anti-violence support group counseling was led by the two court advocates who had offices inside the crisis center. Group counseling not only consisted of understanding the different dimensions and layers of DV and SA but also was a crash course in how the law can remedy all of those problems. As Lee Ann S. Wang argues, undocumented women are heavily pressured to pursue orders of protection against their abusers,[14] and if clients refused to take legal action against their abusers, counseling services were scaled back and the women were then informed that their lack of action could put both them and their children in greater danger either at the hands of their abuser or by the state in the form of deportation.

Anti-violence advocacy actively connected survivors to state-sanctioned violence through "protective" forms of surveillance and threats of carceral violence through deportation. Court advocates with the support of the crisis center carried a tremendous weight when it came to community outreach and fundraising strategies, and they intentionally aligned themselves with the police department and police presence. Indeed, police involvement was highly visible within the Pilsen organization, specifically the crisis center's work with Chicago Alternative Policing Strategy (CAPS).[15] CAPS is a Chicago community-based program that has been functioning since 1993 and identifies itself as a policing strategy that brings police, local government agencies, and the community together in the "fight against crime." The Chicago Police Department website describes CAPS as

> a new weapon in the fight against crime. . . . What makes CAPS innovative is that it brings the police, the community, and other City agencies together to identify and solve neighborhood crime problems, rather than simply react to their symptoms after the fact. Problem solving at the neighborhood level is supported by a variety

> of strategies, including neighborhood-based beat officers; regular Beat Community Meetings involving police and residents; extensive training for both police and community; more efficient use of City services that impact crime; and new technology to help police and residents target crime hot spots.[16]

The program was initially rolled out in five trial-based police districts, and it is not a coincidence that those districts were communities that were primarily Black and disproportionately targeted by Chicago PD. When the program was revitalized by Rahm Emanuel (ex-mayor of Chicago and previous chief of staff under the Obama administration) in 2013, the program was rolled out in all twenty-five police districts. The city of Chicago's approach to community policing was to make "the community" the police, and it aimed to weaponize its citizens in a way that would allow a surveilling of communities twenty-four hours a day, seven days a week. The website contends "that weapon is you, the community." Cosponsored events between the crisis center and the police department directed the surrounding community's attention to strategies centering carceral remedies.

This was and is anti-violence advocacy administered within a carceral framework and logic; it is anti-violence advocacy that is bound to the nation-state. Anti-violence advocacy gained its legibility only through its connection to the state and its carceral practices. Survivor/victim narratives were guided by the imposed assumption that the state could remedy violence and that violence could be eradicated only if carcerality was part of advocacy frameworks. Carceral practices organized in the form of support services—surveillance, containment, and regulation—were integrated into advocacy for certain bodies through the withholding of information for the purpose of securing funding, required orders of protection, and counseling services that were shaped by carceral logics and literal carceral agents, and finally, the threat of deportation and continued violence was the ultimate way this crisis center advocated for survivor/victims. The law as remedy was also particularly visible at the DV shelter; however, law as remedy really meant remedy as literal carcerality, advocacy as carcerality, community as carcerality.

The DV shelter that primarily served Black victims was located on the West Side of Chicago in the Garfield Park neighborhood, which according to statistics in 2015 had a Black population of over 95 percent with a median household income of a little over $23,000. The shelter was a three-flat apartment building that had been converted into one large space with minimal accommodations. It housed about ten to twelve women and their children at a time. At the time, all the women were Black, and almost all were parents of small children, most under the age of seven. Per shelter policy, boys over thirteen were not allowed at the shelter for a fear (on behalf of the shelter staff) of possible sexual relationships between the boys and the women staying there.

Most of the women were young and had minimal educational opportunities prior to entering the shelter. Additionally, most women were unemployed, but the shelter required them to either have or seek employment with minimal assistance from shelter personnel. They held group counseling sessions (individual counseling was provided only if specifically requested and determined by the staff to be "needed"), required women to check in with their case managers, and offered a résumé building class, mothering/parenting classes, and good-citizenship classes. Whenever I speak about my time working at the shelter, I always say that I essentially acted as a sort of probation officer who would regulate and surveil these adult women during their hours at the shelter. Per *Merriam-Webster's*, a probation officer is an officer appointed to investigate, report on, and supervise the conduct of convicted offenders on probation.

Along with the imposed structure created by the shelter, the status of these women and their families, both inside and outside of the house, was saturated in surveillance. Surveillance or "supervising" within the context of the shelter consisted of making sure that the women and their children were first and foremost out of the house. Per house rules, they were not allowed to be at the shelter during the day. It did not matter if the women were employed or not—the shelter had to be empty from the hours of 8:00 a.m. to 6:00 p.m. This rule applied even during Chicago winters. The women and children living at the shelter were not in a space of community where advocacy and support were possible, but instead they were on probation, where dehumanizing conditions have been languaged to signify care work.[17] *Probation: the release of an offender from detention, subject to a period of good behavior under supervision.* The women and, by extension, their children were involved in deviant behavior that threatened hegemonic social norms, and in turn, these women and their children were labeled as offenders who were disposable but who also required containment, regulating, and constant surveillance.

To receive any type of physical or financial assistance these women were and are required by the state to exhibit good behavior and submit themselves to constant supervision. The law as a form of language had imposed a body of antiblack meaning onto Black women that further subordinated them as DV victims, a category which became interchangeable with offenders.[18] Any form of misconduct could lead to these women being removed from the shelter or denied other services. The shelter not only functioned as the law but also for the law, and it ultimately perpetuated the violence of the law.

Black women at the shelter existed in perpetual containment while becoming symbols of the perpetuation of what Richie calls "the prison nation," or prison beyond the cage. Perpetual containment and surveillance is what anti-violence advocacy looks like here—anti-violence advocacy that intentionally violates Black women.[19] Antiblackness and carcerality normalize the continuous pathologizing of Black women, treating them as undeserving of privacy, space, the ability and right to motherhood, nutrition and health, and the possibility of care and love.

The potential for Black women who identify as victims/survivors of DV is contained to a discourse on bodies who have made poor choices and perpetuate deviant behavior. Staff were directed to confirm that DV victims had made their beds every morning, the rooms were clean (the belongings of the women and their families had to be fully stored in a single box), breakfast and dinner were being cooked daily, communal spaces were clean and toy-free, and that medications for the women and their children were monitored to assure that they were being administered appropriately and safely. "Advocacy" in the space of this state-bound shelter had been transformed into carceral punishment and surveillance, and advocacy and protection for Black women had simultaneously become entangled with the devaluing of Black women's safety.

Instead of receiving community and support, Black women at the shelter were required to submit both themselves and their children to symbolic protection under the state. In this case, protection is not the opposite of violence but a correlation. The Black women who were victims and survivors of DV now symbolized bodies that required containment and surveillance. Surveillance had a continuous presence that reinforced Black women's lack of entitlement to privacy. For example, "protection and advocacy" meant that supervision was required when asking for sanitary pads and tampons, it meant timed restroom usage, and it meant mothers were not allowed to administer their children's medications without their case managers present. Hanging in the basement kitchen of the shelter, a sign read, "All canned foods are expired but still edible." At first glance I didn't believe what I was reading. I remember rereading the sign over and over because there was no way a shelter, especially a shelter for battered and violated women, would serve women and children expired foods. I was informed by the staff that the presence of expired foods was normal for shelters, and I was reassured by the staff that the women and children were happy to just be eating.

GENDERED ANTIBLACKNESS

What is gratuitous violence when it is gendered? Saidiya Hartman has argued that Black women are constructed as unrapeable, writing,

> The rape of black women existed as an unspoken but normative condition full within the purview of everyday sexual practices, whether within the implied arrangements of the slave enclave or within the plantation household.[20]

Antiblackness as gratuitous violence against Black women is materialized in the ceaseless presence of sexual violence, but more broadly, the corporeal illegibility of "victim." As a system of meaning, antiblackness situates Black victims as bodies that require surveillance, containment, regulation, and other forms of gratuitous incarceration. The "black female body" as always signifying and being a space and time of gratuitous violence, specifically and intentionally sexual violence or corporeal violence,[21] is central to why and how anti-violence advocacy is, at its foundation, a carceral antiblack project that disproportionally attacks Black women through the mechanisms of continuous surveillance and containment. Understanding how and why Black victims/survivors experience surveillance, containment, and regulation at the hands of the anti-violence movement requires contending with how antiblackness structures anti-violence advocacy.

The state's shift toward framing DV through poor personal choices and deviant behavior, and the centering of Black women within these neoliberal narratives of blame was, and continues to be, intentional. The presence of antiblackness and the necessity for surveillance within narratives of DV and its forms of redress construct sites of violence that are structural and gratuitous. As many have argued, antiblackness requires Blackness to be positioned outside of humanity, and, therefore, I argue also outside of DV victimhood.[22] Antiblackness forecloses the possibility of Black women occupying the category of proper victims of DV. If DV is defined as a racialized personal problem at the site of the individual or the individual community, DV and its victims are and can become pathologized.

Domestic violence becomes a "Black and Brown issue" as it is reinforced through the individualization and pathologization of DV.[23] This constructs violence as something that is unique and singular—if we understand DV as an isolated subject then, logically, the pathologizing of victims is merited. A pathologized victim indicates the need for "treatment," and the burden of that treatment is then transferred, in some cases, to victims and not the abuser.[24] Through the mechanism of pathology, the violence experienced by women is transformed into a nonviolence but more accurately a nonviolence that is simply a result of an individual's poor choices or deviant behavior.

If we understand pathology through the logics of antiblackness, it clarifies how the treatment of victims is transformed into the surveillance and containment of Black victims. Black women are signified as the "deviant outsider" and ultimately as destruction itself, as Tiffany Lethabo King writes, positioning Black women as profound threats to the nation-state and, relatedly, to the violent colonial project of the "family."[25] For example, the 1965 *Moynihan Report* emerged within a historical continuation of Black surveillance specifically situated at the site of Black women and Black mothers.[26] The report contends that "the United States is approaching a new crisis in race relations,"[27] and at the middle of this crisis is the "Negro family structure." The tethering of Black women and pathology is central to the report's argument that "the Negro community has been forced into a matriarchal structure which, because it is so out of line with the rest of the American society, seriously retards the progress of the group as a whole."[28]

King argues, "The Moynihan Report, like all projects of settler colonialism, must place Blackness. Settler colonialism must manage Black people and Black spaces."[29] As the head of a "tangle of pathology," as Moynihan characterizes Black families, Black women are positioned as an embodied justification for surveillance, containment, and regulation.[30] Centering Black women's positionality within the historical making and transforming of the anti-violence movement provides a genealogy that speaks to not only the current logics but also the material results seen in today's anti-violence advocacy. Anti-violence advocacy reinforces the construction of Black women as threats to the nation-state whose "poor choices" and "deviant behavior" have led them to become victims of DV. For Black DV victims in a carceral feminist, antiblack world, "protection, care, and advocacy" can only be surveillance, containment, and regulation.

TOWARD A THEORY OF SPECULATIVE ADVOCACY

After working at the crisis center and shelter I really questioned whether I was expecting too much from advocacy. After many conversations with people in and out of advocacy work, I was adamantly reassured that I was in fact not expecting too much from what it means to be an advocate. The sign in the kitchen at the shelter addressing the spoiled food was deplorable and unacceptable. The fact that women who had sons that were older than thirteen were unable to live at the shelter for the fear of any kind of sexual activity occurring between the boys and the women at the shelter was intolerable. So again I ask, what does anti-violence advocacy look like when it does not enact violence?

Throughout the years I have been asked why my research centers Black women and their experiences as opposed to Latinx narratives considering I identify as Mexican. Or I am told why I should instead center all women of color who experience DV. My answer: Because something different and intentional is happening when Black women attempt to identify as DV survivors and victims. That something different is found in gratuitous violence leveled against Black women in these forms of dehumanization. Black women are placed, if not made to be, "outside" of our understandings of what it means to be a proper victim of violence. The only survivors being asked and heard within anti-violence advocacy are those farthest away from Blackness. Blackness is not legible as something that deserves or warrants protection under the schema of anti-violence advocacy; instead Blackness ushers in a carceral logic that is understood to be necessary and therefore normalized. Multiple interventions within the field of anti-violence scholarship interrogate the violent structures that inform both gender violence and anti-violence advocacy.[31] Critics have provided the language necessary to understand that the law protecting the batterers is not an accidental shift—it is rooted in the racialized criminality of DV issues/victims/survivors.[32] These interventions exemplify what it means to center those most marginalized in order to produce anti-violence strategies that might actually address the concerns of women of color. Meeting INCITE!'s provocation in its 2006 anthology, *The Color of Violence*, scholars and organizers have shifted their question from, What should DV programs look like? to What would it take to end violence against women of color? These interventions make clear that to depend on the nation-state to redress violence against women of color is to hinge anti-violence to the white colonial structure that is the institutionalized violence women are experiencing. Therefore, shelters and agencies that depend on the nation-state and state funding to correct violence against women are a contradiction that perpetuates violence.

These authors transcend the politics of inclusion and instead create different forms of relationality by pushing back on the anti-violence movement that has been co-opted by the colonial structure that, in turn, now functions as a surrogate for the state. They also recognize the pathologization of women who are victims of violence and understand that the nonprofit-industrial complex functions within the capitalist system in managing dissent and administering state-sanctioned and state-sponsored violence. These authors recognize the complex dynamics of abuse and violence that structure the experiences of women of color. In the process of writing this essay I found myself constantly taking a step back to recenter myself and my argument. I kept asking myself, Am I sure that the advocacy and the community I am arguing for does not already exist? Are people already practicing a radical understanding of advocacy that is moving toward a better beyond, not just for the individual but for everyone? Honestly, I do not know. Regardless of whether it is, a radical understanding and practice of advocacy and community are not available or possible for all.

I do not have a clear, concise definition for the radical manifestations of advocacy or community that I am constantly referencing; however, I do think that we can look back on the critical work that has been done, take fragments of those interventions that have worked and continue to work, and piece them together in hopes of making and knowing a more robust form of caring. Reconceptualizing advocacy with an entirely new language that has the potential to interrupt the uninterrupted line of punitive actions and care is a good start. Care work is not static; instead it is always adapting, growing, and moving.[33]

Critical advocacy can help remedy the now while working toward possible futures. I am left with a series of questions that may help us map a nonviolent form of anti-violence advocacy. How do we begin to reconceptualize advocacy that is not antiblack, carceral, and bound to the nation-state? Decades-long scholarship shows us that violence is at times generational, structural, and systemic, so how can we build a more robust way of advocating and community so that care work does not just begin after the violence has materialized? What steps, what types of conversations, what types of community care work can we implement that will perhaps aid in the days/months/years before the violence occurs? How can we begin to advocate and be in community in a way that has the potential to stop gender violence altogether? Anti-violence advocacy assumes that survivor/victims no longer experience violence once those violent events have passed, and it assumes that community presence and support will not aid in the long process of healing. If we center alternative ways of being and living instead of alternative ways of dealing with violence, advocacy can be more than just a reaction to the co-opted anti-violence movement. A reconceptualization of anti-violence advocacy is essentially a call for a new form of being, a new form of caring, a new form of being community, and new world making.

The long legacy of Black and abolition feminisms encourages us to imagine and create the world we want that is not existentially dependent on antiblackness and carcerality. Additionally, abolition feminisms foreground the significance and power of creating and cultivating strong communities, understanding that community is foundational to living in a better beyond. If we center the most basic foundations of feminist abolitionist work—radical liberation and shared accountability—then creating a new form of advocacy and being is definitely a possibility. Anti-violence work that is not anti-Black, carceral, and nation-state-bound understands that it is not about finding a remedy to a single event in an individual's life based on poor choices or deviant behavior but instead a form of care work that calls on us to reevaluate and recalibrate how we care and love one another. Critical anti-violence work and advocacy also acknowledge that violence is present in the before and after. Violence, anti-Blackness, and carcerality are profound technologies of power. Articulating and most importantly practicing a different kind of imaginary when it comes to the praxis of being is therefore deeply needed. It cannot just be critique and resistance; it must be that and then something else, a space of otherwise.

BIBLIOGRAPHY

Asian American Writers' Workshop, AAWW TV: "Dreaming Disability Justice," with Leah Lakshmi Piepzna-Samarasinha and Cyrée Jarelle Johnson. https://www.youtube.com/watch?v=8UpQVlT2wCQ&ab_channel=AsianAmericanWriters%27Workshop.

Bell, Derrick. *Faces at the Bottom of the Well: The Permanence of Racism*. New York: Basic Books, 2018.

Bierria Alisa. "Missing in Action: Violence, Power, and Discerning Agency." *Hypatia* 29, no. 1 (2014): 129–45.

Bierria, Alisa, and Colby Lenz. "Battering Court Syndrome: A Structural Critique of 'Failure to Protect.'" In *The Politicization of Safety: Critical Perspectives on Domestic Violence Responses*, 91–118. New York: NYU Press, 2019.

Bumiller, Kristin. *In an Abusive State: How Neoliberalism Appropriated the Feminist Movement against Sexual Violence*. Durham, NC: Duke University Press, 2008.

Chicago Police Department. Accessed May 22, 2020. https://home.chicagopolice.org/community-policing-group/how-caps-works/what-is-caps/.

Combahee River Collective. *A Black Feminist Statement*. In *The Second Wave: A Reader in Feminist Theory*, edited by Linda Nicholson, 63–70. New York: Routledge, 1997.

Dixon, Ejeris, and Leah Lakshmi Piepzna-Samarasinha. *Beyond Survival: Strategies and Stories from the Transformative Justice Movement*. Chico, CA: AK Press, 2020.

Fanon, Frantz. *Black Skin, White Masks*. New York: Grove Weidenfeld, 1991.

———. *The Wretched of the Earth*. New York: Grove Press, 1963.

Hartman, Saidiya. *Scenes of Subjection: Terror, Slavery and Self-Making in Nineteenth-Century America*. Oxford, UK: Oxford University Press, 1997.

INCITE! "Critical Resistance Statement on Gender Violence and the Prison-Industrial Complex." *Social Justice* 30, no. 3 (2003): 141–50.

———. *Color of Violence: The INCITE! Anthology*. Durham, NC: Duke University Press, 2016.

———. The Revolution Will Not Be Funded: Beyond the Non-Profit Industrial Complex. Durham, NC: Duke University Press, 2017.

Kim, Mimi E. "The Carceral Creep: Gender-Based Violence, Race and the Expansion of the Punitive State, 1973–1983." *Social Problems*, 2019.

King, Tiffany Lethabo. "Black 'Feminisms' and Pessimism: Abolishing Moynihan's Negro Family." *Theory & Event* 21, no. 1 (January 2018): 68–87.

———. "In the Clearing: Black Female Bodies, Space and Settle Colonial Landscapes." PhD dissertation, University of Maryland, 2013.

Koyama, Emi. "Disloyal to Feminism: Abuse of Survivors within the Domestic Violence Shelter System." In *Color of Violence: The INCITE! Anthology*, 208–22. Durham, NC: Duke University Press, 2016.

Lorde, Audre. *Sister Outsider: Essays and Speeches*. Trumansburg, NY: Crossing Press, 1984.

McDuff, Robin, et al. "Open Letter to the Anti-Rape Movement, 1977." Edited by Mariame Kaba. Project Nia, 2020. https://issuu.com/projectnia/docs/letter-to-the-antirape-movement.

Moynihan, Daniel Patrick. *The Negro Family: The Case for National Action*. Office of Policy Planning and Research. Washington, DC: US Department of Labor, March 1965.

Richie, Beth E. *Arrested Justice: Black Women, Violence, and America's Prison Nation*. New York: New York University Press, 2012.

Ritchie, Andrea J. *Invisible No More: Police Violence against Black Women and Women of Color*. Boston: Beacon Press, 2017.

Roberts, Dorothy. *Killing the Black Body: Race, Reproduction, and the Meaning of Liberty*. New York: Random House, 1997.

Smith, Andrea. *Conquest: Sexual Violence and American Indian Genocide*. Boston: South End Press, 2005.

Vargas, João Helion Costa. *The Denial of Antiblackness: Multiracial Redemption and Black Suffering*. Minneapolis: University of Minnesota Press, 2018.

Wang, Lee Ann S. "Unsettling Innocence: Rewriting the Law's Invention of Immigrant Woman as Cooperator and Criminal Enforcer." *Scholar & Feminist Online: Navigating Neoliberalism in the Academy, Nonprofits, and Beyond*, no. 13.2 (Spring 2016). https://sfonline.barnard.edu/navigating-neoliberalism-in-the-academy-nonprofits-and-beyond/lee-ann-wang-unsettling-innocence-rewriting-the-laws-invention-of-immigrant-woman-as-cooperator-and-criminal-enforcer/.

White, James Boyd. *The Legal Imagination*. Boston: Little, Brown, 1973.

Wilderson III, Frank. "Irreconcilable Anti-Blackness: A Conversation with Dr. Frank Wilderson III." Ask the Theory Question. May 25, 2017. https://www.youtube.com/watch?v=k1W7WzQyLmI&t=2194s.

NOTES

1 Beth E. Richie, *Arrested Justice: Black Women, Violence, and America's Prison Nation* (New York: New York University Press, 2012).

2 Richie, *Arrested Justice*.

3 Kristin Bumiller, *In an Abusive State: How Neoliberalism Appropriated the Feminist Movement against Sexual Violence* (Durham, NC: Duke University Press, 2008); Richie, *Arrested Justice*; Robin McDuff et al., "Open Letter to the Anti-Rape Movement, 1977," ed. Mariame Kaba, Project Nia, 2020, https://issuu.com/projectnia/docs/letter-to-the-antirape-movement; Mimi E. Kim, "The Carceral Creep: Gender-Based Violence, Race and the Expansion of the Punitive State, 1973–1983," *Social Problems* (2019).

4 Bumiller, *In an Abusive State*.

5 Richie, *Arrested Justice*.

6 Richie, 108.

7 Alisa Bierria, "Missing in Action: Violence, Power, and Discerning Agency," *Hypatia* 29, no. 1 (2014): 129–45.

8 Richie, *Arrested Justice*.

9 See Dorothy Roberts, *Killing the Black Body: Race, Reproduction, and the Meaning of Liberty* (New York: Random House, 1997) for a detailed review of

how the narrative of "personal choices and immoral behavior" similarly shaped the history of reproductive politics for Black women in the US.

10 Bumiller, 2008.

11 Other advocates have also analyzed how racist capitalism structures the boundaries of anti-violence advocacy, including "Pursing a Radical Anti-Violence Agenda Inside/Outside a Non-Profit Structure," by Alisa Bierria, and "'We Were Never Meant to Survive': Fighting Violence against Women and the Fourth World War," by Ana Clarissa Rojas Durazo, both published in the INCITE! anthology *The Revolution Will Not Be Funded* (2007), as well as "Disloyal to Feminism: Abuse of Survivors within the Domestic Violence Shelter System," by Emi Koyama, published in the INCITE! anthology *Color of Violence* (2006).

12 Activist-scholar Mimi Kim has troubled this notion of insidious co-optation in her article "Dancing the Carceral Creep: The Anti-Domestic Violence Movement and the Paradoxical Pursuit of Criminalization," arguing that, though anti-violence advocates aimed to control state power rather than collude with it, they were nevertheless consumed by it (2019).

13 Richie, 86.

14 In her article "Unsettling Innocence: Rewriting the Law's Invention of Immigrant Woman as Cooperator and Criminal Enforcer," Lee Ann S. Wang centers the link between anti-violence advocacy and immigration law as a way to illuminate the invention of new legal subjects. Wang argues that undocumented Asian women who experience violence are "shuttled between positions of innocence and culpability and are invented as new kinds of legal subjects who expand criminal enforcement while being marked as objects of legal protection." In this case, undocumented Asian women who experience violence receive advocacy and "protection" only as long as they are willing to contribute to the expansion of the prison nation.

15 Chicago Police Department, "What Is CAPS?" https://home.chicagopolice.org/community-policing-group/how-caps-works/what-is-caps/.

16 Chicago Police Department, https://home.chicagopolice.org/community-policing-group/how-caps-works/what-is-caps/.

17 The intentional conjugation of the word "language" into a verb, *languaged/s*, is meant to signify the capability of action and power within language. As a verb, language is revealed to contain transforming abilities; it can make and unmake something or someone. Drawing from James Boyd White's work in *The Legal Imagination* and Hortense Spillers's intervention in "Mama's Baby, Papa's Maybe: An American Grammar Book," the material consequences of language as a verb are realized. White argues that the law is not only a form of language that is capable of constructing and containing but also a site where different possibilities can be created. Similar to the language of the law, Spillers contends that the captive (female) body is marked as "a kind of hieroglyphic" that renders it as flesh available for torture and naming. Spillers is calling attention to the language that contains and regulates Black women as continuous sites of state violence—"Peaches, Brown Sugar, Sapphire, Earth Mother, Aunty, Granny, etc." Drawing from Spillers and White, I argue that anti-violence work as it functions within an anti-Black world is also a

language that is capable of constructing, containing, but more importantly creating different realities. Meaning and understanding are transformed within the context of anti-Blackness specifically for Black women—for example, "protection," "victim," and "advocacy" are reconstructed to mean carcerality, criminal, and surveillance.

18 James Boyd White, *The Legal Imagination* (Boston: Little, Brown, 1973).

19 While the word "violence" is typically used and understood as a noun, I believe within the context of anti-Blackness, violence more accurately functions as a verb. "Violences" implies that it is continuous, always moving, shifting, transforming, remaking itself perpetually, and most importantly, innate and never ending.

20 Saidiya Hartman, *Scenes of Subjection: Terror, Slavery and Self-Making in Nineteenth-Century America* (Oxford: Oxford University Press, 1997).

21 This argument is drawing from Saidiya Hartman's *Scenes of Subjection* and her analysis of the "black female body" and the conditions of illegible violence and Tiffany Lethabo King's argument in her dissertation "In the Clearing: Black Female Bodies, Space and Settle Colonial Landscapes" regarding the Black female body and its function as a site where we can observe the power of slavery and settler colonialism simultaneously.

22 Derrick Bell, *Faces at the Bottom of the Well: The Permanence of Racism* (New York: Basic Books, 2018); the work of Frank Wilderson, more specifically his talk in Ask the Theory Question, "Irreconcilable Anti-Blackness: A Conversation with Dr. Frank Wilderson III"; Saidiya Hartman, *Scenes of Subjection*; João Helion Costa Vargas, *The Denial of Antiblackness: Multiracial Redemption and Black Suffering* (Minneapolis: University of Minnesota Press, 2018); and Tiffany Lethabo King, "In the Clearing."

23 Bumiller, *In an Abusive State.*

24 Bumiller, 67–70.

25 Tiffany Lethabo King, "Black 'Feminisms' and Pessimism: Abolishing Moynihan's Negro Family," *Theory & Event* 21, no. 1 (January 2018): 68–87.

26 Daniel Patrick Moynihan, *The Negro Family: The Case for National Action*, Office of Policy Planning and Research (Washington, DC: US Department of Labor, March 1965).

27 Moynihan, introduction.

28 Moynihan, 29.

29 King, "In the Clearing."

30 King, "Black 'Feminisms' and Pessimism."

31 Kim, "Dancing the Carceral Creep"; Bierria, "Missing in Action"; Rojas Durazo, "Reimagining Community Accountability"; Koyama, "Disloyal to Feminism"; Richie, *Arrested Justice*; Smith, *Conquest;* INCITE! "Critical Resistance."

32 Alisa Bierria and Colby Lenz, "Battering Court Syndrome: A Structural Critique of 'Failure to Protect,'" in *The Politicization of Safety: Critical Perspectives on Domestic Violence Responses*, 91–118 (New York: New York University Press, 2019).

33 Asian American Writers' Workshop, AAWW TV: "Dreaming Disability Justice," with Leah Lakshmi Piepzna-Samarasinha and Cyrée Jarelle Johnson, https://www.youtube.com/watch?v=8UpQVlT2wCQ&ab_channel=AsianAmericanWriters%27Workshop.

kai lumumba barrow, "Aunt Hester's Scream" (photo by Shana M. griffin)

"Aunt Hester's Scream" is part of the installation *The Moment of Sale*. This work considers the bitter history of Louisiana's largest cash crop. Embracing historian Stephanie Camp's rival geographies thesis, the work imagines the resistance of enslaved women in the face of constraint. Auction houses, private showrooms, holding cells, slave quarters, and fields all served as carceral locations where the enslaved came to expect displacement and dehumanization. Nonetheless, these public and private sites of sex and violence were also places where the enslaved actualized their agency and control. From being uncooperative and "artful" to misrepresentation and self-harm, from organizing work stoppages to escapes and revolts, the rival geographies of the enslaved provided the space for private and public creative expressions, rest and recreation, community and self-care, coded communication, and defiance. Persistent noncompliance was built into the social and human fabric of plantation life. In this sense, *The Moment of Sale* reads the auction block, the bedroom, and the Black body as sites of political performance where the enslaved recast themselves beyond the point of sale.

STAY CONNECTED AT ALL COSTS

Alisha Walker in conversation with Red Schulte

This May 2020 interview stems from the project Archiving Abolition, a collaboration between Interference Archive, a collective that produces the *Audio Interference* podcast cultivating critical and creative engagement with archives of social movements via audio projects and podcasting, and Survived & Punished New York, an abolitionist collective that organizes to end the criminalization of survivors of domestic and sexual violence and the culture of violence that contributes to it.[1] Archiving Abolition bridges the information gap created by prisons by sharing the experiences of survivors behind prison walls with those on the outside. Red Schulte is a member of Support Ho(s)e, a small leftist formation of sex workers based in Chicago and New York that organized the Justice for Alisha Walker Defense Campaign.

Red Schulte: Alisha Walker is a twenty-nine-year-old former sex-working person originally from Akron, Ohio. In January 2014, Alisha was contacted by a returning client who agreed to pay her and another sex worker for sex in his Orland Park [Illinois] house. When Alisha and the other sex worker arrived, the client was very intoxicated and demanded that the sex be unprotected. Alisha and her fellow worker refused what they saw as unsafe services, asserting that he had to stick to their agreed upon terms. He became violent and punched Alisha in the face, then threatened both women with a knife. Alisha struggled with him and managed to wrestle the knife away, stabbing him in self-defense. Both she and the other worker fled. Alisha was arrested and charged with second-degree murder despite no physical evidence ever being recovered. She was held without trial for twenty months in Cook County Jail. At her trial, the prosecutor portrayed Alisha as a manipulative criminal mastermind, calling her a monster and speaking disparagingly about her family and her profession as a sex worker. Her defense attorneys sexually harassed her and never requested bond. A jury convicted her of second-degree murder, and Alisha was sentenced to fifteen years in prison. She was incarcerated at Decatur Correctional Center in Decatur, Illinois, at the time of this interview. Due to her self-advocacy and the organizing of the #FreeLeLe campaign led by Support Ho(s)e, Alisha was released in July 2021.

Alisha Walker: I'm a lot of different things. I'm an unapologetic survivor. I'm a fighter fiercely loyal to my community. I'm a Black multiethnic woman. I'm an artist, a poet, a zine maker, and an inside organizer. I'm queer and I was a sex worker for several years. The criminalization of sex work and survival is why I'm locked up. I'm currently incarcerated in Decatur, Illinois. I want people to know about the amazing work that's being done to fight back. I'm proud to be in that work however I can from inside. I'm deeply grateful for my friends and family who started organizing alongside me through my defense campaign. My comrades and Support Ho(s)e, Survived & Punished, the Uptown People's Law Center, Moms United against Violence and Incarceration, and Love & Protect. When I'm out, get ready.

RS: How do you access information? What information do you feel you're missing? What information are we missing?

AW: I access information by watching what little news we have access to, the four channels basically, but mostly through my support networks and outside friends. When the Wi-Fi works, I get emails and access to information that way. Calls are the most important method of communication for me. I rely on Red and Erica* a lot for these. I know we are missing a lot in here. We can't easily fact check the rumor mills that exist and circulate inside. I understand why people do it, start rumors I mean, but it can be a real obstacle to tackling problems we face in

---

* Red and Erica are founding members of Support Ho(s)e and the Justice for Alisha Walker Campaign.

here. I know the media that we do get access to on TV is controlled by the wealthy and by people in power. So, I know that, without getting real news from my friends and family outside, I'm only getting part of the story or some twisted version of it from the regular news. My mail is censored and read, confiscated, or lost. My emails are looked through and approved or denied. I can't get copies of newsletters like *Free: Survivors* regularly because I got a target on me in here,[2] because they know I stand up for myself and others. There's just the surveillance, you're being watched all the time. It means what we can and can't say or do or discuss is always monitored. Y'all are probably missing how we're really treated in here. Even if COs [correctional officers] are wrong, they're right. The way the prison officers herd us and treat us like we're children or cattle. The way the prison deliberately withholds information, like we don't even know when they know or what they know. That's what scares me. When will they actually tell us if the pandemic or another crisis gets in? Will I find out from you, Red, first? Probably, even if they knew something, they keep it from us. I know it. The other day I was confronting a lieutenant about my personal safety and the poor sanitary conditions here. And I asked him point blank, would you be straight with me? Would you tell me if this virus was in here? He just stared at me and was like, I don't know if I could.

RS: How has access to information and your loved ones changed since the COVID-19 outbreak?

AW: It's scary. I have to ask five different people in here to try and fact check as best I can when news starts circulating. In-person visits have been canceled. Those were lifelines to us. Phone lines are ridiculous. Sometimes you're waiting an hour to use a phone, then you're only allowed to do that maybe twice a day now. No new resources have been added. We still get bleach water to clean with. That's it. There are delays in meals. Only 50 people are allowed in chow hall at a time. And we've got 110 people on my unit. We're not getting to shop fully. There's limited commissary. Women are going to seg left and right because things are escalating.[3] CEOs are going hard against people as fears and anxieties take over. Tensions are running high. The prison administration is not telling people about these related policies, or these release policies. Everything feels random, made up. We're all just reeling.

RS: What do you think are effective models for solidarity across boundaries?

AW: Listen to us. Solidarity comes from building relationships, connecting with other advocates, and the drive to keep fighting and not give up. I'd say, to be effective, you must stay connected at all costs. Letter-writing campaigns need to be responsive to our needs. The newsletters! Newsletters let me know what's going on outside. This organizing news is so crucial. Getting report backs on actions and campaigns, it keeps us all going.

RS: "Access" comes from the Latin *accessus*, meaning "a coming to" from the adjective "to" + "*cedere*" – go, move, to move to, toward. What would you like to see our world moving toward? What do you think is preventing that movement?

AW: I want to see a better world. I want acceptance without judgment and hate. I want real joy. I want sex workers to be truly safe. We should move toward a world without prisons and police that really only hurt us. I don't fit easily into categories. I don't fit into boxes. I want a world without boxes. I want to live in a world that doesn't criminalize our survival. My faith tells me to love and forgive and that's what I want for all of us. I want us to really love our neighbors. The ego and desire of people in power control us, preventing us from moving forward like we need to. Sometimes we prevent our own moving forward because we're tripping on each other. There's a lot standing that has been built to be in our way. We want a better world, but that's not cheap. So how do we get the people what they need to keep fighting? How do we get us out so that we can fight as free people? What keeps all of us from being truly free? I'm left with so many questions. I hope we can overcome all that stands between us and get that world that we want.

NOTES

1 *Audio Interference* is produced by Interference Archive, a volunteer-run social space, exhibition venue, and open stacks community archive based in Brooklyn, New York, that explores the relationship between art production and social movements. See https://interferencearchive.org/. Survived & Punished NY is a collective dedicated to ending the criminalization of survival. See https://www.survivedandpunishedny.org/.

2 Survived & Punished New York publishes the newsletter *Free: Survivors* and circulates copies to incarcerated survivors throughout New York State and across the country.

3 "Seg" is short for Segregated Housing Units, where incarcerated people are punished by isolating them in a cell, sometimes for twenty-three hours a day.

when he dies

Jasmine Tabor

when our brother dies, we tie pretty ribbons to our hats
sit in the back of the parlor and pet the funeral home cat
wait til the hot pie is pulled from the oven, baking hot
and touch the fork to our tongue, heat producing snot
running down the front of our cardigans
because it's better to make a mess than cry again

when our father dies, we press flowers to his casket
listen to the pastor tell us eternal sins await us
while we toss quarters from the ground into the basket
we hold his handkerchief in our hands, must
sniffle into the initials—being ladylike enough to mask it:
the sadness while we adjust

when our husband dies, we lose a sense of self
as we fade impolitely into the wallpaper,
the grievances left for them while i think, too,
did my mother not die last year? her shelf
of books left to me as her mind turns to vapor
and my tears lost to the moon's view

when i go, it will be nothing of the ceremonies
i witnessed in my life as my passing was peaceful
(ulcers here, stress scars in my brain,
my knees needed replacing, my hands are coarse)
in comparison to all the bullet holes, the broken necks
because longevity beats short term somehow

PART TWO

REFUSING REFORM, RESISTING CAPTIVITY

Shana M. griffin, "The Precarity of Crossing," SOIL Project (photo by Shana M. griffin), 2021

"The Precarity of Crossing," taken at the levee by Nottoway Plantation facing the Mississippi River near White Castle, Louisiana, is part of a soil collection and photographic series documenting the violent subjugation and dispossession of Black people on former and current sugarcane plantations lining the East and West Banks of the Mississippi River in Louisiana.

Spanning fifty-five sites, including abandoned and vacant houses, slave cabins, museums, tourist destinations, levee landings, private residencies, and sugarcane fields across fifteen parishes, the Nottaway Plantation is symbolic of the violence of slavery, the dangers of "crossing" to escape, and the precarity of fugitivity and freedom. SOIL traces the carceral spaces of what is left behind in and on the grounds of sugarcane plantations, mapping the forgotten scars of past and present disappearances through the soil. It interrogates the history of a crop marked by slavery, conquest, and confinement, bringing attention to the marginalized lives of enslaved people who worked, died, created families, and witnessed loved ones born and sold into servitude on the grounds from which the soil is collected, objects assembled, and photos taken.

SOIL is an exercise in Black feminist geographic thought and grounded theory, making visible the violence of slavery, its carceral afterlife, and remnants of loss bearing witness in the soil. The geographies of Black extraction, displacement, and disposability, shaped by a carceral landscape and colonial enterprise, congeal fragments of life, blood, tears, despair, and memories of resistance recorded in the soil.

DOMESTIC TERROR

WOMEN'S PRISONS AND ASSATA SHAKUR'S ABOLITIONIST REFUSAL

Jess Issacharoff

In 2013 Assata Shakur had the dubious honor of becoming the first woman named to the FBI's Most Wanted Terrorists list, with a million-dollar reward listed for "information leading to her capture."[1] Shakur's addition to the list was prompted by the fortieth anniversary of the death of a New Jersey state trooper that she was convicted for in 1973, before escaping prison in 1979 and finding political asylum in Cuba. It was far from the first time Shakur was portrayed as exceptional by either her critics or her supporters. In making an example of Shakur as a "domestic terrorist," the Federal Bureau of Investigation primarily succeeded in sealing her legacy as a revolutionary icon whose radical politics of Black liberation, played out in a very public sphere. Today Shakur's words are a rallying cry for Black liberation, and the phrase "Assata taught me" is omnipresent at Black Lives Matter protests.

I take advantage of the multiple resonances of the term "domestic terrorism" to read the triple threat Shakur posed to the state, to the conception of the white domestic family, and to the domestic forms of discipline enacted against her during her incarceration. Shakur is not traditionally read as a critic of the family or domesticity, and her status as a revolutionary figure is generally understood primarily as a critique of the violent domestic state. I argue that Shakur incisively reads the significance of particularly domestic forms of discipline enacted on

Black families by the state in relation to "smaller" forms of familial violence and "larger" forms of global hegemony. She also makes explicit connections between legacies of slavery and racial capitalism and refers to her current status as that of a maroon or fugitive slave.

Shakur documents her experience and analysis of the role played by the women's prison and its relationship to "the tenements, the shooting galleries, and the welfare hotels" in "Women in Prison: How We Are," an essay published in the *Black Scholar* in 1978, the year before she escaped from Clinton Correctional Facility for Women in New Jersey.[2] Shakur's essay, born out of her experience at the Rikers Island Correctional Institution for Women, forms the central theoretical framework of this essay. In it I foreground Shakur's experience to analyze the forms of discipline levied against her and explore the political and theoretical mode of refusal she enacts. Through Shakur's analysis I read the women's facility on Rikers Island as both a descendant of and a departure from previous iterations of women's incarceration and domestic forms of discipline.*

The Rikers Island Correctional Institution for Women was dedicated in 1971 with great fanfare. As Mayor John Lindsay looked on in approval, Corrections Commissioner George F. McGrath claimed, "This is the first time we have had a physical facility to match what has been our philosophy for decades."[3] The same *New York Times* article in which McGrath's optimistic quote appeared wholeheartedly condemned the previous central jail facility for women in NYC, the House of Detention: "The old house of detention, built in 1932, was overcrowded almost from its opening. It came in for frequent criticism and calls for its replacement, and a new one first appeared in the 1955

* I am slightly eliding a distinction between jail and prison here. Rikers Island, and the institutions it replaced, are jails, in that they were primarily meant for pretrial confinement and short sentences of less than a year, though in actuality people may be held for far longer depending on trial delays and other failings. Though there is a distinction, I am reading this particular institution as emblematic of certain shifts in the ideological framing of the "women's prison" writ large. While the women incarcerated primarily served relatively short sentences at Rikers and its predecessors, the language used to describe and justify them still relies heavily on the broad aims of prison as "rehabilitative" institutions that produce particular reformed subjects.

capital budget."[4] The irony of this account is almost unbearable given that forty years earlier the same paper had breathlessly covered the opening ceremony for the House of Detention, and the closing of the similarly derided Blackwells Island, heralding its incredible strides in rehabilitation. Now it noted that the new Correctional Institution for Women "reflects the change from punitive incarceration to rehabilitation."[5] The improvement over the old, overcrowded facility naturally included an expanded holding capacity with 750 cells to replace the 500 at the House of Detention.

In its expanded capacity, the new facility offered "private rooms," another promised innovation of the House of Detention that was quickly undermined by overcrowding. However, though the House of Detention was heralded as "the most modern and best-equipped penal institution for women in the world" and a "school for citizenship," Commissioner McGrath opened the dedication ceremonies for the Correctional Institution for Women by stating, "Welcome to New York's newest and perhaps best hotel."[6] No longer just a model and pedagogic penal institution, the new facility was portrayed as a temporary housing complex, and better than many that New York City had to offer, suggesting a more damning picture of the city than had perhaps been intended. Although many of these trumpeted reforms could have been plucked from the same paper's description of the previous maligned institution, McGrath's triumphant likening of the prison to a hotel signals a shift. The Correctional Institution for Women offered temporary housing rather than the moral training of the domestic home, more akin to the welfare hotel or the tenement than a "school for citizenship."* This temporary housing model marks a point of

---

* The section of this essay titled "Women's Prisons and Welfare Hotels" explores the phenomenon of welfare hotels. In short, they were squalid hotels used as temporary housing for unhoused populations in New York City in the 1970s and 1980s. As with the distinction between jails and prisons, the "temporary" nature of the stays was often stretched past the limit. The practice was publicized to great public dismay, and a majority of the hotels were vacated by the early nineties, though the practice has remained in other forms. See Jonathan Kozol, *Rachel and Her Children: Homeless Families in America* (Crown Publishers, 1988), a revised collection of his *New Yorker* series on the phenomenon.

departure for the women's prison and one that Shakur illustrates in her writing about her own experience. Shakur stayed at "hotel" Rikers for just over eight months during her trial in 1973. If previous eras marked strategic containment to and exclusion from an idealized home, this period marks the beginning of a strategy of warehousing excess populations.

Shakur's experience and her analysis of that experience illuminate the nature of mass incarceration at the moment of its birth. In the year 1974, President Richard Nixon declared war on drugs, which inaugurated a steep rise in incarceration.[7] From 1973 to 1974, the year identified by the Consensus Study Report as the beginning of a period of sustained growth, the population of men incarcerated in state and federal institutions increased from 204,211 to 218,466 (a 7 percent rise) while that of women grew from 6,004 to 7,309 (a 22 percent rise).[8] While it is the massive nominal growth of men's incarceration that is usually traced to Nixon's war on drugs, these policies would have an immediate and sharp effect on women, effecting a growing women's prison population. That growth would accelerate sharply in the early eighties, as policies and programs initiated in the early seventies took full effect. The Drug Enforcement Agency was created in 1973, institutionalizing the war on drugs, which would in turn justify the massive increases in policing and sentencing in the coming decades.[9]

The year 1973 also saw one of the major instigating events of a global project of privatization and neoliberalism: the American-backed coup in Chile, which toppled democratically elected Salvador Allende and installed the brutal dictator Augusto Pinochet. In linking the massive expansion of domestic policing and state intervention with the project of promoting privatization and a shrunken welfare state abroad, I follow Shakur, who connects intimate forms of violence to structural state projects as well as global colonial ones. In *Assata: An Autobiography* Shakur asserts that "prisons are part of this government's genocidal war against Black and Third World people."[10] Through Shakur's work, I offer an abolitionist feminist framework for analyzing the nascent structure of mass incarceration and the evolving disciplinary modes of women's incarceration. This abolitionist feminism provides scaffolding for a critique of carcerality that illuminates the experiential and spatial nature of confinement; the interwoven histories of sites and practices of social reproduction, race, and housing policy; and the structuring discipline of the home in shaping and justifying women's confinement.

BLACK LIBERATION AND THE ORIGINS OF MASS INCARCERATION

Shakur's trial and incarceration were, from the start, political flashpoints. Her arrest was, and continues to be, understood as part of a wholesale attack on Black radicals by the state. One of these attacks was the 1969 murder of Fred Hampton, the twenty-one-year-old leader of the Illinois chapter of the Black Panther Party (BPP). The Chicago Police Department, under the orders of the FBI, assassinated Hampton in his bed where he slept beside his pregnant girlfriend. He was shot twice in the head at point-blank range. Hampton's assassination represented a targeted murder designed to undermine the operations of the Chicago Black Panthers. Hampton, in particular, had been a remarkably effective young organizer who prioritized solidarity and social welfare programs. He had introduced the Panthers' free breakfast program to Chicago, successfully created a multiracial "rainbow coalition" in city politics, and brokered a ceasefire between local gangs. It was Hampton's demonstrated aim and ability to foment and develop networks of community and kinship that proved so dangerous.[11]

Through the murder of Fred Hampton and many more, COINTELPRO decimated a generation of Black political leaders throughout the 1960s and 1970s. Shakur, too, was targeted in this assault on Black radical leaders, leading to her 1973 arrest. She had been the subject of several investigations by the NYPD and FBI in 1971 and 1972. In 1973 Shakur, along with Zayd Malik Shakur and Sundiata Acoli, was pulled over on the Jersey Turnpike by a New Jersey state trooper for driving with a broken taillight, a common justification for search and seizure used by police. Shakur was arrested as a result of this encounter and accused of the murder of a state trooper, for which she was convicted and incarcerated.*

Shakur's position within the Black liberation movement and her deployment as a threat in state propaganda are both incredibly particular to her as an individual and representative of a large-scale attack on Black women in the 1970s. Joy James notes in "Framing the Panther: Assata Shakur and Black Female Agency" that Assata "stands alone" among the women of the Black Panther Party as "a recognizable female revolutionary, one not bound to a male persona."[12] Shakur was politicized individually and without connection to a Black male counterpart, a status amplified by her "outlaw status." According to James, "Her hybridity is a confluence of masculine and feminine (stereotypical) characteristics."[13] Shakur was at once the prototypical revolutionary and the "revolutionary mother hen" of the Black Liberation Army (BLA).[14] Shakur thus functions as a domestic terrorist both in her threat to the national family and in her position as political mother figure for the militants.

In a third sense she literalized this threat when she became pregnant by her codefendant while preparing for trial. Initially worried for the future of her child, she refused the state's attempt to foreclose her future children—"I'm not letting these parasites, these oppressors, these greedy swine make me kill my children in my mind before they are even born."[15] In choosing to become pregnant by her codefendant, at precisely the moment she was being ripped from her family and political community, Shakur refused absolutely to accede to the state's attack on her reproductive futurity. Shakur ends the chapter

* I am explicitly uninterested in the innocence or guilt of Assata Shakur—a political dissident targeted for violence, incarceration, and death by a violent state cannot be stacked up equally to the power of the state that was levied against her. Shakur's own words in a 1987 interview in Cuba, where she resides to this day, remain informative: "In reality, armed struggle historically has been used by people to liberate themselves. But the question lies in when do people use armed struggle. . . . There were people [in the BLA] who absolutely took the position that it was just time to resist, and if Black people didn't start to fight back against police brutality and didn't start to wage armed resistance, we would be annihilated." Shakur's answer to the question of her own guilt redirects the question to the guilt of the state. Shakur quoted in Ron Howell, "On the Run with JoAnne Chesimard," *Newsday*, October 11, 1987.

in her autobiography in which she finds she is pregnant with a poem, "love," that ends, "We are pregnant with freedom / We are a conspiracy," firmly aligning her literal motherhood with her revolutionary practice.[16]

In a broad sense, Shakur is the perverse mother who reproduces revolution rather than citizen-laborers.* In this way she embodies at once the threat of both Black radicalism and Black motherhood. Patricia Hill Collins notes the ways in which the white nuclear family is linked to the "American national family" as a eugenicist project.[17] Collins argues that Black women are registered as threats to this project biologically and socially through their status as mothers of Black children and culture, which is understood to be ideologically at odds with the US domestic project. Shakur connected this "domestic" threat to the public political threat of the Black power movement. While racism has been a central feature of the criminal justice system since its inception in the US, the use of incarceration as the primary tool of social control and housing of excess populations emerges in the 1970s as the Black mother begins to signify a primary threat to social order.

Cultural myths of the inherent social malfunction of the Black family had circulated since the end of slavery, but in the 1960s these myths calcified into a social scientific discourse of a "culture of poverty," with Black women bearing much of the blame. The *Moynihan Report*, released in 1965, located the "fundamental problem" of social unrest in a fundamental disorder of the "Negro family."[18] Moynihan couched his analysis in a Black intellectual tradition, citing W. E. B. Du Bois's 1908 *The Negro American Family* and, more significantly, Franklin Frazier's 1939 *The Negro Family in the United States*, which offered an analysis of the development of the Black family in the US in the aftermath of slavery. Moynihan's productive misuse of Du Bois and Frazier lent his analysis legitimacy and a progressive veneer, even as he provided the roadmap for the devastation of Black communities through welfare

* Angela Davis frames the resonances of slavery and the violent seizure of Black women's bodies and reproductive capacity for "alien and predatory economic interests" in "Reflections on the Black Woman's Role in the Community of Slaves" (1972). Davis sets this history against contemporary discussions of Black kinship structures and the perverse rhetorical framing of "matriarchies."

reform and policing. Moynihan, a sociologist, Democratic senator, and adviser to Nixon, offered a pathology of the Black family, stemming from the perceived problem of absent fathers and "matriarchal" family structure. The problematizing of maternal discipline and the clear implication that the state should intervene, creates a doubly precarious and pathologized Black maternal figure. She is at once the disciplinarian and the locus of state's disciplining of the Black family—the bad mother (of the domestic home) and the bad child (of the state).

The pathologies of the Black family coalesced in the figure of the welfare queen who was imagined to be both a threat to the social order and a drain on state resources. In her analysis of the Anita Hill hearings, Wahneema Lubiano argues that the *Moynihan Report* is "in many ways the Urtext for the simplistic 'culture of poverty' discussions," positions the "welfare-dependent single mother" as the "synecdoche, the shortest possible shorthand, for the pathology of poor, urban, Black culture."[19] Given that she is, as Lubiano emphasizes, "responsible for creating and maintaining a family that can only be perceived as pathological compared to the normative (and thus allegedly 'healthy') family structure in the larger society, the welfare mother is the root of greater Black pathology."[20] In *Family Values: Between Neoliberalism and the New Social Conservativism*, Melinda Cooper demonstrates Moynihan's prefiguring of the welfare queen, highlighting his framing of the "militant Black mothers" of the National Welfare Rights Organization as the "aristocracy of welfare recipients."* In militant Black mothers, Moynihan unites the threat of the Black radical and the Black mother under one sign.

In naming them "aristocracy," Moynihan provided the template for the myth of the welfare queen, which would form a cornerstone of Reagan's 1976 presidential campaign. The myth of the welfare queen,

* Melinda Cooper, *Family Values: Between Neoliberalism and the New Social Conservatism* (MIT Press, 2017), 46. The National Welfare Rights Organization (NWRO), here maligned by Moynihan, emerged in 1966 to fight for the rights of the poor, demanding a say in welfare regulations, and combatting attempts to restrict access to welfare, particularly directed at Black mothers. As chair of the NWRO, Johnnie Tillmon made the connection between poverty, welfare reforms, and motherhood—particularly Black motherhood—explicit, claiming that "welfare is a women's issue" in a piece in *Ms.* magazine in 1972.

through which Reagan launched his attacks on welfare, was based on the supposedly true story of a Black woman who "used 80 names, 30 addresses, 15 telephone numbers to collect food stamps, Social Security, veterans' benefits for four nonexistent deceased veteran husbands, as well as welfare. Her tax-free cash income alone has been running $150,000 a year."[21] The narrative's implication—that welfare was primarily for poor Black people and allowing them not just to live, but to live well without a job—touched a live wire of racial resentment and allowed Reagan to begin systematically dismantling the welfare state. In a 1996 review of recent scholarship on welfare reform, legal scholar Dorothy Roberts writes that "racial politics has so dominated welfare reform efforts that it is commonplace to observe that 'welfare' has become a code word for race."[22]

Moynihan's reformulation pathologized the Black mother in a double bind as both an inadequate and excessive mother. The form of domestic discipline that the state adopts becomes its own twisted form of familial "care." As a "domestic terrorist" Shakur represents both an object and refusal of this form of care and an epochal threat to state power. Shakur's form of Black motherhood, tied inextricably to a political community, unites the predominant anxieties surrounding Black motherhood and radical projects of Black liberation. COINTELPRO was a concerted attack on forms of community making and political organizing, aimed specifically at undermining solidarity within and between groups that functioned as a refutation of kinship networks outside the traditional family. The attempt to undermine the BPP and BLA framed them as primarily aggressive and militaristic. But the Panthers had centered communal forms of care and social reproduction in its free breakfasts, medical clinics, and education programs. Additionally, by 1969, "two thirds of the members of the Black Panther Party were women."[23] That number, from a survey by Bobby Seale, contradicts the image of the Panthers promulgated by the contemporary media. Kathleen Cleaver highlights the attention paid to "how many Panthers got arrested or killed."[24] For Cleaver, the erasure of the image of the Black women as revolutionaries and the emphasis on the capture and killing of Black men was part of a strategy to portray the state's conflict with the BPP as a masculinized, military struggle and a one which the state was winning.[25]

COINTELPRO sought to erase and neutralize the influence of the role of Black women in revolutionary struggle. As a public face of the struggle and a "mother hen," Shakur was a provocation and an all-consuming threat. Her arrest and prison sentence served to remove her from a social world rather than inculcate in her a sense of social and domestic responsibility. Shakur represented not a failed mother but a dangerously successful one. Her sentence therefore served to sever connections to the family and community rather than produce them, as previous women's prisons, particularly reformatories that housed primarily white women, had promised was their pedagogical and rehabilitative aim.

WOMEN'S PRISONS AND WELFARE HOTELS

With Shakur's incarceration the state attempted in multiple ways to cut her off from her own political community. She was moved frequently and held in multiple jails, including a men's facility, in which she was held in solitary confinement. When she was not in solitary, many of the facilities sought to inoculate their population by segregating Shakur as a political prisoner.* In her eight months at Rikers, however, Shakur found herself among the residents of "New York's newest and perhaps best hotel."[26] In "Women in Prison: How We Are," Shakur details her experience at Rikers and offers an analysis of the form and aims of

* A note on terminology: The use of the term "political prisoner" is contested. Mumia Abu-Jamal echoes Fred Hampton in alleging that "all prisoners are political prisoners" in *Still Black, Still Strong* (1993), and the sentiment is prominent in abolitionist circles. While legal and punitive structures are political and the decision to punish and remove people from society is inherently a political one, I use the term in this text because Assata Shakur has identified herself as a political prisoner and later as an ex–political prisoner in multiple writings. Many have also argued against the use of the term "prisoner" as it identifies a human being primarily through their entanglement within the criminal justice system. Activists and academics alike have called for person-first language. In this essay I do not refer to any individuals who are incarcerated as "prisoners," though I do use the term in discussing quoted materials and as a theoretical subject.

the women's prison. Throughout the essay, Shakur stresses the overwhelming presence of nonwhite women at Rikers, connecting systemic abuse of Black and Latina women to histories of domestic abuse and their overrepresentation in prisons. Shakur asserts, "There are no criminals here . . . only victims. Most of the women (over 95 percent) are Black and Puerto Rican. Many were abused children. Most have been abused by men and all have been abused by 'the system.'"[27] The portrait painted by Shakur, illustrating the overwhelming racial disparity of the prison population in the 1970s, is the final act in the prehistory of mass incarceration as applied to women. It is also a critical turning point for the project of the women's prison and public housing.

The incarcerated women Shakur describes—not themselves radicals but all subject to the same anxieties—are caught in the center of an intricate, connected web of economic exploitation, racial oppression, and domestic violence. Shakur connects this shared history to the kind of crimes most of the women at Rikers were charged with: sex work, petty theft, and drug charges, many of which are accessory charges stemming from a male partner. These crimes are, as Shakur notes, intimately connected to the economic insecurity of poor women of color, especially mothers. "The women see stealing or hustling as necessary for the survival of themselves or their children because jobs are scarce and welfare is impossible to live on."[28] Having sketched out the gendered dynamics of the crimes most frequently committed, Shakur comments on the ways in which the prison itself is constructed to reinforce a feminine reproductive subject, even as it serves primarily to rip women from their families and disrupt relationships.

Shakur details the design of the women's prison, which is distinctly different than the model of the men's prison. "One gets the impression," she comments, "when first coming to Riker's Island [Women's Prison] that the architects conceived of it as a juvenile center."[29] Nicole Hahn Rafter's historical account of the construction of women's prisons affirms this: "In both theory and design, the reformatory model was influenced by previously established institutions for children," especially in their "deliberately anti-institutional" architecture.[30] In the case of the Rikers Island women's facility, the architects were specifically inspired by a "new" trend in prison architecture. In the punningly titled "Prison Architects Break Tradition's Bars," the *New York Times* covered this trend in 1971, writing that the "fortress" model, with its "Bastille-like structure with bleak gray boxes of stone and iron piled one upon the other like rat cages" had fallen out of favor.[31] These new-age architects "have begun producing a variety of new designs" including "invisible jails . . . that look like the other buildings in their neighborhoods, or jails whose cells have brightly colored walls, barless windows, retractable beds or access to education, recreational or even kitchen facilities."[32]

In fading into the background of the other buildings in the neighborhoods, the dispersed and shared disciplinary function of the urban center as highly policed and surveilled becomes clear. But the prison's seamless integration into the landscape also serves to normalize its function as part of this apparatus. The *Times*'s exploration of the new-age architecture of the prison cites, in particular, "New York City's spacious new Women's House of Detention, which opened last month on Riker's Island" as "typify[ing] the new approach."* Rikers is not invisible through camouflage, but through segregation, situated on a dedicated carceral island. However, the women's facility adopts many of the "anti-institutional" features of these new style prisons: "With its sleek two-story chevron design, large windows, and brightly colored interior, it looks more like an Eastern girls' college than a detention facility. The buildings are sprawled across the northern end of the island, giving the inmates a commanding view of the East River."[33]

The new facility is endlessly other-than-prison—a hotel, a junior college, apartments. As with the coverage of the dedication, this *Times* piece uncritically reproduces what amounts to free publicity for the Department of Corrections. Shakur depicts this anti-institutional décor: "Instead of bars the cells have doors which are painted bright, optimistic colors with slim glass observation panels. . . . The cells are called rooms by everybody. . . . The prison distributes brightly colored

* Most likely a residual effect of the last House of Detention, reports on the new Correctional Institution for Women often refer to it as the "House of Detention" for the first few years. ("Prison Architects," *New York Times*, August 11, 1971.)

bedspreads and throw rugs for a homey effect."[34] The approximation of a "homey" atmosphere in the prison has the dual effect of infantilizing the women while re-creating the domestic atmosphere they are expected to inhabit properly as wives and mothers. But even more so than the House of Detention, this domestic fantasy is not one that the women of Rikers are expected or even allowed to occupy.

While the architects associated with this newer, kinder prison asserted "we are trying to create an environment that is as much like the outside world as possible," Shakur points out that the lives of the women incarcerated at Rikers are more likely to be defined by movement between institutions and forms of violence than "homey effect."[35] And despite the attempts at dressing it up, Rikers becomes, for these women, just another institution:

> For many the cells are not much different from the tenements, the shooting galleries, and the welfare hotels they live in on the street. Sick call is no different from the clinic or the hospital emergency room. The fights are the same except they are less dangerous. The police are the same. The poverty is the same. The alienation is the same. The racism is the same. The sexism is the same. The drugs are the same and the system is the same. Riker's and is just another institution. In childhood school was their prison, or youth houses or reform schools or children shelters or foster homes or mental hospitals or drug programs and they see all institutions as indifferent to their needs, yet necessary to their survival.[36]

The women's prison did, as it turns out, resemble the domestic lives of the outside world, but the outside world of the largely poor, largely Black and Latina population was not that of an "Eastern women's college" (think Radcliffe), but the increasingly decrepit public housing projects of New York City. The prison was like the tenement, was like the shooting gallery, was like the welfare hotel—a carceral archipelago of poverty. While the jubilantly self-congratulatory words of Commissioner McGrath announced the construction of the Correctional Institution for Women as "New York's newest and perhaps best hotel," Shakur compares it to the welfare hotel, the perfect symbol of the exclusionary project of public housing.

When Shakur compares the women's prison to the welfare hotel, she is observing a shift from a project of domestication to one of warehousing subjects deemed surplus. The welfare hotel had emerged in New York in 1965, when faced with "desperate shortage of low-cost housing" the city "began locating homeless families on welfare 'temporarily' in hotels."[37] As a 1971 *Time* article put it, "What started as an emergency measure has burgeoned into a monstrous problem, a squalid way of life."[38] By 1971 the number of families housed in welfare hotels had risen to over a thousand from under three hundred in 1969. The phenomenon of the welfare hotel was partly a product of New York City Housing Association's (NYCHA) explicit aims and policies, which sought out middle-class families and largely barred welfare recipients from accessing public housing. The distinction could not be clearer. Public housing was to provide entry into the middle class through the domestic home, while the welfare hotel was merely to provide temporary housing for excess populations.

The Housing and Urban Development Act of 1968 precipitated a shift in the policy of exclusion and the ways in which public housing was conceived in New York and nationally. In stating its purpose, the 1968 act reiterates the Housing Act of 1949, which set as its goal "a decent home and a suitable living environment for every American family" and recognizes that "this goal has not been fully realized for many of the Nation's lower income families; that this is a matter of grave national concern."[39] The grave national concern had, as the *Time* article illustrates, not abated with the extension of public housing to lower-income families on welfare, and in fact precipitated a stark downturn in the quality of public housing and an uptick in its policing. The extension of public housing to the working poor in New York City, along with the highly racialized face of this working poor (prior to the 1970s, the face of NYCHA was a white middle- or working-class family) fueled political campaigns to dismantle the programs that utilized racial resentments to undermine the logic of welfare altogether. Michael Katz indicates a turning tide in the 1960s from Johnson's "war on poverty" to a "war on welfare."[40] Katz notes, "By the early 1960s, the theory of delinquency, which had emerged as a national issue in the preceding decade, had shifted from individual to community pathology."[41]

This shift occurred, as Katz emphasizes, in conjunction with a growing civil rights movement. To be blunt, when public housing became associated with Blackness it came under political attack. Theories of the "culture of poverty" located the Black family as the source of social dysfunction and the housing project as a breeding ground. This image allowed opponents of welfare to simultaneously slash funding for public housing projects and vastly increase funding for policing of those same housing projects. In the 1970s the housing project and the prison were connected both ideologically (housing populations considered socially unfit, locked down) and literally in that the increased policing of public housing projects, particularly as part of the war on drugs, provided the prison with its steeply growing population.

Connecting the prison to the tenement house and the welfare hotel, Shakur also points to the peculiar position of the prison and the public home. Forms of public housing are simultaneously private domestic spaces and state-operated public services. As such, familial and state discipline are intimately wrapped up in each other. NYCHA housing had been governed by the Housing Authority Police Department (a separate city police than the NYPD) since 1952 and, as such, the houses under its jurisdiction were subject to extreme forms of surveillance. The pre-1968 public moral codes disallowing single mothers, drunkenness, and other coded behaviors granted the housing authority the right to ensure that these behaviors were not occurring. After 1968, as the demographics of public housing became distinctly less white, the surveillance and policing of the properties became more sharply racialized and aggressive. The threat of state discipline hangs over public housing, connecting it to the prison in myriad ways—one can lose access to public housing through a prison sentence and one can be sent to prison for violations committed on public housing grounds. Your home may be your private sphere, but it is also the public property of the state. The logic of the welfare state proposes that the state is responsible for some limited forms of care, but for Black families, that "care" has been punitive. That punitive care of the state overwhelmingly falls on Black women, who had been pathologized as both "over mothering" and incapable of proper domestic reproduction.

Shakur witnesses the effect of this pathology at Rikers. She expounds on her theory that the women's prison, in addition to reproducing the welfare hotel, adopts the architectural and disciplinary modes of the juvenile center, both violently subjugating and infantilizing the women it confines. The "homey" atmosphere of the domestic cells is reinforced in the reproduction of familial hierarchy and gender roles in the guard-inmate relationship.* "This image is further reinforced by the pseudo-motherly attitude [taken by] many of the guards; a deception which all too often successfully reverts women to children. The guards call the women inmates by their first names. The women address the guards either as Officer, Miss—or by nicknames (Teddy Bear, Spanky, Aunt Louise, Squeeze, Sarge, Black Beauty, Nutty Mahogany, etc.)."[42]

Shakur notes the ways in which even the naming rituals approximate familial power structures. Shakur is deeply aware of the importance of names as signifiers of relationality—she had changed her own name and referred to her given one as her "slave name." "Assata" is a West African variant of the Arabic "Aisha," "she who struggles," and "Shakur," in Arabic, means "thankful one." By contrast, in Rikers, the women are stripped of their own familial marker (their last name) and only referred to by their first names while the guards are either referred to by a title or a familiar nickname, masking the division between the two.

> Frequently, when a woman returns to Riker's she will make the rounds, gleefully embracing her favorite guard: the prodigal daughter returns. If two women are having a debate about any given topic the argument will often be resolved by "asking the officer." The guards are forever telling the women to "grow up," to "act like ladies," to "behave," and to be "good girls." If an inmate is breaking some minor rule like coming to say "hi" to her friend on another floor or locking in a few minutes late, a guard will say, jokingly, "don't let me have to come down there and beat your

* See note 28 about terminology re "prisoner" and "inmate."

> butt." It is not unusual to hear a guard tell a woman, "What you need is a good spanking." The tone is often motherly, "didn't I tell you, young lady, to . . ."; or "you know better than that"; or, "that's a good girl." And the women respond accordingly. Some guards and inmates "play" together. One officer's favorite "game" is taking off her belt and chasing her "girls" down the hall with it, smacking them on the butt.[43]

The discipline here is both masked by and produced through the appeal to familial kinship. The incarcerated are exhorted to "grow up" and be "good girls" even as they are forcibly positioned as children in relation to their benevolent motherly guardians. Even as it reproduces the roles of the domestic home, the prison seeks to produce the women not as mothers but as children, petty and divided. The "play" of domestic discipline—exemplified here by the game of "spanking" the "girls"—manages at once to reproduce the violence of the home as play in the prison and mask the violence of incarceration through reference to the "loving" environment of the home, even in the highly sexually charged discipline of chasing and smacking women on the butt. In the play between the two spaces, the "deception" Shakur notes is doubled, negating both the violence of the home and prison by marking them as one and the same through playful mockery.

The familial play of the relationship between guards and incarcerated women also served to triangulate relations between the women themselves, routing all sociality through the "mother" figure of the guard, as with the "caring" state intervening in the Black family. The unidirectionality of these relationships was, ironically, noticed by the very guards who maintained them. In an article published in the *New York Times* only three weeks after their coverage of the dedication ceremony, both incarcerated women and guards aired grievances with the new facility. In an article titled "Rikers Island May Be Posh, but They Miss House of Detention," the quotes from incarcerated women highlighted the poor food and lack of contact with men as the primary complaints. The portrait offered by the guards was a little different: "The girls liked the old place better—it was more like home." And, "The girls like being closer together; this place is too big."[44] A superintendent (the country's only Black female superintendent at that time) recalled that "there was more friendliness and warmth at Greenwich Avenue. . . . I miss the closeness of the girls. They had more freedom to move around in the building. It was smaller and they didn't have to be escorted."[45] The unstated reason for the lack of closeness is the massive expansion from one prison to the next. There was simply more space, and in the first year of its life, Rikers Correctional Institution for Women had not yet filled to, or over, capacity.

There is a tension here between the homeyness described by the guards and the environment described by Shakur that has to do with both the retreat of the domesticating mission and the object of familial relationality. The article also mentions the former House of Detention's central location and the possibility of calling out to people on the street below, "a form of street theater that Greenwich Village residents didn't always appreciate."[46] The curious invocation of the homelike environment of the former institution even as the current one celebrates the modern domestic amenities and forms of training offered speak to a particular distinction that Shakur's essay illustrates. While the previous institution allowed for forms of sociality outside of the prisoner-guard relation, the current one disallows these and re-anchors the familial home in the figure of the guard and the matron as emblems of the state as domestic disciplinarian, severing relationships between women.

Shakur particularly bemoans the lack of solidarity and radical political organizing in the women's prison in comparison with the men's prison. "There is no sense of class struggle."[47] While the women "verbalize acute recognition that amerika is a racist country where the poor are treated like dirt, they, nevertheless, feel responsible for the filth of their lives."[48] According to Shakur, the women at Rikers internalize injustices as individual failures, which produces a twisted sense of self. "The air at Riker's is permeated with self-hatred. Many women bear marks on their arms, legs and wrists from suicide attempts or self-mutilation. They speak about themselves in self-deprecating terms. They consider themselves failures."[49] Without a collective politics of solidarity, the women, according to Shakur, direct inward the anger that she insists should be productively projected outwardly. She diagnoses this as a form of false consciousness. I would add that in demanding a particular genre of revolutionary subjectivity, Shakur may miss the private and intimate forms of collective care and survival between women who are incarcerated, which may be illegible as public political praxis. But the production of these women as isolated and atomized subjects is a product of the prison itself. The individuation of the homey rooms and the unilateral relationality with guard-mother figures exacerbates this alienation. The woman of the domestic prison becomes petty and inward facing, refusing a larger world both architecturally and socially.

This form of discipline runs counter to the expectations of the US reader, saturated with images of brutal physical violence through autobiographical accounts and fictional representations of the men's prison. To Shakur, the women incarcerated at Rikers seem to take note of the difference in their own situation and the presumed physical brutality that the image of the prison conjures. She points out the danger of the apparently successful mission to render the women's prison "gentle" in comparison to the "harsh" men's prison.

> The guards have successfully convinced most of the women that Riker's Island is a country club. They say that it is a playhouse compared to some other prisons (especially male): a statement whose partial veracity is not predicated upon the humanity of correction officials at Riker's Island, but, rather, by contrast to the unbelievably barbaric conditions of other prisons. Many women are convinced that they are, somehow, "getting over." Some go so far as to reason that because they are not doing hard time, they are not really in prison.[50]

As Shakur asserts, the portrayal of the women's prison as a "country club" as compared to men's prisons rests on the assumption that the men's prison with its "unbelievably barbaric conditions" provides a normative baseline and that the lack of that barbarity constitutes some kind of allowance or benevolent dispensation. Furthermore, this comparison flattens the forms of discipline without attention to the ways in which gendered discipline is violent in divergent and insidious ways. The women's prison, even as it consistently fails to live up to its rehabilitative ideals, succeeds in projecting an image of softer and more humane punishment.

This critique mirrors Michel Foucault's assertion that the modern penitentiary prides itself on a "gentle" punishment and rehabilitative mission as opposed to the barbarity of torture and the public spectacles of death sentences.[51] This is particularly true of women's prisons. The success of the women's reform movement was precisely in the production of new women's prisons. Successive generations of reformers have likewise managed to justify the construction of new prisons through the malfunction of the old and, in this regard, the women's prison reform project was pioneering.

Along with its adoption of the "gentle" discipline of the domestic home, Shakur points to another intimate form of violence enacted by the women's prison. In her autobiography, Shakur recalls her arrival at Rikers and the conversation she has with the other women regarding the strip search: "'You mean they really put their hands inside you, to search you?' I had asked. 'Uh-huh,' they answered. Every woman who has ever been on the rock, or in the old house of detention, can tell you about it. The women call it 'getting the finger,' or, more vulgarly, 'getting finger-fucked.'"[52] The violence of the strip search has been addressed by many critics. The sexual violation as part of a simultaneous impersonal "search" calls up images of both rape and the auction block, with the searching hands feeling all parts of the slave to check their value as "livestock." The description of the strip search as a violation and explicitly as a form of sexual assault ties the discipline of the women's prison to a regime of sexual violence that unites "domestic" violence in the home and the state.

In a 2001 interview with political prisoners, Marilyn Buck and Laura Whitehorn frame this form of sexual violence as a tactic of the prison and one which exacerbates histories of abuse. At the time of the interview, Whitehorn had been released two years earlier on parole, fourteen years into a twenty-year sentence for a series of 1983 bombings at the US Capitol in protest of US domestic and international policies. No one was injured. Buck had been arrested on multiple charges including her involvement in Shakur's escape from prison, which she participated in while underground after escaping her own sentence while on furlough. Both Buck and Whitehorn highlight the techniques of absolute control and the scrutiny of behavior, dress, appearance—and the effect of reducing women to powerless objects.

They cite the strip searches (often by men) and their invasive violence enacted upon women who often have histories of sexual and domestic abuse. Both women emphasize the oft-cited statistic that an enormous percentage of incarcerated women have histories of abuse (over 80 percent by most accounts). The prison, according to Buck, acts as another form of abusive relationship.* Whitehorn notes the medicalized trauma that the prison clinic further inflicts. She recounts the request of one woman to be sedated during an operation on her cervix since her history of sexual abuse means she will have a panic attack if asked to "lie on my back with my legs spread and chained in front of strangers."[53] The image is horrifying on its own, even more so with the specter of sexual abuse present. Whitehorn recalls that her doctor simply laughed and refused to perform the surgery. Whitehorn suggests that the experience of being "cared for" by "someone who sees you as the enemy is completely deleterious to your health."[54] This image of care performed by the enemy is haunting. The image again calls up the specter of domestic abuse, of the veiling of violence as care, but recalling that it was Shakur's depiction of the strip search that opened the discussion, there is a sense that the Black radical, as an enemy of the state, experiences a particular brand of hatred. In the domestic terrorist, geopolitical, national, and familial anxieties converge.

Buck was eventually released in 2010, due to her advanced uterine cancer. She died one month later. Both Buck and Whitehorn point to the broader effect that the incarceration of women has on their

* Dorothy Roberts makes similar claims about disciplinary functions of welfare regulation and their racialized and sexual forms of abuse. In *Killing the Black Body* (1997) she argues that "regulating Black women's reproductive decisions has been a central aspect of racial oppression in America" writ large (6). This is manifestly true in prisons where Black women have been sterilized without their consent. Erika Cohn's documentary *Belly of the Beast* (2020) addresses the continuation of the practice in California prisons, despite having been made illegal almost forty years ago.

communities. Whitehorn cites the high incidence of incarceration for mothers as severing collective bonds in the communities they come from and continuing a cycle of incarceration. But the cases of Buck and Whitehorn themselves, as well as Shakur, point to another loss to communal forms of solidarity and support. The incarceration of these women represents an incredible loss of a generation of political leaders and organizers, and one which was explicitly the strategy of the US criminal justice system in the 1960s and 1970s. As prison reform becomes mainstreamed, an abolitionist feminist approach must track the ways in which carceral forms adapt and appropriate feminist formations in service of dislocating and disciplining women.

On March 31, 2017, the *New York Times* covered a press conference with Mayor Bill de Blasio, who "vowed . . . to close the troubled jail complex on Rikers Island, which has spawned federal investigations, brought waves of protests and became a byword for brutality, in a move he said was intended to end an era of mass incarceration in New York City."[55] The dissonance between that promise and the title of the article—"Mayor Backs Plan to Close Rikers and Open Jails Elsewhere"—emphasizes that when it comes to prisons, the more things change the more they stay the same. The women's prison at Rikers opened to declarations that it marked a new phase of humane punishment and an end to a barbaric past. The Women's House of Detention emerged out of the ashes of its own disavowed past of barbarity. Each successive iteration of the women's prison has justified itself through this act of refusal and rebirth. And each iteration, like the spores of a weed, disseminates the reach of the prison further and opens new avenues and new rooms to house more prisoners.

On the heels of de Blasio's announcement another initiative was launched, headed by his wife, Chirlane McCray. "Building on efforts to reduce the jail population at Rikers Island, Mayor Bill de Blasio will announce on Thursday a $6 million plan intended to help rehabilitate female inmates and lessen the chance that they return."[56] The $6 million plan comes at a significantly lower price point than the $10 billion plan to replace the men's facility on Rikers with several smaller jails located around the city. Both are premised on an end to mass incarceration and a more humane form of correction. In the words of Andrew Cuomo's chief counsel, Alphonso David, "a fair, safe and humane criminal justice system is essential for our state, and we will make it happen."[57] Even in the constant failure of the rehabilitative mission and the evacuation of many of its central tenets, the logic of reform remains largely the same. The presumption that incarceration is a necessary form of justice remains and serves to open the potential for many more jails, to say nothing of new forms of carceral control like ankle monitors. The same article notes that the city is in dire need of public housing but does not include any promise for more of that.

The opening of the first women's facility on Rikers Island in 1971 followed closely on the heels of the 1968 Housing and Urban Development Act, and the explicit push for NYCHA to serve low-income and welfare-receiving families. In connecting these developments to the historical narratives of the prison, I insist on the connection of the women's prison to forms of home and housing and the state policy of women's punishment with state housing policy. Rikers correctional institution for women was heralded for its grand step forward in rehabilitation (just as the imagined future of Rikers is already being sold). The fantasy projection of the humane prison is even more powerful for the portrait of the prisoner it conjures. In this way, new reforms, necessarily portrayed as domestic and "soft" forms of discipline, are smuggled into the public consciousness, reiterating the prison itself as a form, and often spreading this normalization to men's institutions.

As much as George H. W. Bush's promise of a "kinder, gentler nation" in the late 1980s concealed neo-imperial exploits like the first Gulf War and the Iran–Contra scandal, as well as a ramping up of hyper-policing and the war on drugs, the kinder, gentler women's prison provides cover for more intrusive forms of domestic discipline, exploitive expansions in the name of "rehabilitation," and more diffused forms of carceral control. Consider the disappeared history of the House of Detention, and it is significant that it was introduced not only as a model institution for women, but New York's model prison.

I submit that the women's prison often offers a model of prison reform while simultaneously operating as a model of prison expansion.

If we are to track the growth and diffusion of the prison, it is vital to understand the growth and diffusion of the women's prison. What do we do with the potentially disappearing Rikers? Will Rikers go the way of previous iterations (reborn in a familiar if adapted form)? To answer this question, it is important to remember Rikers's past while we still consider its future. If we do not demand an end to prison on our terms, reforms will take place on the terms of the criminal justice system and real estate developers.

FUGITIVITY AND FREEDOM

In a 1973 taped message, "To My People," reproduced in full in her 1987 memoir, Shakur makes clear the inextricability of her own fight for freedom from larger struggles:

> Black brothers, Black sisters, i want you to know that i love you and i hope that somewhere in your hearts you have love for me. My name is Assata Shakur (slave name joanne chesimard), and i am a revolutionary. A Black revolutionary. By that i mean that i have declared war on all forces that have raped our women, castrated our men, and kept our babies empty-bellied. I have declared war on the rich who prosper on our poverty, the politicians who lie to us with smiling faces, and all the mindless, heartless robots who protect them and their property.[58]

Shakur begins with a message of love and kinship that transcends the nuclear family. Her refusal of her "slave name" recalls slavery's imposition of names signifying ownership, and the violent fracturing of Black families under the name of the white patriarch. Shakur's love then demands a declaration of war against all the forces that immiserate her sisters and brothers, among whom she counts Black Americans as well as the victims of imperialism in "Vietnam, Cambodia, Mozambique, Angola, and South Africa."[59]

Shakur connects slavery, capitalism, and imperialism to the violence of everyday life. "We are burned alive in fire-trap tenements. Our brothers and sisters OD daily from heroin and methadone. Our babies die from lead poisoning. . . . This is murder."[60] Shakur reframes the crimes she and her comrades have been accused of, calling attention to the slow murder of poverty. Shakur asserts that the Black Liberation Army (BLA) will continue to exist "until every Black man, woman, and child is free."[61] The BLA will continue to exist, insists Shakur, as long as it is needed because the same conditions that the BLA fights to end produce new revolutionaries: "Black revolutionaries do not drop from the moon. We are created by our conditions. Shaped by our oppression. We are being manufactured in droves in the ghetto streets, places like attica, san quentin, bedford hills, leavenworth, and sing sing. They are turning out thousands of us. Many jobless Black veterans and welfare mothers are joining our ranks. Brothers and sisters from all walks of life, who are tired of suffering passively, make up the BLA."[62]

The reproduction of Black revolutionaries, Shakur elaborates, is both an effect of violence and a form of antidomestic reproduction. Forged in struggle and suffering, this form of procreation cannot be violently repressed as it is precisely that repression which produces it. Shakur promotes a project of love and liberation that embraces not-yet-born revolutionaries.

The BLA will, she promises, continue "to struggle for Black freedom, and to prepare for the future. We must defend ourselves and let no one disrespect us. We must gain our liberation by any means necessary."[63] The preparation for the future, with the knowledge that sisters and brothers will join, is to some degree a utopian project, demanding current struggle for a future that others will likely see. Shakur ends with the mantra that has become her most well-known quote and a protest standard:

> It is our duty to fight for our freedom.
> It is our duty to win.
> We must love each other and support each other.
> We have nothing to lose but our chains.[64]

This call to arms poses revolutionary love as a charge. It imagines love as an active and political project, and one that is essential to liberation. Love here nurtures for the purpose not of reproducing the present but making possible the future.

Shakur ends her memoir with her own escape to freedom. As she reaches Havana, she can finally breathe free: "Freedom. I couldn't believe that it had really happened, that the nightmare was over, that finally the dream had come true. I was elated. Ecstatic. But i was completely disoriented. Everything was the same, yet everything was different."[65] Her freedom is tempered not only in the fact that not all are free but also because her years in prison have altered her. Even as she celebrates her escape, she recalls the "the horrors of prison and every disgusting experience that somehow i had been able to minimize while inside."[66] Shakur tries to convey the psychic and bodily effects of prison on her: "I had developed the ability to be patient, calculating, and completely self-controlled. For the most part, i had been incapable of crying. I felt rigid, as though chunks of steel and concrete had worked themselves into my body. I was cold. I strained to touch my softness. I was afraid that prison had made me ugly."[67]

While Shakur notes the ways in which prison honed her ability to compartmentalize and strategize, she fears its deadening effect. She does not celebrate cold calculation but warm and soft revolutionary love. Shakur recognizes here that the women's prison has served not to produce in her a form of domestic affect but to deaden. Shakur recalls the other lessons prison has taught her, namely that collectivity and internationalism are central to revolutionary theory and practice: "Any community seriously concerned with its own freedom has to be concerned about other peoples' freedom as well."[68] As Shakur reminds us, it is our duty to win. Shakur wins by surviving and escaping. But what is it to be free in an unfree world?

For Shakur, that freedom lives in fugitivity, or escape not as removal from captivity but as active and lasting evasion. In *Stolen Life*, the second volume in his trilogy, consent not to be a single being, Fred Moten defines fugitivity as "a desire for and a spirit of escape and transgression of the proper and the proposed. It's a desire for the outside, for a playing or being outside, an outlaw edge proper to the now always already improper voice or instrument."[69] Shakur's fugitive status, one that remains today, is premised on an active and continual refusal of captivity, but not as an individual project.

Shakur's vision of collective and international socialism is premised upon an expansive love and refusal of the boundaries placed on that love, insisting that true love is revolutionary love, and that revolution is ineffective without softness and support.

> It is our duty to fight for our freedom.
> It is our duty to win.
> We must love each other and support each other.
> We have nothing to lose but our chains.[70]

I restate this affirmation to return to Shakur's particular vision of revolutionary love, which stands in direct opposition to the parodic form of familial care she saw inside the prison. But it also refuses the deadening effect she recognizes in herself as a result of her time in prison. This deadening is an indication of a burgeoning women's prison that does not actually seek to position women as (re)productive members of society but to cut them off from it. The project of COINTELPRO and, more broadly, the inception of the war on drugs and mass incarceration represented a new frontier in social control. In lingering on a prehistory of our current moment (of both mass incarceration and critiques of mass incarceration), I aim to remember previous reformist reorganizations of the carceral landscape of the city to make space for abolitionist demands in the present. Echoing the rallying cry, "Assata taught me," it is imperative now more than ever to learn the lessons she taught us in an expansive way: both in her fierce critique and her revolutionary affirmation.

BIBLIOGRAPHY

Cleaver, Kathleen Neal. "Women, Power, and Revolution." *New Political Science* 21, no. 2 (June 1, 1999): 231–36.

Collins, Patricia Hill. "Will the 'Real' Mother Please Stand Up?: The Logic of Eugenics and American National Family Planning." In *Revisioning Women, Health and Healing: Feminist, Cultural and Technoscience Perspectives*, edited by Adele E. Clarke and Virginia Olesen. Routledge, 1999.

Cooper, Melinda. *Family Values: Between Neoliberalism and the New Social Conservatism*. MIT Press, 2017.

Cunningham, David, and John Noakes. "What if She's from the FBI? The Effects of Covert Forms of Social Control on Social Movements." In *Surveillance and*

Governance: Crime Control and Beyond, 175–97. Sociology of Crime, Law and Deviance, vol. 10. Emerald Group Publishing Limited, 2008.

Davis, Angela Y. *Are Prisons Obsolete?* Seven Stories Press, 2011.

———. "Reflections on the Black Woman's Role in the Community of Slaves." *Massachusetts Review* 13, no. 1/2 (1972): 81–100.

———. *Women, Race, and Class*. 1st Vintage Books edition. Vintage, 2011.

Davis, Angela Yvonne, and Bettina Aptheker, eds. *If They Come in the Morning: Voices of Resistance*. Third Press, 1971.

Elliott, Anne, et al. "Women of Color in Prison." *Souls* 2, no. 1 (January 2000): 79–83.

Federal Bureau of Investigation, "Most Wanted Terrorists: Joanne Deborah Chesimard." FBI.gov, 2013. https://www.fbi.gov/wanted/wanted_terrorists/joanne-deborah-chesimard.

Ferré-Sadurní, Luis. "The Rise and Fall of New York Public Housing: An Oral History." *New York Times*, June 25, 2018.

Foucault, Michel. *Discipline and Punish: The Birth of the Prison*. New York: Vintage Books, 1977.

Freedman, Estelle B. *Their Sisters' Keepers: Women's Prison Reform in America, 1830–1930*. University of Michigan Press, 1984.

Goodman, J. David. "Mayor Backs Plan to Close Rikers and Open Jails Elsewhere." *New York Times*, February 14, 2018.

Haas, Jeffrey. *The Assassination of Fred Hampton: How the FBI and the Chicago Police Murdered a Black Panther*. Chicago Review Press, 2011.

Haley, Sarah. *No Mercy Here: Gender, Punishment, and the Making of Jim Crow Modernity*. Chapel Hill: University of North Carolina Press, 2016.

Harris, Sara. *Hellhole: The Shocking Story of the Inmates and Life in the New York City House of Detention for Women*. New York: Dutton, 1967.

Hinton, Elizabeth Kai. *From the War on Poverty to the War on Crime: The Making of Mass Incarceration in America*. Cambridge, MA: Harvard University Press, 2016.

Howell, Ron. "On the Run with JoAnne Chesimard." *Newsday*, October 11, 1987.

James, Joy. "Framing the Panther:" In *Want to Start a Revolution?*, edited by Dayo F. Gore, Jeanne Theoharis, and Komozi Woodard, 138–60. Radical Women in the Black Freedom Struggle. New York: NYU Press, 2009.

———. *States of Confinement: Policing, Detention, and Prisons*. Palgrave Macmillan, 2002.

Kaba, Mariame. "What Abolitionists Do." *Jacobin*, August 24, 2017.

Katz, Michael B. *In the Shadow of the Poorhouse: A Social History of Welfare in America*, 10th anniversary ed. New York: Basic Books, 1996.

Kozol, Jonathan. *Rachel and Her Children: Homeless Families in America*. New York: Crown Publishers, 1988.

Kunzel, Regina G. *Criminal Intimacy: Prison and the Uneven History of Modern American Sexuality*. Chicago: University of Chicago Press, 2010.

Levin, Josh. "The Real Story of Linda Taylor, America's Original Welfare Queen." *Slate*, December 19, 2013.

Lubiano, Wahneema. "Black Ladies, Welfare Queens, and State Minstrels: Ideological War by Narrative Means." In *Race-Ing Justice, En-Gendering Power:*

Essays on Anita Hill, Clarence Thomas and the Construction of Social Reality, edited by Toni Morrison. New York: Pantheon, 1992.

"'Luxury' Jail Here for Women Ready; Prison without Bars, Costing $2,000,000, to Have Official 'Housewarming' Today. Windows Casement Type but Door Panels Are Bullet-Proof Glass—Residents to Be Known as Inmates, Not Prisoners." *New York Times*, March 29, 1932.

"Mayor Lays Stone of Women's Prison; Terms New House of Detention the Most Humane Building Ever Erected in City. Lauds Patterson's Work Correction Commissioner Asserts Each Prisoner Will Receive Individual Study." *New York Times*, April 4, 1930.

Mays, Jeffery C. "Chirlane McCray to Lead Effort to Help Female Inmates at Rikers." *New York Times*, July 18, 2018.

McCarthy, Thomas C. *New York City's Suffragist Commissioner: Correction's Katharine Bement Davis, a Mini-History about the First Woman to Head a Major NYC Municipal Agency*. New York: Department of Correction, 1997.

Minor-Harper, Stephanie. "Prisoners in 1982." *Bureau of Justice Statistics—Bulletin*. US Department of Justice, 1983. www.bjs.gov/index.cfm?ty=pbdetail&iid=3488.

Montgomery, Paul. "Jail for Women Dedicated Here." *New York Times*, June 19, 1971. https://www.nytimes.com/1971/06/19/archives/jail-for-women-dedicated-here-mcgrath-on-rikers-island-calls-it.html.

Moten, Fred. *Stolen Life*. Durham, NC: Duke University Press, 2018.

"Prison Architects Break Tradition's Bars." *New York Times*, August 11, 1971.

Rafter, Nicole. *Partial Justice: Women, Prisons and Social Control*. New York: Routledge, 2017.

———. "Prisons for Women, 1790-–1980." *Crime and Justice* 5 (1983): 129–81.

Rankin, Rebecca. "Department of Public Welfare of the City of New York." NYC Department of Records & Information Services, June 7, 2018.

Roberts, Dorothy E. *Killing the Black Body: Race, Reproduction, and the Meaning of Liberty*. New York: Vintage Books, 1999.

———. "Welfare and the Problem of Black Citizenship." Faculty Scholarship at Penn Law, January 1, 1996.

Rothstein, Richard. *The Color of Law: A Forgotten History of How Our Government Segregated America*. New York: Liveright Publishing, 2017.

Shakur, Assata. *Assata: An Autobiography*. London: Zed Books, 2001.

Shakur, Assata, with Dhoruba Bin Wahad and Mumia Abu-Jamal. *Still Black, Still Strong: Survivors of the U.S. War against Black Revolutionaries*, edited by Jim Fletcher, Tanaquil Jones, and Sylvere Lotringer. Los Angeles: Semiotext(e), 1993.

Shakur, Assata. "Women in Prison: How We Are." *Black Scholar* 9, no. 7 (1978): 8–15. Available at http://www.jstor.org/stable/41066477.

Taylor, Angela. "Rikers Island May Be Posh, but They Miss House of Detention." *New York Times*, July 9, 1971.

Travis, Jeremy, Bruce Western, and F. Redburn. *The Growth of Incarceration in the United States: Exploring Causes and Consequences*." Publications and

Research—John Jay College of Criminal Justice. Washington, DC: National Academies Press, 2014. Available at https://academicworks.cuny.edu/jj_pubs/27.

Weiser, Benjamin. "$1.2 Million City Settlement with Rikers Inmates Who Accused Guard of Rape." *New York Times*, December 22, 2017.

"Welfare: Hotels without Hope." *Time*, January 4, 1971.

Williams, Jakobi. *From the Bullet to the Ballot: The Illinois Chapter of the Black Panther Party and Racial Coalition Politics in Chicago*. Chapel Hill: University of North Carolina Pres, 2013.

NOTES

1 Federal Bureau of Investigation, "Most Wanted Terrorists: Joanne Deborah Chesimard," FBI.gov, 2013, https://www.fbi.gov/wanted/wanted_terrorists/joanne-deborah-chesimard.

2 Assata Shakur, "Women in Prison: How We Are." *Black Scholar* 9, no. 7 (April 1978): 13, available at http://www.jstor.org/stable/41066477.

3 Paul Montgomery, "Jail for Women Dedicated Here," *New York Times*, June 19, 1971, https://www.nytimes.com/1971/06/19/archives/jail-for-women-dedicated-here-mcgrath-on-rikers-island-calls-it.html.

4 Montgomery, "Jail for Women."

5 Montgomery, "Jail for Women."

6 Montgomery, "Jail for Women."

7 According to a report by the National Academies of Sciences, Engineering, and Medicine, "in 1973, after 50 years of stability, the rate of incarceration in the United States began a sustained period of growth." Jeremy Travis, Bruce Western, and F. Redburn, *The Growth of Incarceration in the United States: Exploring Causes and Consequences*." Publications and Research—John Jay College of Criminal Justice (Washington, DC: National Academies Press, 2014), available at https://academicworks.cuny.edu/jj_pubs/27.

8 Stephanie Minor-Harper, "Prisoners in 1982," *Bureau of Justice Statistics—Bulletin* (US Department of Justice, 1983), www.bjs.gov/index.cfm?ty=pbdetail&iid=3488.

9 See Katherine Beckett, *Making Crime Pay: Law and Order in Contemporary American Politics* (New York: Oxford University Press, 2000); Elizabeth Kai Hinton, *From the War on Poverty to the War on Crime: The Making of Mass Incarceration in America* (Cambridge, MA: Harvard University Press, 2016); Julilly Kohler-Hausmann, "'The Attila the Hun Law': New York's Rockefeller Drug Laws and the Making of a Putitive State," *Journal of Social History* 44, 2010); Doris Marie Provine, *Unequal under Law: Race in the War on Drugs* (Chicago: University of Chicago Press, 2007).

10 Assata Shakur, *Assata: An Autobiography* (Chicago: Lawrence Hill, 1987).

11 See Jakobi Williams, *From the Bullet to the Ballot: The Illinois Chapter of the Black Panther Party and Racial Coalition Politics in Chicago* (Chapel Hill: University of North Carolina Press, 2013).

12 Joy James, "Framing the Panther: Assata Shakur and Black Female Agency," in *Want to Start a Revolution?: Radical Women in the Black Freedom Struggle* (New York: NYU Press, 2009), 138.

13 James, "Framing the Panther," 138.

14 James, "Framing the Panther," 138. This particular nickname was a pejorative one given by the FBI in a propaganda campaign leading up to her arrest.

15 Shakur, *Assata: An Autobiography*, 93.

16 Shakur, *Assata: An Autobiography*, 130.

17 Patricia Hill Collins, "Will the 'Real' Mother Please Stand Up?: The Logic of Eugenics and American National Family Planning," in *Revisioning Women, Health and Healing: Feminist, Cultural and Technoscience*, eds. Adele E. Clarke and Virginia L. Olesen (New York: Routledge, 1999), 266–82.

18 Daniel Patrick Moynihan, *The Negro Family: The Case for National Action*, Office of Policy Planning and Research (Washington, DC: US Department of Labor, March 1965).

19 Wahneema Lubiano, "Black Ladies, Welfare Queens, and State Minstrels: Ideological War by Narrative Means," in *Race-Ing Justice, En-Gendering Power: Essays on Anita Hill, Clarence Thomas and the Construction of Social Reality*, ed. Toni Morrison (New York: Pantheon, 1992), 335.

20 Lubiano, "Black Ladies, Welfare Queens, and State Minstrels," 335.

21 Josh Levin, "The Real Story of Linda Taylor, America's Original Welfare Queen," *Slate*, December 19, 2013.

22 Dorothy E. Roberts, "Welfare and the Problem of Black Citizenship" *Yale Law Journal* 105 (1996): 1563.

23 Kathleen Neal Cleaver, "Women, Power, and Revolution," *New Political Science* 21, no. 2 (1999), 125.

24 Cleaver, "Women, Power, and Revolution," 125.

25 See Elaine Brown, *A Taste of Power: A Black Woman's Story* (Anchor Books, 1994); Kathleen Cleaver and George Katsiaficas, *Liberation, Imagination and the Black Panther Party: A New Look at the Black Panthers and Their Legacy* (Routledge, 2014); Ashley D. Farmer, *Remaking Black Power: How Black Women Transformed an Era* (UNC Press, 2017); Robyn C. Spencer, *The Revolution Has Come: Black Power, Gender, and the Black Panther Party in Oakland* (Duke University Press, 2016).

26 Montgomery, "Jail for Women."

27 Shakur, "Women in Prison," 8.

28 Shakur, "Women in Prison," 12.

29 Shakur, "Women in Prison," 12.

30 Nicole Hahn Rafter, *Partial Justice: Women, Prisons and Social Control.* (New York: Routledge, 2017), 147.

31 "Prison Architects Break Tradition's Bars," *New York Times*, 1971. This is strikingly similar to perceived trends of the 1930s and the shift from the fortress-like Blackwell's penitentiary to new and similarly "anti-institutional" institutions like the House of Detention that replaced it for women and preceded the Rikers women's facility.

32 "Prison Architects."
33 "Prison Architects."
34 Shakur, "Women in Prison," 9.
35 Shakur, "Women in Prison," 9.
36 Shakur, "Women in Prison" 11.
37 "Welfare: Hotels without Hope," *Time*, January 4, 1971.
38 "Welfare: Hotels without Hope."
39 The Housing and Urban Development Act of 1968, Pub.L. 90–448, 82 Stat. 476 (United States Department of Housing and Urban Development, 1968).
40 Michael B. Katz, *In the Shadow of the Poorhouse: A Social History of Welfare in America*, 10th anniversary ed. (New York: Basic Books, 1996), 262.
41 Katz, *In the Shadow of the Poorhouse*, 264.
42 Shakur, "Women in Prison," 12.
43 Shakur, "Women in Prison," 12.
44 Angela Taylor, "Rikers Island May Be Posh, but They Miss House of Detention," *New York Times*, 1971.
45 Taylor, "Rikers Island May Be Posh."
46 Taylor, "Rikers Island May Be Posh."
47 Shakur, "Women in Prison," 12.
48 Shakur, "Women in Prison," 12.
49 Shakur, "Women in Prison," 12.
50 Shakur, "Women in Prison," 11.
51 Michel Foucault, *Discipline and Punish: The Birth of the Prison* (New York: Vintage Books, 1977).
52 Shakur, *Assata: An Autobiography*, 83
53 Marilyn Buck and Laura Whitehorn, "Cruel but Not Unusual: The Punishment of Women in U.S. Prisons," in *New Abolitionists, The: (Neo)Slave Narratives and Contemporary Prison Writings*, ed. Joy James (Albany: SUNY Press, 2005), 264.
54 Buck and Whitehorn, "Cruel but Not Unusual," 264.
55 David J. Goodman, "Mayor Backs Plan to Close Rikers and Open Jails Elsewhere," *New York Times*, 2018.
56 Jeffery C. Mays, "Chirlane McCray to Lead Effort to Help Female Inmates at Rikers," *New York Times*, February 1, 2018.
57 Goodman, "Mayor Backs Plan to Close Rikers."
58 Shakur, *Assata: An Autobiography*, 49–50.
59 Shakur, *Assata: An Autobiography*, 50.
60 Shakur, *Assata: An Autobiography*, 51.
61 Shakur, *Assata: An Autobiography*, 250.
62 Shakur, *Assata: An Autobiography*, 52.
63 Shakur, *Assata: An Autobiography*, 52.
64 Shakur, *Assata: An Autobiography*, 52.
65 Shakur, *Assata: An Autobiography*, 266.

66 Shakur, *Assata: An Autobiography*, 266.
67 Shakur, *Assata: An Autobiography*, 266.
68 Shakur, *Assata: An Autobiography*, 267
69 Fred Moten, *Stolen Life* (Durham, NC: Duke University Press, 2018), 131.
70 Moten, *Stolen Life*, 65

From a knife

Yola Gómez

It's about six am started drinking with my friend The one who had a shootout with the cops and lived We're here talking about a flask paper bag some kind-of gettin' in trouble talked about gin whiskey or about that bum jug of Carlo Rossi Pacific Northwest Green Scare how they tortured our friend into wearing a wire locked him up while coming down Yeah We call him a Snake now We exchanged street stories and scars That one from a knife fight that looks like a centipede Proud scars Raised skin through mispronunciations and slurred speech talked about the weather and the feel of the place without ever really speaking ` I was twenty family had lots of run-ins with the law Held down Strapped in Screamed at Stripped down It could have been
Morning could have been Noon but turns out it was dusk Me with my friend we're on the porch and we're sipping and struggling to make sense of the world without ever saying as much Someone calls us Native or foreign My friend laughs, "Ojibwa" he says sips passes it to me I say "I'm nothing" But I am Or I was And we have the feeling of being on display Us on the porch and them staring from the grass "Man, white anarchists are a trip" We say with a glance And my white old man boyfriend comes they say I'm acting up "The pigs" they say the bum jug pulls up we get outta hand

I'm feral They say "she's wild" I say I'm nothing
So he chases me down Drags me in My friend gets away
He knows better
He fought a gun battle and won here comes the law Flashing
lights Welfare
check they say I say something in Span-
ish But they know what I mean they give chase
I'm caught for "being a concern for my own safety" Cop
pulled his gun pointed it close range at my head Said
something like he "didn't take a shot officer in his line of
fire" through the thin worn fibers of a grayish purple pillow-
case pulled over my head Slow motion beating by five I'm
kicking wailing but the sound is gone my head is ringing Kill-
ers in my house they beat me till I can't see out my left eye my
hands are black and blue I spit and lady cop laughs I'm caught
Stripped down Bent over Thrown out inspected inside
my kennel I'm groped by a guard that offers extra food for a hand
job Another gives me a bible fifteen to twenty They say Hit
that cop with his own baton they say Wild girl they say I say I'm
nothing But I guess I was The threat of existence We all were
me and the others Inside we look at each other and talk about
the feel of the place Without saying as much white girls sit
over there we sit some place else but you know I get up and
walk around I put my hair in braids and my pro bono lawyer says
"she has promise" I'm 21 Just found out I'm pregnant
by my white old man boyfriend judge looks at me
tells me "just put another girl in for fifteen for something less
You know, he says her skin was darker than mine without sayin'
as much I just look at him I got out didn't give birth locked
up cuffed held down didn't have my baby taken Didn't get
shot in the head Got to live another day got friends that
died in here Died out there too Shot dead in front of a school Shot
dead had folks call it suicide by cop I'm here Survivor's guilt
But that one time I was 20 started drinking round six am with
my friend The one that had a shootout with the

cops and lived   we plan in whispers   of backpacks   weapons some
kind-of "government surveillance"   and gin or whiskey   or that
bum   jug of Carlo Rossi Through mispronunciations and slurred
speech talked about why   life is worth
living and of   the feel of the place without ever really   knowing
run-ins with truth and reality Born   as though dead   Spoken of
as numbers   Grieved through clenched fists Buried   still alive
I'm still alive   Still on the   outside and we   all look at
each other and know   why   without saying as much

BAD APPLES, ROTTED ROOTS, AND THE THREE Rs OF REFORMIST REFORMS

Ren-yo Hwang

While you're worried about "bad apples" we're wary of the roots. Because no healthy tree naturally bears strange fruit.

—Jessica Foster (@gindaanis)

Letting a few bad apples ruin the bunch.
Don't minimize the fight comparing apples to cops.
This is about the orchards poisoned roots not loose fruits in a box.
Once the soils been spoiled the whole crop's corrupt.
That's why we need the grassroots working from the ground up . . .

—Kimya Dawson, "At the Seams"

I, like many abolitionists, came to abolition because we were tired of harm and we wanted to see something else happening in our communities and in the world. We didn't come idealistically thinking that there was no such thing as harm. Rather, we looked at the political category of crime and wanted to take it apart.

—Ruth Wilson Gilmore

In late May 2020, the United States saw a resurgence of Black Lives Matter rallies and protests following the street execution of Ahmaud Arbery by white nationalists on February 23, the March 13 murder of sleeping Breonna Taylor in her home by plainclothes officers of the Louisville Metro Police Department, and most notably, the death of George Floyd on May 25 in broad daylight on the streets of Minneapolis—the choice of weapon: nine and a half minutes of asphyxiation by knee when Derek Chauvin of the Minneapolis Police Department kneeled on his neck. From mid-2020 onward, we witnessed a remarkable call to challenge the very presence of policing, as discussions of prison and police abolition remarkably moved into the mainstream with hashtags such as #DefundPolice, #AbolishPolice, #FreeThemAll, #CareNotCops, and #CareNotCages. As a strategy to limit the scope of this movement and appear pragmatic in an attempt to achieve "immediate deliverables," to borrow from the nonprofit-industrial complex lexicon, #DefundPolice was interpreted by some to be one of many perfunctory, reformist reforms that seek to advance a more humanist model of policing and but only reproduce the status quo. Abolitionist scholar Liat Ben-Moshe writes, "Reformist reforms are situated in the discursive formation of the system as is, so that any changes are made within or against this existing framework."[1]

Most emblematic of reformist reform in 2020 is DeRay Mckesson's Campaign Zero platform called #8CantWait. "A campaign to bring immediate change to police departments," the project levied eight demands upon police officers, one of which included that police give "a verbal warning in all situations before using deadly force."[2] Such demands are simply a request for a less-lethal (nonlethal) or "more humane" practice, where the system of policing is left largely undisturbed.* A statement and counterdemand under the banner of #8toAbolition was offered to recontextualize the call to #DefundPolice and challenge its deployment as a potential reformist reform policy, ridding the demand of procedural jargon that only requested the most modest version of accountability. In most cases, this only amounted to a temporary shift in practice and perhaps some resources that, again, leave policing as an institution intact. In countering #8CantWait, some organizers of #8toAbolition argue that "the end goal of these

---

* Dylan Rodríguez writes, "#8CantWait attempts to convince those questioning and rebelling against a violent, misery-making system that policing is reformable—that it can be modified and refurbished to protect and serve the very same places, communities, and bodies it has historically surveilled, patrolled, intimidated, and eviscerated." Dylan Rodríguez, "Reformism Isn't Liberation, It's Counterinsurgency: You Can't Abolish Systemic Anti-Blackness and Racial-Colonial Violence by Protecting the System Itself," in *Abolition for the People: The Movement for a Future without Policing and Prisons*, eds. Kaepernick Publishing and *LEVEL*, October 20, 2020, https://level.medium.com/reformism-isnt-liberation-it-s-counterinsurgency-7ea0a1ce11eb.

[#8toAbolition] reforms are not to create better, friendlier, or more community-oriented police or prisons. Instead, we hope to build toward a society without police or prisons, where communities are equipped to provide for their safety and wellbeing."[3]

Indeed, non-reformist reforms require a rewriting of safety altogether, where changes to the penal and police systems must "reduce the power of an oppressive system while illuminating the system's inability to solve the crises it creates."[4] As Ben-Moshe suggests, "Non-reformist reforms imagine a different horizon that should be realizable for the improvement of humanity, and are not limited by a discussion of what is possible at present."[5] To challenge this sense of limitation, the research initiative "Interrupting Criminalization" launched toolkits and campaigns breaking down how and why the call to #DefundPolice was urgent, necessary, and long overdue, however radical and impossible it seemed.[6] In response to a narrow interpretation of the verbiage of *defund*, they remarked,

> #DefundPolice is a strategy that goes beyond dollars and cents—it is not just about decreasing police budgets, it is about reducing the power, scope, and size of police departments. It is about delegitimizing institutions of surveillance, policing and punishment, and these strategies, no matter who is deploying them, to produce safety. It is a strategy (part of the HOW) to advance a long-term vision of abolition of police through divestment from policing as a practice, dismantling policing institutions, and building community-based responses to harm, need, and conflict that do not rely on surveillance, policing, and punishment.[7]

On a policy level, reformist reforms reflect the interior motive of state institutions to reproduce themselves and the logics by which they are informed. In "Razing the Carceral State," Marie Gottschalk offers a critique of how the last decade of penal reform conceived of its initiatives and "best practices" by emphasizing the Three R approach: reinvestment, recidivism, and reentry, which fundamentally framed reform as a cost-benefit analysis. Treated as simply a "dollar-and-cents problem," a solely economic penal reform approach of the Three Rs would in the end, Gottschalk notes, never reduce prison expansion via the tools located within and of the criminal justice system.* The focus on reinvestment, recidivism, and reentry was ultimately a reinvestment in the expanding power of penal practices as the exclusive pathway to abrogating recidivism, allowing only a recalculation of the costs of reentry. Such an additive model of carceral capital, to be determined and used by and for jailers and their partners, would be a consummate example of penal reformist reform.

With Gottschalk's critique in mind, this essay aims to critique what I consider the Three Rs of carceral reform within contemporary prison and police culture. A remix of the neoliberal Three R approach to penal reform policy (reinvestment, recidivism, and reentry), this article uses an abolitionist feminist framework to position the Three Rs of police reform—rebranding, recruitment, and retraining—as a reformist reform recycled from and emboldened by the logics of carceral feminism.†

CARCERAL FEMINISM AND REFORMIST REFORM

Reformist reform, whether it be penal reform or police reform, induces the cyclical reproduction of what Lena Palacios calls the "transcarceral continuum," a continuum that "blurs the boundary between the prison's outside and inside, extending its control through stigmatization and the embodied markers of imprisonment of criminalized girls who have spent the majority of their lives under some form of state control."[8] The transcarceral continuum, like militarism abroad and domestically, requires an unambiguous investment in a logic of enforcement

* Gottschalk writes, "Recasting the problem of mass incarceration in econometric or cost-benefit language does little to challenge the excessively punitive rhetoric that has left such a pernicious mark on penal policy over the last half century. It also is no match for the considerable economic interests that are now deeply invested in the perpetuation of the carceral state." Marie Gottschalk, "Razing the Carceral State," *Social Justice* 42, no. 2 (2015): 22.

† Likewise, Naomi Murakawa describes three traps of reform in policing in the *Abolition for the People*: The first trap is "rewarding police" as a mode of reforming the police. The second trap is, "Reformers try to enhance people's procedural rights as if arming individuals with legal protections might slow the churn of criminalization." The third trap is, "Because reformers refuse abolition, they can only tinker with the techniques of police violence."

and domination as an objective necessity, in the name of a supposedly ungendered and dispassionate—but ultimately *highly* gendered, *highly* passionate—apparatus called the law and, its successor, order. As scholars have traced the connections between militarism and militarization of domestic law enforcement agencies in the United States, abolition feminism connects militarism and imperial war abroad to "everyday" quotidian sites of anti-Black, anti-Indigenous, and xenophobic domestic warfare.[9] The race-gender analysis of abolition feminism provides a view into the machinations of the transcarceral continuum more clearly. Abolition feminism also asserts an unapologetic collective investment in a world without policing, prisons, and patriarchy is possible, real, and a future within reach.

Indeed, abolition feminism recognizes that at the root of state violence is an overwhelming practice and ideology of sexual and gender-based violence. Historically and in the present, sexual and gender-based violence have been used both formally and informally as the modus operandi of state-sanctioned militarized violence by the US domestically and overseas, including countless documented patterns of sexual violence committed by police and military members on and off duty.[10] The rising visibility of gender and sexual violence in the 1980s and 1990s led to the advancement of a feminist mainstream movement that found partnership with the state. Formed with the leadership and assistance of anti-violence and domestic violence organizers, many of whom were white women and belonged to the managerial class, this movement, ultimately described as "carceral feminism," was seduced by the promise of safekeeping by US legal apparatuses and often participated willfully or unwittingly in the expansion of criminalization and imprisonment.[11]

Abolition feminism and anti-carceral feminists have amplified how such partnerships with the very interlocking state systems that enact and exacerbate gender and sexual violence, serving to reproduce the kinds of institutions and infrastructures that undermine efforts to empower survivors as well as community-driven work to preempt and end cycles of harm.[12] As reformist reforms, these carceral feminist formations invested in legal punishment rather than other forms of accountability and consequence, and they hinged this call for punishment on a racialized narrative of safety. As exemplified in the 1989 Central Park jogger case, state-based discourse and de facto practice ushered white women and girls into the cultural imaginary of safekeeping within a protectable public. Black and brown women and girls, on the other hand, were not afforded the same protections against patriarchal, gender, and sexual violence. In the name of the dual prongs of "protection" (state-based claims of safety) and "punishment" (state-sanctioned violence), mainstream anti-violence reformist reforms favored the reproduction, unlimited power, force, and application of law enforcement to sustain the sovereign (settler) state and associated patriarchal regimes that require it. As Denise Ferreira da Silva writes, "Though both referents of juridical-political power have the dual task of protecting and punishing their subjects, the state (the sovereign) also has the obligation to preserve itself."[13]

Because protection (for some) and punishment (for others) form the basic calculus for state preservation, state-based claims to "public safety" have long been affixed to the punishment of the individuated figures of the "criminal" and the "innocent." Anti-carceral feminists highlight how mainstream public safety narratives drive the commitment to prison, policing, and the incrementalization of carceral reform precisely because they rely on highly charged narratives of "dangerous others" that situate law enforcement as "necessary" to protect the innocent. Indeed, abolition feminism reminds us that safety is promised only to those who can access or preemptively assume the category of innocence. As Prentis Hemphill writes,

> The use of innocence is violence. Innocence refuses responsibility, care, and reflection. It is why blame will always be planted on a Black body. Innocence is the psychological desperation of a history too big to face. Innocence is insatiable. . . . Innocence and exceptionalism sit at the core of white identity and will only be undone in responsibility, action, risk, and care. It will only be undone through a systemic uprooting of all that enforces its myth making violence.[14]

The idea of "innocence" as myth making violence troubles the very objectivity of law and status quo demands for "public safety," which are amplified within conservative political climates that emphasize "law and order" and "tough-on-crime" approaches to addressing social problems.[15] Anti-carceral feminists, primarily queer/trans people and feminists of color, thus call for transformative and restorative justice above and beyond a penalties-first view of public safety and individual innocence.

Beth E. Richie explains the importance of comprehending gender and sexual violence (and with it safety and innocence) beyond a narrow, individuated exchange. Richie's concept of the "violence matrix" requires readers to understand the impacts of multiple scales of violence on Black women. She offers us a lens from which to understand anti-violence and "safety" measures as always requiring an analysis of violence as something that transpires on a reverberating scale—never solely divisible and contained in one person, one unit, one household, one neighborhood, one demographic, and so forth. Additionally, the violence matrix, like other contributions by Black, Indigenous, and feminists of color, highlights how harm and abuse exist in multiple overlapping contexts, but also how they are exacerbated by the law-enforcing institutions and actors that are considered too sacred and too necessary to unmake.[16] Richie's vision of an anti-violence practice operationalizes holistic models of community safety that center survivorship and healing and disrupt the root issues of violence. These models defy a foundational faith in top-down masculinist saviorship and ask, What could be possible if granted the resources, time, energy, and collective commitment to explore possibilities for community-based safety outside of the patriarchal figuration of the state as it is manifested in and emboldened by prisons and policing?

To address the lack of imagination and impoverishment of carceral culture, this article unpacks three contemporary trends in mainstream police and carceral reform—rebranding, recruitment, and retraining—marking the ways that they bear the trappings of carceral feminist ideology and practice, and their seeming inevitability. In bringing attention to these other Three Rs if you will, I ask, How might a shared analysis of abolitionist non-reformist reforms provide pathways and principles that prevent us from becoming entrapped within cycles of "betterment" that reproduce systems of incarceration and policing? Though not exhaustive in capturing the totality of neoliberal and progressive reformist reforms that have been central to mainstream criminal justice reforms, the Three Rs offer a pulse of the contemporary range in strategies and tactics used to ameliorate public discontent to juridical oversight and the threats of defunding that come with it. The reformist reform of "rebranding" is used here to describe the superficial veneer of shallow, sometimes even temporary, cosmetic changes used to paint over, reframe, or recuperate policing and imprisonment and rally positive public sentiment. These veneer-like alterations can exist via legislation, policy, practice, or simply external propaganda. Rebranding as a reformist reform strategy is wholly detached from any semblance of structural change and dangerously traffics in tactics of diversification, multiculturalism, feminism, and LGBTQ tokenism. As abolition feminism makes plain, this tactic not only fails to upend the racist, sexist, homophobic, colonialist, genocidal, and patriarchal violence of policing in practice, but the attempt to identify specific actors (i.e., "bad apples") and swap them out with other actors that are representative of "inclusivity" also perversely obscures the ways such death-making ideologies serve as premise to policing itself.

Connectedly, the reformist reform of "recruitment" is used here to describe models of participatory diversification and enlistment via white-supremacist multiculturalism in the shape of community policing—a conscription of minority representation but not "minority-driven politics," to quote Robin D. G. Kelley.[17] Recruitment, as explored by Ruth Wilson Gilmore, Dylan Rodríguez, Alex Vitale, Angela Y. Davis, and others, is used particularly as a tactic of counter-revolutionary pro-statist political maneuvering to quell and extinguish the possibility of life-affirming and liberatory mobilization. Carceral recruitment also corrupts the vision of community care and the possibility of collective responsibility toward disrupting violence that abolitionist feminists, especially those working at the cross sections of gender violence (in all its forms), demand as cornerstone to any forms of meaningful political work based in life-affirming community-building.

Lastly, the reformist reform of "retraining" is used to describe the methods in which police, penal, and carceral reformist reforms have sought to remediate and recalibrate how we measure or what is considered too lethal. Retraining suggests, to borrow from Rose Braz, a kinder and gentler model of carcerality—a "more sensitive" practice of policing and imprisonment.[18] Retraining, like recruitment and rebranding, assumes that reformation is simply the perfecting and "betterment" of systems and practices of law enforcement of policing and imprisonment. Much like the penal reform Three R approach of reinvestment, recidivism, and reentry, the policing reform Three R approach is also devised as policy-driven economic additive models that, in sum, regenerate carceral resources and capital, reinforcing state-based measures of law enforcement as public safety. As I will show, the Three Rs of carceral feminist reformist reform employ neoliberal, multicultural logics that uphold the very systems they claim to intervene upon.

COPAGANDA* AND REBRANDING OF THE BAD APPLE THEORY

In a 1973 conversation occurring in the midst of Black power and third world pro-revolutionary liberation movements, James Baldwin and Nikki Giovanni discuss the issue of pro-police benevolence campaigns in response to active calls against the enterprise of policing and police altogether. Giovanni and Baldwin together offer a profound reading against ubiquitously circulated and self-authorizing pro-police campaigns rebranded as a wholly humanistic endeavor.

Baldwin: A cop is a cop.

Giovanni: Well, cops are white.

Baldwin: Yeah, and he may be a very nice man. But I haven't got the time to figure that out. All I know is, he's got a uniform, and a gun, and I have to relate to him that way. That's the only way to relate to him, at all, because one of us may have to die.

---

* "Copaganda" is a portmanteau of "cop" and "propaganda." The originator of this term is unattributed, though it became popularized in mainstream and social media in 2019 and 2020.

Giovanni: You know in New York there's a big campaign going on to humanize the policemen. They have posters, billboards, upstate and they have a picture of a BIG cop bending over this little blonde girl—

Baldwin: Uh-huh.

Giovanni: And the sign says: "And some people call him pig."

I wanted to rent a billboard, I told a friend of mine, and show this big cop and this fourteen-year-old kid, with thirty bullets in him and say, "And some people call him peacemaker."[19]

Giovanni's reading of pro-police benevolence campaign reveals an attempt to counter the derogatory moniker of "pig" as a term, which has origins in British slang from as early as 1811.[20] Shifting away from the police-centered anxiety of being seen as self-serving, greedy, and contemptible, Giovanni poses a countercampaign. Her campaign invokes the deadly horrors that remain intact with policing today, where the very semantics of police officer as "peacemaker" paint over of what is death in plain sight, best revealed in a juxtaposition of the text next to the image of a lifeless unnamed young person, riddled with bullets from a state-sanctioned, tax-funded, law-enforcing deadly weapon. Giovanni rewrites and flips a historically uninterrupted script that relies on the figure of the "little blonde girl" as weaponized white feminine innocence in contrast to the lifeless body of what is likely a Black or brown masculine youth. Giovanni poses to us, both in 1973 and today, even in a post-Trump and Biden-era presidency, that such campaigns to "humanize" police remain an ongoing project of the state in rebranding its image as a benevolent protector.

Rebranding policing overall is defined here as a mode of superficial reframing of the enterprise of policing and its cooperating agencies and institutions, as inclusionary, tolerant, and a vehicle to aid the diversification of its agents and oversight. A tactic that has appealed to those seeking piecemeal neoliberal police reformist reforms from the left, rebranding can range for calls like less-lethal or more gender-affirming or minority-inclusive forms penalization, incarceration, and policing. Rebranding cleverly hides how progressive reform tactics have simply retrofitted multiculturalism onto the lethal legacy of colonial, white-supremacist institutions. Unlike the association of "pigs" as a moniker for any and all police, the shift to compartmentalizing police violence as bad apples re-trended in 2020 in the wake of the COVID-19 pandemic and #DefundThePolice. Prior to the 1990s, the metaphor of bad apples was associated mainly with exposing police corruption. The metaphor has been studied under the designations of "rotten apple theory," "rotten apple doctrine," "bad apple theory," "bad apple hypothesis," and "bad apple syndrome." For instance, in 1974, political scientist Wesley Skogan wrote,

> The standard explanation which is advanced when policemen are discovered to be on the take is the "rotten-apple" theory of corruption: every big barrel is sure to have a few, but we can bob for them if we have the public behind us. . . . The real effect of rotten-apple rhetoric, the commission argues, is to forestall unpleasant but meaningful reform.[21]

It is in the 1990s, particularly at the height of the 1992 Los Angeles uprisings following the brutal police beating of Rodney King, that the concept of bad apples becomes used more closely in association with police violence or, euphemistically, police "misconduct."[22]

The bad or rotten apples theory as a reformist reframing, seeks to isolate and reduce the problems of police violence to single, misbehaving, rogue, and even sometimes simply ignorant cops. A collective critique of the bad apple cop, a parochial reformist metaphor, has reemerged in recent abolitionist to liberal reform calls to #DefundThePolice, noting the problems of excluding said apple from the barrel, tree, orchard, and the very stolen land it rests on—bloodied roots make for brutal branches and rotting fruit.[23] The call to defund the police requires a shift from individuation of the violence of policing and instead demands a commitment to defending Black lives, all Black lives, beyond the prosecution, sentencing, or disciplining of particular murderous police officers. As our Black, trans, queer, disability justice, feminist organizers and activists have repeated, defunding policing is a call for feminist anti-violence community-based anti-carceral strategies of transformative justice no less.

As criminal punishment relies on the letter of the law, the deployment of state violence is made computable and interpretable through juridical systems of control. That is, how we comprehend and thus intervene on violence via law and law-enforcing state agencies remains woefully amiss when only seen as worth combatting if measured properly on an extractable and isolated scale of the individual (sexual assault, domestic abuse, interpersonal to street-based violence as largely isolated events that must be trackable to be prosecutable). The law relies on its ability to prove itself useful in quantifying violence as that which can be relegated to individual acts and bad actors—that is, persons who can somehow be simultaneous surveilled and neglected through the carceral euphemisms of correction and rehabilitation, or rather, those who can be isolated and forgotten behind walls.*

Following the death of Ahmaud Arbery, Breonna Taylor, George Floyd, and less-named Tony McDade, a Black trans man, in late May to mid-June 2020, marches, protests, and actions gathered under the banner of Black Lives Matter would center collective calls to abolish the police state to the immediate divestment tactic of "defunding police." Meanwhile, alongside platforms such as #8toAbolition in counter to reformist calls revising policing via Mckesson's Campaign Zero platform of #8CantWait, viral videos circulated in which frontline protestors pled with patrolling police officers to display a shared gesture of disapproval of police killings—a call to "take a knee."[24] In the spirit of Colin Kaepernick's 2016 protest of state violence against Black communities by kneeling during the US national anthem performed during the broadcast of the NFL preseason, kneeling has been taken up by Kaepernick-inspired NFL players as well as those in other major sports leagues and at college and high school games despite threats of professional penalty and inflammatory criticism by the conservative right wing.[25]

The transference of this gesture from those protesting policing to asking police to participate should be troubled. Such a gesture was considered by onlookers and protestors as a tactic of forcing officers to indict their colleagues or themselves in a moment of public pressure

* Literally in the sense that the California Department of Corrections and Rehabilitation, the largest public prison system in the world, uses such terms as ultimate euphemisms for penalty, sentencing, and caging as the modes of rehabilitation of the criminal justice system.

and protest, far from an acknowledgment of the very long history of policing as foot soldiers of state violence. Unfortunately, kneeling has been used to retool the still presiding reformist logic of good cops versus bad cops. Such a logic relies on the concept of rooting out the bad apples or simply applying more "restrictive use of force policies" without addressing structural and systemic violence.[26]

The gesture of kneeling manufactures the optics of officers acknowledging, if not also protesting, the misapplication of force. Perhaps, however momentarily, it feels like a win, that orders can be taken from elsewhere, disrupting policing's hierarchical chain of command. Meanwhile, such a rewriting of kneeling is particularly curious, as Chauvin, the officer who suffocated Floyd with his knee to his neck, inspired several circulated social media posts of white men parroting the deadly scene of Floyd's murder.* These short, viral video reenactments consistently showcase an eruption of jubilation by those protesting police violence when police officers, following the plea of the very protestors they are there to control, elect to kneel. However, when police officers bend their knees, even if as a token of respect, or so it reads, activists on the ground have reported and captured footage of these very officers soon after employing violent tactics of dispersal. Using a range of "less-lethal" riot control—pyrotechnic chemical projectiles, advanced tasers, chemical disbursers, pepper spray, tear gas, stun grenades, rubber ball munition, expulsion grenades, and brute force—is yet another tactic to quell anti-police critique. In the same vein, for-profit weapons manufacturers of this less-lethal riot control gear very audaciously market their weapons and ammunition using names like "peacekeeper." This also parallels interchangeability of public sector law-enforcing agents

---

* Bystander-reported incidents that made headlines include one of a New Jersey correctional officer and another of a Pennsylvania police officer. See Morgan Winsor, "New Jersey Corrections Officer Suspended after Being Filmed Mocking George Floyd's Death," *ABC News*, June 10, 2020, https://abcnews.go.com/US/jersey-corrections-officer-suspended-filmed-mocking-george-floyds/story?id=71168455, and Sam Ruland, "York City Police Officer Accused of Reenacting George Floyd's Death on Administrative Leave," *York Daily Record*, June 4, 2020, https://www.ydr.com/story/news/2020/06/04/george-floyds-death-allegedly-mocked-york-city-officer-investigation-ongoing/3142937001.

such as police, sheriffs, constables, Border Patrol, immigration officers, marshals, deputies, and their categorization under the umbrella term of "peace officers."*

Rebranding police as largely "good" cops is a recurring phenomenon through the decades. For example, *Cops*—arguably one of the first cinéma verité–style reality television series as well as one of the longest running (1989 to this writing)—is a three-segment, thirty-minute show that glorifies police officers as tough-on-crime heroes combatting "societal blight" of Black, brown, and working-class white communities.[27] Demonstrated by the targeted enforcement of those working in survival economies and coping with poverty via substance use, the criminalization of poverty in *Cops* is revealed in the absence of police responses to illicit drug dealing, use, and experimentation that undoubtedly occurs in gated and affluent communities and college campuses, not to mention unprosecuted class-war transgressions like wage theft or "white collar" crime.† In response to the George Floyd–inspired protests in the summer of 2020, *Cops* production came to a temporary and brief halt, another superficial gesture that aimed to intervene in the problem of criminal representation among the Black, brown, and poor communities, but more likely served to rehabilitate the reputation of police by taking its brutalities out of primetime view.

The "sensitivity" of removing a show like *Cops* from the air is akin to the fleeting act of police kneeling with protesters, wherein the police take on a new strategy of social and cultural "peacekeeping." Such liberal feel-good moments of police and communities "coming

---

* For instance, a 12-gauge Peacekeeper round is described as "designed to provide temporary incapacitation through kinetic energy impact and to mark the target." See *Department of Defense Nonlethal Weapons and Equipment Review: A Research Guide for Civil Law Enforcement and Corrections*, US Department of Justice, October 2004, https://www.ojp.gov/pdffiles1/nij/205293.pdf, 39. See also law enforcement supplier US PeaceKeeper, based in Chino, California, https://www.uspeacekeeper.com/pages/testimonials.

† As seen in a parody segment called "Corporate Cops" in *Bowling for Columbine*, director Michael Moore pitches a reality cop show that polices white-collar crime instead of Black and brown communities. "Corporate Cops," *Bowling for Columbine*, directed by Michael Moore (Santa Monica, CA: Metro-Goldwyn-Mayer, 2002).

together" have been touted by mainstream press as the most respectable and, thus, preferred form of civil disobedience and police protest, where police officers are not "demonized" but asked to participate in a critique of themselves and their colleagues, much of which is wholly disingenuous and misleading.

This was demonstrated in media celebration of the copaganda released by the National Fraternal Order of the Police in their October 29, 2020, social media post of a white woman police officer holding a young Black toddler characterized as "lost" during the "lawlessness" and "violent riots in Philadelphia." The caption reads, "We are not your enemy. We are the Thin Blue Line. And WE ARE the only thing standing between Order and Anarchy."[28] It soon surfaced via social media and the lawyers defending the mother of the child that the mother's car had been swarmed by a dozen cops, her windows bashed in, and her child, a witness to this violence, removed from the car. In other words, as the child was both forcibly removed from the car, the fraternal order used this picture of the white woman cop holding the child as propaganda to demonize the protests, reinforce a fake narrative of "absent" Black parents, and make heroic their efforts to "rescue" a Black child and control the anarchy. Meanwhile, many independent and rogue journalists have filmed and documented the riotous and violent militarized police response to protestors.

Despite the ubiquity of live social media reporting, police officers can still be found using hostile and violent tactics of dispersal. Rehabilitating the image of lethal policing does not make paramilitaristic law enforcement any less deadly. If anything, it has been in the midst of riot control police efforts that we see a shared culture of fulfillment in dominance articulated most clearly. As Minneapolis residents were shot with what looked to be PepperBalls—a trademarked nonlethal round for automatic and semiautomatic rifles that shoot this "3-gram marble-sized ball that explodes into a cloud of oleoresin capsicum (OC) on impact"—killing field phrases such as "light 'em up" were routinely heard.[29]

Against a discourse that imagines police can "do better," or themselves root out the bad apples, radical queer and feminist of color abolitionists continue to uproot such liberal investments and hollow promises of police reform. Abolitionist feminist analysis recognizes how the reframing and rebranding of police as "more sensitive" law-enforcing foot soldiers amounts to only more reformist reforms that strengthen reinvestments in the carceral apparatus.

COMMUNITY POLICING AS RECRUITMENT AND THE WEAPONIZATION OF DIVERSIFICATION

As both consequence and fuel for the reformist tactic of reframing, the similar reformist strategy of recruitment has been put forward as a model of progressive inclusionary police and penal reform. Recruitment of more minoritarian subjects, particularly people of color, women, and LGBTQ persons, has been rationalized as necessary to the proposed philosophy and eventual institutionalization of community policing through the US Department of Justice's Community Oriented Policing Services (COPS). Under the auspices of the Clinton administration, and in the same year as the Violence against Women Act (VAWA), the 1994 Violent Crime Control and Law Enforcement Act (VCCLEA) was enacted as the largest crime bill in the history of the United States, and in an attempt to reduce crime through what is termed "community policing," the VCCLEA created such institutions as COPS. COPS defines community policing as "a philosophy that promotes organizational strategies that support the systematic use of partnerships and problem-solving techniques to proactively address the immediate conditions that give rise to public safety issues such as crime, social disorder, and fear of crime."*

In *Our Enemies in Blue*, Kristian Williams discusses a Department of Justice (DOJ) report by a Community Policing Consortium from the VCCLEA era that describes "the two 'core components'" of community

---

* COPS states that community policing "concentrates on preventing crime and eliminating the atmosphere of fear it creates. Earning the trust of the community and making those individuals stakeholders in their own safety enables law enforcement to better understand and address both the needs of the community and the factors that contribute to crime." Community Oriented Policing Services, "Community Policing Defined," US Department of Justice, 2014, https://cops.usdoj.gov/RIC/Publications/cops-p157-pub.pdf.

policing as "community partnership and problem solving."[30] Citing sociologists Jerome Skolnick and David Bayley's study of six police departments that innovated, piloted, and tested community policing, Williams describes community policing as a strategy in which "police and the public are co-producers of crime prevention."[31] In these situations, the already limited resources devoted to community-driven and survivor-centered—meaning defined or led by those most impacted by violence—projects fighting violence are aggressively usurped and repackaged via methods and metrics related to community policing, such as COPS. The strategies, policies, and research of COPS alongside the recruitment of multicultural police and jailers remain heavily focused on the expansion of apparatuses of punishment itself, ensuring that methods of carceral surveillance, criminalization, and imprisonment be viewed as the only possible trajectory toward achieving "public safety." Recruitment of "diverse" police, community members, and local social service agencies or members of community organizations predetermines the roles of police and community members in defining what makes and means safety and what is defined as violence and crime. This reformist method stands in stark contrast to abolitionist feminism's practice of reparative and transformative justice and community accountability, where defining collective safety requires the recognition of the impact of state violence and the coercive nature of collaborating with state agencies. Community-policing partnerships simply fail to center those most impacted by quotidian and intersecting violence. The top-down approach and penal prerogative of community policing is defended by police claiming that they are a perpetually underfunded institution with limited resources in need of recruitment, buy-in, and bolstering by minoritarian subjects. This narrative continues to be paraded as a tool to be trotted out and perfected among economically starved and resource-divested neighborhoods and communities who are touted as needing the most *control* from *within*.

The reformist form of recruitment is seen throughout most militarized state agencies—the armed forces, local police, Central Intelligence Agency, and Federal Bureau of Investigation—where the recruitment and retainment of minoritarian subjects is driven by a desire to attract those who are more capable of blending into the communities they seek to surveil, making it easier to extract information and intelligence from those communities. The euphemism of "community partnerships" is shorthand for recruitment of community insiders to direct how the expansion of policing can be made more possible, more seamless. That is, recruitment is made possible and is seen as a positive through its association with civic duty and a shared investment in the ideology that better training, better representation, and better understanding between those policed and those doing the policing make for peacekeeping. This amounts to a recruitment not just into the police force but into a fictive ideology of community policing *as* akin to community safety.

Following collaborations among the DOJ agencies and select law enforcement and participating NGOs, the political climate of "distrust" of law enforcement by Black communities in the wake of late 1980s civil unrest and the Los Angeles uprising of 1992 also shaped this model of community-oriented community control, rebranded as "community invested," "community collaborating," "community partnerships," and most notably, "community policing" as a form of recruitment of diverse officers and community partners.

Following the Watts Rebellion of 1965, the Los Angeles Police Department (LAPD) and many other surrounding agencies in the county understood the advantage of law enforcement as setting a lowered yet tolerable bar for "serving and protecting," pinpointing then community insiders and collaborators willing to toe the line of law and enforcement. Such modes of reform were considered a progressive move to strategically curtail backlash from the very failures, negligence, and outright violence and abuse from various arms of the DOJ—minimal to no sentences in high-profile cases of law enforcement abuse (Rodney King) to outright harassment and profiling by law enforcement on individual and large scales (Virginia Beach; Washington, DC; Chicago). In the decades to follow, the strategies of recruitment have been exceedingly normalized as models of encouraging community participation and input. Task forces and advisory committees geared toward the recruitment, retention, and collaboration of historically marginalized groups have unfortunately been an incredibly effective tool by establishmentarian state politics, institutions, and law enforcement agencies. In reference to the digital and billboard campaigns and initiatives by the LAPD as "multiculturalist policing as remarshaled domestic war," Dylan Rodríguez writes, "Join LAPD signifies the formation of a visual curriculum that attempts to decontextualize, deflect, and disavow the racist state's dense ensembles of anti-Black and racial-colonial power. . . . The Join LAPD initiative reflects the racist state's concession that white supremacist policing must undergo substantive reform to remain politically and institutionally viable."[32] Multiculturalist policing as a form of recruitment weaponizes diversification and manipulates the "value of diversity" to that which is merely representational, an identarian state politics that relinquishes any political identity and anti-authoritarian political stance. In response to the reformist reform of community policing, the authors of 8toAbolition.com state, "The end goal of these reforms is not to create better, friendlier, or more community-oriented police or prisons. Instead, we hope to build toward a society without police or prisons, where communities are equipped to provide for their safety and wellbeing."[33] In discussing how diversification as a form of dogmatic reformism does little to disturb the violent order of militarized statecraft, Rodríguez asserts,

> The reformist counterinsurgency pivots on a fervent belief that the spirit of progress, national improvement, and patriotic belief will prevail over a fundamentally violent order. In practice, this belief approximates a form of dogmatic liberal faith—a kind of pseudo-religion. Thus, increased "diversity" in personnel and bureaucratic infrastructure, shifts in the legal and policy apparatus, and individualized "anti-bias trainings" ascend as some of the principal methods for alleviating state violence.[34]

Recruitment of diverse soldiers, tacticians, and keepers of war does little to change the nature of war itself: death.

The diversity recruitment strategy of the FBI—the principal law enforcement agency of the United States—shares parallels with the progressive policing strategies of local law enforcement agencies.* With taglines such as "The FBI Values Diversity," "At the FBI, everyone is welcome!" to "A FAMILY LIKE NO OTHER" (printed in boldface and in all capital letters), the multicultural representation of actual diverse agents remains aspirational, as the bureau continues to employ a general majority of white men.† Even if law enforcement could suddenly become majority people of color, as we have seen over time in certain cities and geographies, diverse law enforcement agents have actually become *more* effective in wielding tools of criminalization, surveillance, and capture, and they distract from real structural change.[35]

Such tactics of reform are reflected in similar strategies of community policing as a mode of progressive policing in cities such as Los Angeles, Boston, and New York. At the height of community policing, a 1994 DOJ report reveals the connections between diversity recruitment and community policing:

---

* The nine diversity advisory committees of the FBI include American Indian and Alaska Native Advisory Committee; Asian Pacific American Advisory Committee; Black Affairs Diversity Committee; Hispanic Advisory Board; Lesbian, Gay, Bisexual, Transgender and Allies Advisory Committee; Near and Middle East Advisory Committee; Persons with Disabilities Advisory Committee; Veterans Affairs Advisory Committee; and Women's Advisory Committee. See "Diversity at the FBI," Federal Bureau of Investigation, accessed September 27, 2021, https://web.archive.org/web/20200729133722/https://fbijobs.gov/working-at-FBI/diversity.

† The FBI's diversity recruitment page says, "To effectively accomplish our mission, the FBI needs people from different backgrounds, experiences and perspectives. The FBI values and leverages human differences, opinions and perspectives to empower our FBI community to achieve its greatest potential. The FBI's commitment to fostering diversity and inclusion is integrated into every facet of employment." In the next section, titled "Repeatedly Recognized as a 'Best Place to Work' for Diversity," the text continues: "Did you know that the FBI was recently named as one of Diversity Jobs' Top Employers for 2020 in government? That's not surprising given our concerted efforts in promoting diversity throughout our workforce and ensuring fairness and equality for all employees. . . . This consistent recognition further emphasizes our commitment to diversity and equality within the workplace—be it in the field, in the lab or within our Washington, DC Headquarters. At the FBI, everyone is welcome!" See "Diversity at the FBI."

> The social fabric of our country has changed radically. The family unit is not as stable as it once was. Single working parents find it extremely difficult to spend enough time with their children, and churches and schools have been unable to fill this void. Immigrants, ethnic groups, and minorities, while adding to the diverse nature of American communities, often have different interests and pursue disparate goals.[36]

The deterioration of the "social fabric," especially among minorities, provides a rationalization for community policing, and thus the continuance of "reformed" policing as a benefit to community; it is cast as "a collaboration between the police and the community that identifies and solves community problems." Such evaluations of communities *in need* of policing rely on the racialized sociological cohering logic that communities of color require tailored forms of minoritized policing, a logic of saving while surveilling "broken" Black and brown families. In this way, community policing builds upon the anti-Black principles of the highly controversial but influential 1965 *Moynihan Report*.[37]

Community policing as a mode of carceral feminism similarly echoed in the spirit of women and LGBT recruitment in law enforcement agencies, that is the carceral feminism of "female representation" and women of color in agencies such as the FBI. If searching online for "FBI recruitment of women," a top result leads to "Female Special Agents at the FBI."[38] These search results may well reflect the growing cultural interest in female representation in law enforcement stoked by iconic "strong female leads" in fictional stories like *The Silence of the Lambs*, the first cinematic adaptation of Thomas Harris's 1988 psychological horror novel. In this film, mainstream audiences are introduced to FBI agent Clarice Starling. Director Jonathan Demme and his team were allowed unprecedented access to the FBI Academy in Quantico, Virginia, for the film. In this partnership the fictional portrayal of Agent Starling would come to symbolize the need for strong women to join law enforcement. Such methods of recruitment through mainstream representation influenced the feminist cultural imagination into a shared belief that such inclusion was a marker of progress, a carceral feminist fantasy in which ending gender and sexual violence would require more female agents like Starling (never mind the caricature of the cross-dressing/trans-menacing serial predator, Buffalo Bill).*

Much like the fictional detectives Grace Rasmussen and Karen Duvall in Netflix's critically acclaimed true crime series *Unbelievable*, adapted from investigative Pulitzer Prize–winning collaborative news article between ProPublica and the Marshall Project, "An Unbelievable Story of Rape," one might find themselves rooting for feminist cops over sexist cops who uphold a culture of rape and sexual violence. Rasmussen and Duvall are positioned as the "good feminist cops," rescuing survivors of sexual violence from the re-traumatization experienced by way of commonplace police procedural processes that demand proof, that is, a re-accounting of sexual violence in order to materialize incontrovertible and object-oriented evidence. The trauma and testimonies from survivors, particularly if marked as less than innocent, are treated as dubious in nature. Most of the survivors portrayed in the show, particularly Marie Adler, the main young, white woman, require the persistent and investigative woman-led policing in order to be saved.

From Starling to Rasmussen and Duvall, Hollywood offers a constancy of women's empowerment in law enforcement as a mode of recruitment and reform. Carceral feminism invests in the promise of simply kinder and more gender competent policing and imprisonment via representation, too. But as seen in *Unbelievable*, it is also the supposed "survivor-centered procedural protocols" that Duvall and Rasmussen follow that reveal the co-optation of actual community-

---

* Trying to locate further insight into the FBI's early 1990s recruitment strategy was in vain, other than some nods to the rarity of the cooperation between Demme's *The Silence of the Lambs* production team and the FBI. It is reported,

> In what was a rare act of cooperation at the time, the FBI allowed scenes to be filmed at the FBI Academy in Quantico; some FBI staff members even acted in bit parts. . . . The FBI, in a move rare for this bureaucratic and self-conscious agency, cooperated in the making of the film version of *The Silence of the Lambs*. (See Carl N. Edwards, *Responsibilities and Dispensations: Behavior, Science, and American Justice* [Dover, MA: Four Oaks Press, 2001], 132.)

driven and survivor-centered procedures.* At the end of the TV series, only when the sexual predator's stack of polaroid photographs from his attacks are discovered is Adler's case reopened. Thanks to the teaming of Duvall and Rasmussen.

There is an opening for a counter-evaluation of the series beyond one of carceral feminist pro-policing, as Adler turns to Duvall in the end and says, "More than him going to jail, more than the money, it was knowing there were these two people out there trying to do something."[39] The doing of *something* is where abolition feminism offers the possibility of creative interventions to prosecution, jailing, and punishment—a call to overhaul completely the very systems in which we have laid so much wasted labor and resources. Carceral feminism, in its recruitment into the criminal punishment system, perhaps offers the possibility of less re-traumatization, but abolition feminism negates the fact that re-traumatization is a necessary evil in the first place.

RETRAINING AS KINDER AND GENTLER PROGRESSIVE POLICING AND JAILING

Retraining is a policy and practice-based penal reform that, like the bad apple theory, believes officers who have somehow breached protocol or procedures simply need to be given more "tools" to be less lethal (nonlethal). Retraining is also often a call made by those invested in progressive policing as a constant trajectory toward more inclusionary penal practices of the "betterment" of systems and practices of law enforcement of policing and imprisonment. Trying to make "kinder and gentler" enforcers of state violence, or more sensitive cops and jailers, is premised on the individual actor versus the overall system,

* Not coincidently, Marc Patrick O'Leary, the serial sexual predator portrayed in the series, was an Army veteran, who at his trial stated, "I'm standing here because I need to be in prison. . . . I know that probably more than anyone in this room. I've known it for a while." His admission of needing confinement in prison, as well as use of terms such as "alpha" predatory sexual behavior, is testimony to a masculinist, patriarchal imagination where ending cycles of sexual violence are only possible in a world where patriarchal, inhumane confinement is a necessity, and no other intervention or discouragement is possible prior to the sexual violations themselves.

the apple versus the orchard once again. Retraining, like recruitment, relies, too, on the reformist calls for sensitivity training, community policing, and diversity recruitment to soften police practice and behavior. These efforts often hinge on ensuring that the labor of law enforcement is not "disrespected." But why would anyone respect those who are paid, from our collective pockets, to police and violate those whom we love?

Police, in themselves, do not constitute a people, a social identification personified perhaps, but to echo Baldwin, "A cop is a cop." Policing and police are not a people, and "blue lives matter" is simply an anti-Black misnomer—an overidentification with a uniform that posits and employs authoritarian power to enforce law. This does not mean people do not identify wholly, fraternally, and supremely through and through as the blue, the badge, as unified force are themselves the "good" cops; but this is how patriarchal cultures of violence often remain so unshakable. One cannot simply selectively distance themself from a history and culture that has been entrenched in violence of all sorts and on all scales. For example, to acknowledge that there are individual officers and soldiers who choose not to use sexual violence as part of their everyday conduct does not imply that sexual violence is not embedded in the very fabric and quotidian abuse of power that underwrites the police and military-industrial complex.

Indeed, the patriarchal kinship of military and police culture (never mind the heavy-handed recruitment of veterans into law enforcement) is the very institutionalization of white supremacist and ableist patriarchy. Consider the issue of police who are domestic abusers. The oft-cited statistic that 40 percent of police officers are domestic abusers largely refers to the National Center for Women and Policing's "Police Family Violence Fact Sheet," which notes various studies throughout the 1990s, sympathetically geared in favor of highlighting the stressors police officers face that inhibit them from making less-violent choices off the clock. Many of the prevailing statistics still in use originate from *On the Front Lines: Police Stress and Family Well-Being*, a 1991 landmark hearing before the House of Representatives Select Committee on Children, Youth, and Families.[40] Research that followed included an exposé in 1995 by then Field Operations Lieutenant Lonald D. Lott of the Turlock, California, Police Department. Entitled "Deadly Secrets: Violence in the Police Family," Lott's article appeared in *FBI Law Enforcement Bulletin* and centered on law enforcement officers' "high exposure" to street-based violence and environments of violence, arguing that this exposure caused them to be more likely to commit violence in their domestic lives.[41]

The 1991 statistic only manages to tell us that 40 percent of officers *admitted* to enacting violence within their families. The overall, wholly sympathetic tenor of the committee, as documented in this report, was to locate resources to support and train law enforcement simply to do better by their families. Additionally, it is the impulse of both those who collect, distinguish, and discern violence to not simply evaluate violence but also to stop its constant reproduction. This requires pushing past an idea of violence and harm as something that occurs individually. Data-driven reformist interventions fail to grapple with the less calculable structural and ongoing historical violence shaped by white supremacist settler heteropatriarchy. The reformist perspective of studies like the one conducted by Lott suggests something dangerous about the racialized logic of "street violence"—code for urban, houseless, Black, brown, and poor. These perspectives suggest that the structural and structuring violence that exists as part of enduring intergenerational systemic, and systematic, violence is normal and only troubling when "the chickens come home to roost."

Similarly, a decade later in 2000, the dedication page of the *Domestic Violence by Police Officers: A Compilation of Papers Submitted to the Domestic Violence by Police Officers Conference*, a report issued by the FBI, emphasizes that the overwhelming statistics regarding police officer family abuse should not discredit those on the force who do not do the same. It reads, "We sympathize with all the victims in domestic violence situations and honor the vast majority of police officers who, on a daily basis, absorb the worst toxins our society produces without poisoning their beloved families."[42] This institutional admittance and promise of both attempting to retrain and rehabilitate their image says little about the direct impact and changes needed to repair and address the intergenerational and interpersonal violence experienced directly by police and military families. This again is testimony to how such violence is treated as an "unfortunate consequence" of being enforcers of the law or, rather, the nonliability of enforcers of criminalization.

In a 2013 *New York Times* exposé "Departments Are Slow to Police Their Own Abusers," Sarah Cohen, Rebecca R. Ruiz, and Sarah Childress make note of a particular form of carceral feminism that indicates the need for better reporting:

> With no central reporting system and little definitive research, there is no accurate way to measure the problem—how often officers abuse their domestic partners and how severely abusers are punished. In some instances, researchers have resorted to asking officers to confess how often they had committed abuse. One such study, published in 2000, said one in 10 officers at seven police agencies admitted that they had "slapped, punched or otherwise injured" a spouse or domestic partner.[43]

Much of the data that has been collected to account for the overwhelming evidence of domestic interpersonal violence at the hands of law enforcement is pulled from self-reported testimonies by law enforcement officers themselves. Importantly, statistical data based on reported domestic violence by police officers is likely an undercount because families who have experienced domestic violence by an officer fear reporting these instances of violence due to the threat of retaliation as well as the consequences of placing their domestic partner's job in jeopardy. After all, the people they would report the violence to are the friends and colleagues of their abuser. This resembles, in a different way, why marginalized communities do not always seek support from law enforcement in the context of intimate-partner violence. However, in the case of marginalized communities, the fear and mistrust are usually situated in a historical context in which survivors fear being further harassed, violated, questioned, humiliated, or even killed by police, such as in cases of "wellness checks" that end in death, such as the police murder of Atatiana Jefferson in 2019.

CONCLUSION

Someone smashed the policeman's radio
And finally silence A Black language infinitely
And blue in a decade where it finally means sky

—Sable Elyse Smith, "Landscape 5"

Unlike the former waves of protests under the banner of Black Lives Matter from 2013 to 2019, BLM's #DefundThePolice conversations on abolition would enter mainstream consciousness and discourse. Commercial enterprises, small and large, with a combination of cultural awakening and disingenuous marketing, donned Black Lives Matter banners at the very top of their homepages. Reduced to the newest liberal articulation of equality or "doing good," marketing and brand strategists had determined that associating with BLM had become mainstream enough to avoid any dire commercial threat, all while glossing over the various commercial ties and contracts to law-enforcing agencies such as US Immigration and Customs Enforcement.* Beyond a surface-level engagement with BLM, the call to #DefundThePolice required an on-the-ground visioning and action-based engagement with what it would mean to defend Black lives, an investment in Black futures. In offering a critique of mainstream carceral reform trends that emphasize faulty reformist practices such as rebranding, recruitment, and retraining, there is a case to be made for, at the very least, the exploration of abolitionist feminist possibilities for anti-carceral, social, political, and cultural transformation. This critique of neoliberal and multicultural reformist reform disrupts individualized approaches to reform to signal

---

* Jeff Bezos took to Instagram to share a post of a white supremacist comment about boycotting Amazon with anti-Black words redacted. Bezos responded, "And Dave, you are the kind of customer I am happy to lose." See Jeff Bezos (@jeffbezos), "There have been a number of sickening but not surprising responses in my inbox since my last post. This sort of hate shouldn't be allowed to hide in the shadows. It's important to make it visible. This is just one example of the problem," Instagram, June 7, 2020, https://www.instagram.com/p/CBJrhdzHKNt. See also Kari Paul, "Amazon Says 'Black Lives Matter.' But the Company Has Deep Ties to Policing," *Guardian*, June 9, 2020, https://www.theguardian.com/technology/2020/jun/09/amazon-black-lives-matter-police-ring-jeff-bezos.

the limitations and ultimate impossibility for transformation and liberation under the proliferation of militarized policing regimes under the architectonics of a transcarceral continuum.

In response to BLM protesters in the summer of 2020, former US president Donald J. Trump deployed a "shoot-first" militarized police response of active-duty military units. Under the Insurrection Act of 1807, last used in the 1992 Los Angeles uprisings, he authorized deployment of the National Guard, tanks, armored military patrols, tear gas, rubber bullets, electric tasers, long-range acoustic devices, and water cannons faster and more enthusiastically than any life-saving medical gear, personal protective equipment, or necessary ventilators for those dying or vulnerable to death by COVID-19. Police departments and their supporters, as representative in hashtags such as #DefendPolice, #BlueLivesMatter, #ThinBlueLine, and #LawAndOrder, sought to portray police as the benevolent sole protectors against all violence, anarchy, and lawlessness, a recasting that is neither new nor surprising. A benevolence campaign of "your friendly neighborhood cop" was opportunistically resurrected to counter virally circulated portrayals of rogue cops.

This cycle of police violence, protest of police violence, and the draconian law-and-order response from the state to anti-violence protests is the very manifestation of what Ruth Wilson Gilmore describes as the "application of violence—the cause of premature deaths—produc[ing] political power in a vicious cycle."[44] In other words, the abolitionist call to rethink the institution of policing altogether would trigger a call for additional and expanded violent police and state responses, only adding cogency to the demand of #DefundThePolice.

Abolition and feminism, as bonded together, highlight the shared political discourse and action surrounding the interlocking oppressive systems of cis-heteropatriarchal, settler-colonial control manifested in institutions and practices of policing, prisons, militarism, and empire-building. In other words, abolition feminism is the emphatic naming of the connection between the abolition of policing and prisons as necessitating the abolition of colonial, cis-heteropatriarchal violence. Abolition feminism argues that duty and responsibility to those we imagine as most vulnerable or in need of institutional protection, care, and safety require a robust and collective discernment of the law and the death-driven patriarchal impulses and applications carried out through its enforcers via the US criminal punishment system. The work of organizing and building localized efforts toward safety, defined for and by community, must resist assimilation into the current capitalist punishment system of selective and ableist self-responsibility.

The success and promise of even neighborhood and community safety are, unfortunately, still defined through individuated (isolationist) safety as always reasonably the best possible model for public safety, thus predicated on a tacit agreement that all anti-violence strategies remain in lockstep with the will of law enforcement and state collaboration, an omniscient body. Dean Spade shared in a "Queer Abolition" webinar, "It almost feels like we are being 'parentified' by the state. It's like, I just want somebody to come in who's going to solve things, and we're going to be disempowered.'"*

The call to abolish the cycle of penal and police reformist reform, recycled and reproduced through a transcarceral continuum of policing, prison, and militarism domestically and abroad, is not simply hashtag clicktivism but a new world breaking open, blooming from sweat, blood, ash of a carceral world no more. To rupture the perpetual wheel of reformism that we are witness to time and time again, abolitionist feminism offers us insight, analysis, vision, and pathways to challenge the bloody repetition of reformism of state patriarchal violence. Whether it be the rebranding of policing as the white woman cop pretending to save a small Black child from danger, or the recruitment of that very same white woman or a transgender cop as evidence of progressive politics for all, or the retraining of minoritarian figures of law enforcement to better police their counterparts, these modes of

---

* Spade continued, "It's actually that we need to empower ourselves to solve problems on the block, to step in when a fight is happening, and to have the training and support that we need. I'm not going to do that by myself. But I'm like, 'Oh, the people I keep going out with, we're going to figure it out together.' . . . Actually skilling us all up, rather than we call on some faraway expert to come—that is the police model." Dean Spade, "Queer Abolition," (webinar, July 2, 2020, 57:45–58:16), available at https://www.facebook.com/BlackAndPinkMA/videos.

reformist reform still, at their core, embody and embolden the mantle of policing as "public safety."[45]

Whether it is rainbow decals on police vehicles or LGBT community-police liaisons, coincidentally or not unveiled in the years following the rise of BLM, such gestures remain grossly perverse in all that they hope to conceal.[46] More colorful law-enforcing institutions have only cosmetically modified the appearance of such agencies through tactics of diversification in recruitment, but the carceral and penal conditions remain largely unchanged.[47] Cleverly hidden is how progressive tactics of rebranding, recruitment, and retraining have simply retrofitted multiculturalism as a veneer on the lethal legacy of colonial, white supremacist institutions.[48]

With the continued proliferation of policing as an ongoing reformist project of reinvention and revision, the naturalization of policing has retained its stronghold as a necessary pre-fixture of everyday life. Adopting models of neoliberal multicultural inclusion, policing now is a prime example of multicultural white supremacy as inclusionary diversification into institutional legacies of state violence. Abolition and feminism together, as the utter undoing and rebuilding of our very conceptions of safety and how and what we define as violence, requires that we dismantle cis-heteropatriarchal violence as foundational to the reproduction of state legitimacy as exploitation and abuse of power—that is, its ability to usher in social control through a fiction of democratic participation in juridical objectivity.[49]

To imagine safety as possible without policing and prisons—that is, criminalization and punishment—abolitionist organizers and scholars Mariame Kaba and Shira Hassan have repeatedly posed and responded to the question, "What about public safety?" In *Fumbling Towards Repair,* they write,

> Safety derives from healthy relationships with other people. Prisons are focused on isolation and therefore foster violence rather than safety. People are safe when they have what they need, when they are not desperate, when they have spaces to heal from trauma, and when traumas are prevented in the first place. Bottom Line: We do need to build safety, and we can do that through making sure

people have what they need and building connective relationships and communities—not relying on cops and cages.[50]

Perhaps an alternative to the Three Rs of carceral reformist reform outlined here are instead the redefining, reinvesting, and reimagining of public safety as always relational, communal, survivor-centered—a collective practice requiring the unapologetic resistance to reinventing the deadly wheel of policing, prisons, and punishment.

NOTES

1 Liat Ben-Moshe, "The Tension between Abolition and Reform," in *The End of Prisons: Reflections from the Decarceration Movement*, eds. Mechthild E. Nagel and Anthony J. Nocella II (Amsterdam: Rodopi Press, 2013), 87.

2 "#8CantWait," Campaign Zero, last modified June 2021, https://8cantwait.org.

3 Mon Mohapatra et al., "#8toAbolition," accessed September 27, 2021, https://www.8toabolition.com.

4 Dan Berger, Mariame Kaba, and David Stein, "What Abolitionists Do," *Jacobin*, August 24, 2017, https://www.jacobinmag.com/2017/08/prison-abolition-reform-mass-incarceration.

5 Ben-Moshe, "Tension between Abolition and Reform," 87.

6 Andrea J. Ritchie, Mariame Kaba, and Woods Ervin, "#DefundPolice, #FundThePeople, #DefendBlackLives: Concrete Steps toward Divestment from Policing and Investment in Community Safety," *Interrupting Criminalization and Movement 4 Black Lives*, 2020, https://filtermag.org/wp-content/uploads/2020/06/Defund-Toolkit.pdf.

7 Ritchie et al., "#DefundPolice," 3.

8 Lena Palacios, "'Ain't No Justice . . . It's Just Us': Girls Organizing against Sexual and Carceral Violence," in *Girlhood and the Politics of Place*, Mitchell Claudia and Rentschler Carrie, eds. (New York: Berghahn Books, 2016), 282, accessed February 4, 2021, https://doi.org/10.2307/j.ctt14jxn16.21.

9 Christopher J. Coyne and Abigail R. Hall, *Tyranny Comes Home: The Domestic Fate of U.S. Militarism*, 2018 (Stanford, CA: Stanford University Press, 2018); Radley Balko, *Rise of the Warrior Cop: The Militarization of America's Police Forces* (New York: PublicAffairs, 2014); American Civil Liberties Union, *War Comes: The Excessive Militarization of American Policing* (New York: ACLU, 2014); Peter B. Kraska, "Militarization and Policing—Its Relevance to 21st Century Police," *Policing: A Journal of Policy and Practice* 1, no. 4 (2007): 501–13; Michael S. Sherry, *In the Shadow of War: The United States Since the 1930s* (New Haven: Yale University Press, 1997).

10 See *On the Front Lines: Police Stress and Family Well-being, Hearing before the Select Committee on Children, Youth, and Families, House of Representatives*, 102nd Cong., First Session, 32–48 (1991) (statement of Leanor Boulin Johnson, Associate

Professor of Family Studies, Department of Family Resources and Human Development, Arizona State University, Tempe), https://files.eric.ed.gov/fulltext/ED338997.pdf; Peter H. Neidig, Harold E. Russell, and Albert F. Seng, "Interspousal Aggression in Law Enforcement Families: A Preliminary Investigation," *Police Studies* 15, no. 1 (1992): 30–38; M. A. Straus and R. J. Gelles, *Physical Violence in American Families: Risk Factors and Adaptations to Violence in 8,145 Families* (New Brunswick: Transaction Publishers, 1990); P. H. Neidig, A. F. Seng, and H. E. Russell, "Interspousal Aggression in Law Enforcement Personnel Attending the FOP Biennial Conference," *National FOP Journal* (Fall/Winter 1992): 25–28; A. Levinson, "Abusers behind a Badge," *Arizona Republic*, June 29, 1997, F9; J. Feltgen, "Domestic Violence: When the Abuser Is a Police Officer," *Police Chief* 63, no. 10 (October 1996): 42–49; and L. D. Lott, "Deadly Secrets: Violence in the Police Family," *Law Enforcement Bulletin* 64, no. 11 (November 1995): 12–16.

11 For more see Kristin Bumiller, *In an Abusive State: How Neoliberalism Appropriated the Feminist Movement against Sexual Violence* (Durham, NC: Duke University Press, 2008); Elizabeth Bernstein, "The Sexual Politics of the 'New Abolitionism,'" *Differences* 18, no. 3 (2007): 128–51; Elizabeth Bernstein, "Militarized Humanitarianism Meets Carceral Feminism: The Politics of Sex, Rights, and Freedom in Contemporary Antitrafficking Campaigns," *Signs* 36, no. 1 (2010): 45–71; Brady T. Heiner and Sarah K. Tyson, "Feminism and the Carceral State: Gender-Responsive Justice, Community Accountability, and the Epistemology of Antiviolence," *Feminist Philosophy Quarterly* 3, no. 1 (2017): 3; and Anna Terwiel, "What Is Carceral Feminism?" *Political Theory* 48, no. 4 (2020): 421–42, doi:10.1177/0090591719889946.

12 For more see Mimi E. Kim, "From Carceral Feminism to Transformative Justice: Women-of-Color Feminism and Alternatives to Incarceration," *Journal of Ethnic & Cultural Diversity in Social Work* 27, no. 3 (2018): 219–33; Emily L. Thuma, *All Our Trials: Prisons, Policing, and the Feminist Fight to End Violence* (Champaign: University of Illinois Press, 2019); Victoria Law, "Against Carceral Feminism," *Jacobin*, October 17, 2017, https://www.jacobinmag.com/2014/10/against-carceral-feminism; INCITE! *Color of Violence: The INCITE! Anthology* (Cambridge, MA: South End Press, 2006).

13 Denise Ferreira da Silva, "No-Bodies: Law, Raciality and Violence," *Griffith Law Review* 18, no. 2 (2009): 215, accessed September 27, 2021, https://doi.org/10.1080/10383441.2009.10854638.

14 Prentis Hemphill (@prentishemphill), "The use of innocence is violence. Innocence refuses responsibility, care, and reflection. It is why blame will always be planted on a Black body. Innocence is the psychological desperation of a history too big to face," Instagram, May 27, 2020, https://www.instagram.com/p/CAsNq6nATo3.

15 Beth E. Richie, *Arrested Justice: Black Women, Violence, and America's Prison Nation* (New York: New York University Press, 2012).

16 Kimberlé Crenshaw, "Mapping the Margins: Intersectionality, Identity Politics, and Violence against Women of Color," *Stanford Law Review* 43, no. 6 (July 1991): 1241–1299; Beth E. Richie, 2000; Sarah Deer, *The Beginning and End of*

Rape: Confronting Sexual Violence in Native America (Minneapolis: University of Minnesota Press, 2015); Emi Koyama, 2006; Andrea J. Ritchie et al., 2017.

17 "New World Coming: Racial Capitalism with Robin D. G. Kelley," People's Forum NYC, October 16, 2021, https://www.youtube.com/watch?v=-5UhJYavbA8.

18 Rose Braz, "'Kinder, Gentler, Gender Responsive' Cages: Prison Expansion Is Not Prison Reform," in *Women and Girls in the Criminal Justice System: Policy Issues and Practices*, vol. 2, edited by Russell Immarigeon, 87–91 (Kingston, NJ: Civic Research Institute, 2006).

19 James Baldwin and Nikki Giovanni, "A Dialogue" (London: M. Joseph Ltd., 1975).

20 Francis Grose and Hewson Clarke, *1811 Dictionary of the Vulgar Tongue: A Dictionary of Buckish Slang, University Wit, and Pickpocket Eloquence*, unabridged ed. (Northfield, IL: Digest Books, 1971).

21 Wesley G. Skogan, "Review Essays: Policy-Making and Police Taking; Controlling Behavior on the Beat," *Urban Affairs Quarterly* 9, no. 4 (1974): 520–28.

22 For more, see Marc Cooper, "Violence, Lies and Videotape," *Washington Post*, March 1, 1998; Jerome H. Skolnick, "It's Not Just a Few Rotten Apples: The Beating of Rodney King Reignites Los Angeles' Debate on Police Conduct. How High Does Responsibility Go?" *Los Angeles Times*, March 7, 1991; "The Simpson Legacy / Los Angeles Times Special Report: Trial & Error: Focus Shifts to a Justice System and Its Flaws: Weighing the Necessity of Change: How One Case May Reshape Criminal Justice in America: The Police / 'It's Not a Bad Apple. The Barrel Itself Is Rotten,'" *Los Angeles Times*, October 8, 1995; Ed Timms, "A Plague of Bad Cops: The Fuhrman Affair Is One among a Wave of Apparent Cases of Misconduct," *San Francisco Examiner*, October 8, 1995; Gregory J. Boyle, "Commentary: LAPD Must Drop CRASH in Order to Regain Public's Trust: The Anti-Gang Units' Method Boils Down to 'Getting the Bad Guy at All Costs.' It's Bad Policing and It Doesn't Work," *Los Angeles Times*, September 27, 1999; and Joe Domanick, "Law Enforcement: Civilian Control of LAPD is Elusive Despite Reforms," *Los Angeles Times*, November 14, 1999.

23 See James Downie, "Time to Toss the 'Bad Apples' Excuse," *Washington Post*, May 31, 2020, https://www.washingtonpost.com/opinions/2020/05/31/time-toss-bad-apples-excuse; Rashawn Ray, "Bad Apples Come from Rotten Trees in Policing," Brookings, May 30, 2020, https://www.brookings.edu/blog/how-we-rise/2020/05/30/bad-apples-come-from-rotten-trees-in-policing; Ruth Marcus, "The Problem of Policing Isn't Bad Apples. It's a Diseased Tree," *Washington Post*, June 5, 2020, https://www.washingtonpost.com/opinions/the-problem-of-policing-isnt-bad-apples-its-a-diseased-tree/2020/06/05/7f110b4c-a757-11ea-b473-04905b1af82b_story.html; and Sean Illing, "Why the Policing Problem Isn't about 'A Few Bad Apples': 'The System Was Designed This Way': A Former Prosecutor on the Fundamental Problem with Law Enforcement," *Vox*, June 6, 2020, https://www.vox.com/identities/2020/6/2/21276799/george-floyd-protest-criminal-justice-paul-butler.

24 Adele Peters, "These 8 Steps for Police Abolition Go Further Than #8Can'tWait: 8toAbolition Is a Response to the Set of Eight

Police Reform Proposals Touted by DeRay McKesson," *Fast Company*, June 10, 2020, https://www.fastcompany.com/90514640/these-8-steps-for-police-abolition-go-further-than-8cantwait.

25 Tom Lutz, "New NFL Rules: Teams Face Fines if Players Kneel during National Anthem," *Guardian*, May 23, 2018, https://www.theguardian.com/sport/2018/may/23/nfl-protest-national-anthem-new-rules-fine.

26 Peters, "Further Than #8CantWait."

27 For more on COPS, see Ofelia Ortiz Cuevas, "COPS and the Visual Economy of Punishment," in *Abolition Now! Ten Years of Strategy and Struggle against the Prison Industrial Complex*, CR-10 Publications Collective, eds. (Chico, CA: AK Press, 2008).

28 Char Adams, "Black woman sues police union over misleading Facebook photo of toddler son," NBC News, September 16, 2021, https://www.nbcnews.com/news/nbcblk/rickia-young-sues-police-union-facebook-post-toddler-son-rcna2057.

29 For more, see National Institute of Justice, "Department of Defense Nonlethal Weapons and Equipment Review: A Research Guide for Civil Law Enforcement and Corrections" (October 2004), 50.

30 Kristian Williams, *Our Enemies in Blue: Police and Power in America*, rev. ed. (Chico, CA: AK Press, 2015). For more see Gary Cordner, "Elements of Community Policing," and Carl B. Klockars, "The Rhetoric of Community Policing," in *The Police and Society* (Prospect Heights, IL: Waveland Press, 1999); Bureau of Justice Assistance, *Understanding Community Policing: A Framework for Action*, INCJ 1484-171 (Washington, DC: US Department of Justice, 1994); and Jerome H. Skolnick and David H. Bayley, *New Blue Line: Police Innovation in Six American Cities* (New York: Free Press, 1986), 213.

31 Williams, *Our Enemies in Blue*, 204.

32 Dylan Rodríguez, *White Reconstruction: Domestic Warfare and the Logics of Genocide* (New York: Fordham University Press, 2020), 49.

33 For more, see https://www.8toabolition.com/resources.

34 Rodríguez, *White Reconstruction*.

35 For more, see work to undo the generational trappings of gang databases by Youth Justice Coalition.

36 Bureau of Justice Assistance, *Understanding Community Policing*, 3.

37 Bureau of Justice Assistance, *Understanding Community Policing*, vii.

38 Federal Bureau of Investigation, "Female Special Agents at the FBI," November 15, 2019, https://youtu.be/7Aw0Hd7dg90.

39 Susannah Grant, Lisa Cholodenko, and Michael Dinner, dirs., *Unbelievable*, season 1, episode 8, September 13, 2019, https://www.netflix.com/title/80153467.

40 *On the Front Lines: Police Stress and Family Well-being, Hearing before the Select Committee on Children, Youth, and Families, House of Representatives*, 102nd Cong. (1991).

41 L. D. Lott, "Deadly Secrets: Violence in the Police Family," *Law Enforcement Bulletin*, NCJ Number: 159194, 64, no. 11 (1995), https://www.ojp.gov/ncjrs/virtual-library/abstracts/deadly-secrets-violence-police-family.

42 Donald Sheehan, ed., *Domestic Violence by Police Officers: A Compilation of Papers Submitted to the Domestic Violence by Police Officers Conference at the FBI Academy, Quantico, VA* (Washington, DC, 2000).

43 Sarah Cohen, Rebecca R. Ruiz, and Sarah Childress, "Departments Are Slow to Police Their Own Abusers," *New York Times*, November 23, 2013, http://www.nytimes.com/projects/2013/police-domestic-abuse/index.html.

44 Ruth Wilson Gilmore, "Fatal Couplings of Power and Difference: Notes on Racism and Geography," *Professional Geographer* 54, no. 1 (2002): 15–24. Gilmore here is citing Allen Feldman, *Formations of Violence: The Narrative of the Body and Political Terror in Northern Ireland* (Chicago: University of Chicago Press, 1991).

45 For more on abolition feminisms, see recent work by Victoria Law (2021), Kaba (2021), and Davis, Richie, Meiners, and Dent (2021).

46 See Johnny Diaz, "South Florida's LGBT Capital Has a New Rainbow Police Car," *South Florida Sun Sentinel*, February 2, 2019, https://www.sun-sentinel.com/local/broward/fl-ne-wilton-manors-rainbow-gay-police-car-20190201-story.html; Joseph Choi, "Nashville Police Unveil New Rainbow Car for Pride," *Tennessean*, last modified June 26, 2019, https://www.tennessean.com/story/news/2019/06/21/nashville-police-debut-new-rainbow-car-pride/1516968001; Logan Rude, "Madison Police Unveil Pride Flag Decal in Honor of Pride Month," Channel 3000, June 3, 2020, https://www.channel3000.com/madison-police-unveil-pride-flag-decal-in-honor-of-pride-month; Avianne Tan, "NYPD Unveils Rainbow-Themed Vehicle before City's Gay Pride March," ABC News, June 23, 2016, https://abcnews.go.com/US/nypd-unveils-rainbow-themed-vehicle-ahead-citys-pride/story?id=40072112; and Fran Spielman, "CPD Unveils Rainbow-Bedecked Squad Car in Advance of Sunday's Pride Parade," *Chicago Sun Times*, June 24, 2019, https://chicago.suntimes.com/news/2019/6/24/18715819/pride-parade-chicago-police-vehicle-lgbtq-lightfoot.

47 For more, see Maya Schenwar and Victoria Law, *Prison by Any Other Name: The Harmful Consequences of Popular Reforms* (New York: New Press, 2020).

48 For more, see Denise Ferreira da Silva, *Towards a Global Idea of Race* (Minneapolis: University of Minnesota Press, 2007). Silva writes, "This liberal appropriation of multiculturalism is especially troubling because it embraces the sociohistorical logic of exclusion as the correct account of social (racial, ethnic, gender) subjection and accepts the emergence of claims for recognition of cultural difference as proof of the failure of assimilation (Mabry 1996; Silva 2005): it simultaneously normalizes claims of cultural difference in arguments that are seemingly critical of the earlier project of 'assimilation' while retaining the earlier sociology of race relations argument concerning the extraneousness of the others of Europe that the biologic of racial difference is superseded by a sociologic of cultural difference to incarcerate the others of Europe in bounded transparency."

49 See Alex S. Vitale, *The End of Policing* (New York: Verso, 2018).

50 Mariame Kaba and Shira Hassan, *Fumbling Towards Repair: A Workbook for Community Accountability Facilitators* (Chico, CA: AK Press, 2019), 20.

REFUSING THE VALUE OF IMMIGRANT FEAR

AN ABOLITIONIST FEMINIST CRITIQUE OF SANCTUARY BY POLICE

Lee Ann S. Wang

This essay is a critical reading of state-sanctioned sanctuary, not the politics put forward by social movements to end immigration detention and deportation but a critical reading of when and why law enforcement mobilized sanctuary for policing and the ease with which this mobilization reproduces anti-Blackness through "public safety" agendas via law. As a legal design, to sanction and to shield evoke terms of protection by *enforcement of law* that too easily engulf organizing efforts to center resources, support, and an imagining of what communities of color, collectives, and peoples need to live and thrive differently. Here, I argue to avoid this conflation we can lean on the work and life of abolition feminisms to think critically about sanctuary's legal manifestation within local policing that has at times sought to distance itself as somehow less violent than the ongoing expansion of federal immigration enforcement.

I thank the editors Alisa Bierria, Jakeya Caruthers, and Brooke Lober for their guidance and patience with my ideas in this piece and their commitment to the authors and their work in this anthology. I thank Megan Francis of the "Sawyer/Mellon Race and Capitalism" conference at the University of Washington and Andrea J. Ritchie, organizer of the "Invisible No More: A Symposium on Resisting Police Violence against Black Women and Women of Color" conference at UC Berkeley, where I had the opportunity to present and have conversations about these ideas. I thank Kento Kobayashi for his research assistance and contributions that helped shape this essay.

For example, California has continued to boast one of the largest law enforcement and prison states across the nation, with the Los Angeles Police Department's (LAPD) long history of racial violence against Black communities.[1] Yet, in the few months leading up to the 2016 presidential election of Donald J. Trump, the LAPD was one of the first major law enforcement agencies to support sanctuary publicly and repeatedly. In a press conference, LAPD police chief Charlie Beck asserted that the greatest cost to a city without sanctuary would be the loss of public safety and not the loss of immigrant life, stating, "Over five-hundred thousand Angelinos are undocumented immigrants, I need them for their cooperation, I need them to work with their local police stations, I need them to be witnesses to violent crime, I need them to be part of the fabric of Los Angeles if we are going to keep this city safe."[2] This initial LAPD press conference was followed by several others throughout the state and the nation launching expressions of support for sanctuary as a police necessity. For the carceral state, sanctuary satisfies a desire and articulates a want to reproduce policing in a form that will allow it to make a liberal claim that policing is on the side of legally vulnerable people of color and, therefore, is not itself a form of racial violence. Beck's expressions—"I need them. . . . I want them . . ."—surface a pledge to do better policing with the coveted cooperation of *good immigrants doing good police work*.[3] The plight of immigration politics, then, may not merely be a question of whether undocumented and immigrant communities can become citizens, but whether, and to what extent, they will need to resist becoming cops.[4]

RACIAL ASSEMBLAGE OF IMMIGRANT FEAR

The increased community organizing and activist calls for sanctuary were a direct response to growing Trump-era anti-immigrant rules and regulations. In the months leading up to the 2016 presidential election, Trump promised to immediately expel undocumented youth, ban Muslims, wage war on bodies and reproduction, and zero in on immigration laws and institutions if he were elected. One recurring promise from the Trump administration focused on increased cooperation between federal immigration agencies and local police to more "efficiently" target, detain, and remove. While such cooperation has long existed in various ways within the racial violence of US immigration history, Trump's immigration agendas triggered even liberal rights-based politics to move against the protection of citizenship, whiteness, and nation-state. This heightened attention mobilized national calls for sanctuary through a broad scope of demands, including community support for every and all undocumented peoples, efforts to end the militarization of borders and state violence toward migrants, and specific efforts to create legislation or ordinances that slowed down cooperation between local police and federal agencies.

Yet, while organizers escalated the call for sanctuary, so did police. Several law enforcement agencies defended sanctuary as a possible means of retaining immigrants who could potentially help "keep the city safe" and come forward to cooperate in the criminalization of other unsanctioned individuals. The LAPD publicly supported sanctuary to recruit immigrants to assist police as well as avoid allocating funds to work they felt should be covered by federal dollars. San Diego's sheriff also announced support for sanctuary, stating, "They [immigrants] are really afraid to report crimes."[5] The San Francisco Police Commission asserted, "We want to assure all residents and visitors of San Francisco that they can report crimes and cooperate with the SFPD [San Francisco Police Department] without fear of any member inquiring into his or her immigration status."[6] In Bakersfield, sanctuary resolutions were passed as distinctly *symbolic* representations in order to express support for immigrant communities and encourage immigrants to continue assisting the police.[7]

To be clear, sanctuary does nothing to decriminalize or end the state violence that monitors legal status, it does not give any institution the power to sanction or prevent a person from being deported, and it does not abolish the grounds for, nor does it end, forcible removal. In this legal scheme, the actual struggles of being without legal status are glaringly absent, while sanctuary is instead thrust into a paradigm of policing historically underwritten by racial punishment. If sanctuary via law can be so limited in keeping immigrants safe, what kinds of work does sanctuary carry on, what kinds of racial subjects must necessarily reside in this space of legal phenomenon, and what labor are these subjects supposed to provide or "do" in a political arena that establishes itself around the idea of sanctuary?

Law enforcement efforts to attach policing to sanctuary push us to pause and work toward theorizations of anti-Black carceral logics that enable the expansion of sanctuary. This violence of carceral humanitarian ease places the burden of keeping the public "safe" on immigrant communities who are denied access to benefits afforded to the public, while their exclusion is maintained so that the very notion of "the public"—who it is and who it is not—can be defined and delineated. In the US nation-state's present history of anti-Black police violence, police desire for sanctuary as a crime-fighting tool organizes a racial assemblage that situates (non-Black) immigrants as valuable police collaborators against "crime," while the racial terms upon which "crime" comes to be recognized as such remains paradigmatically Black.[8]

Don't be afraid to call the police. . . . This reminder and the phrasing around *fear* is cemented in the global history of policing as racial violence and a formation of anti-Blackness that can take up multicultural and multiracial forms and envelop communities into the fold of policing and punishment. The police directive "don't be afraid" was not only prevalent in public spaces, state institutions, police agencies, and so forth but also emerged in community pamphlets and immigrant rights outreach materials contributing to sanctuary efforts. Within ongoing debate, it is the fear of calling and working with police that rests as the object to be corrected by the policy solution to slow down and end cooperation between agencies. Ultimately, sanctuary hinges on a racialized crime-panic that employs the rhetoric of public safety and the power of fear to justify ongoing brutal policing designed to target, police, and control Black people, in particular, while actively encouraging immigrants to police each other. Fear not the police: fear a criminal other.

The California Values Act, or SB 54, established a "sanctuary state" in response to a draconian series of presidential executive orders that increased removals, detentions, and family separation.[9] Alongside SB 54's goals to prevent state and local law enforcement from carrying out mechanisms of immigration effort, the legislation also opened an opportunity for law to broadly configure what or whom immigrants should fear. The law's author justified the bill thusly:

> When local police enforce immigration laws, they rapidly lose the trust of the undocumented community. Crimes go unreported for fear of deportation. The perpetrators roam free to strike again. Our communities become less—not more—safe.
>
> Senate Bill 54, the California Values Act, will prevent state and local law enforcement agencies from acting as agents of Immigration and Customs Enforcement. Instead, it will keep them focused on community policing, rather than rounding up hardworking, honest immigrants who in many instances assist police in solving crimes rather than committing them.[10]

As this defense of SB 54 demonstrates, it is not the welfare, housing, food, water, medical, mental health, education, or well-being of anyone whose lives grapple with immigration status that drives the law's design; it is the expansion of community policing over a public space that marks anyone occupying the legal-subject position without citizenship to be an exception. SB 54 debates brandished "loss of trust" between undocumented communities, immigrants, and police to justify policies aimed at slowing down the sharing of information between local police and federal immigration agencies. Thus, this form of sanctuary that advocates for policing only values immigrants through fear, and *how* they fear, as racial distinctions between what is understood as a rational, "acceptable" fear of the criminalized (such as fear of crime) and what is a misplaced, "correctable" fear of cooperating with cops. Fear of policing, or of the state itself, has no room in this formulation, conveniently disavowing the actual ongoing violence of policing and immigration enforcement together. Furthermore, the law's investment in the legal-subject formation of noncitizen categories continues the tension with the "hard working, honest immigrants who in many instances assist police in solving crimes rather than committing them."[11] This pairing of cooperation between immigrants and police is where abolitionist thinking can advance a politic that interrogates the formation of sanctuary-punishment that ultimately incorporates and engulfs immigrants.

Sanctuary's weaponization of immigrant fear to be of value for policing cannot do so without normalizing the acceptance of racial terms that assemble the unsanctioned immigrants, those "committing crimes," and the sanctioned immigrants who are expected to call law enforcement. Thus, for the sanctioned subject's value to even be a potential *credible* cooperator it must also maintain a *credible* fear that is mistaken yet still accepted. The legal design carries out its promise by inscribing immigrant fear as hesitant and afraid to come forward to the police because of immigration status and federal immigration agencies but never afraid of actual police themselves. The abrasive distinction between the sanctionable and unsanctionable immigrant hinges on a legal fantasy that posits local policing as a seemingly less violent, community-oriented option compared to ICE and federal immigration enforcement. It is important to remember that racial discourses on fear are in excess; they are not necessary, but they are made to seem practical to aid in the normalization of punishment. For example, policing entities that opposed SB 54, rather than supported it, used the same discursive racial terms of fear and the split of the racial subject of sanctioned/unsanctioned. The California Police Chiefs Association's opposition to SB 54 argued that the bill would make it more difficult for police and ICE to work together and "threaten[ed] to create more fear in our communities by forcing federal immigration operations out of our jails and into our communities."[12] We must ask, can there ever actually be a "better" version of sanctuary through law that does not entrench and further deepen such racial terms?

While sanctuary social movements between churches and immigration advocates have been around since before the 1980s and prior, the 2016 postelection "sanctuary" comes into existence as a form of *governance*—a city ordinance, an institutional statement, a state statute. It is a *legal promise* that slows down, but does not abolish, the exchange of information and resources between local police and federal immigration agencies. This incertitude is, in part, where my reading finds its beginnings: the disturbing ease with which sanctuary's promise was able to cast a wide and distinctive layer of its own. There is such variation among what is understood to even count as sanctuary. This variation is not something I seek to clarify or resolve—instead I am suggesting that it should not be understood as a lack of cohesion but rather an assortment that makes a certain kind of promise possible. Sanctuary does not dissolve the relationship between immigration and criminalization; rather its variety of forms hold this relationship in place. Thus, while current debates focus on stopping police compliance with federal immigration, it is the mere existence of the promise that has already begun to give a fleeting voice to the structural burrow of cooperation local law enforcement seeks from "those good immigrants" it aims to retain. To sanction immigrants is not to end the violence of deportations, removals, or nation-state borders themselves; to sanction is to retain a few and establish the relationship with the rest. Why do we even want to just "sanction" immigrants—why don't we want them to be free? How do we all become free from a future that ties undocumented communities to projects of policing rooted in what Alisa Bierria has argued is the conflation of criminality with blackness?[13] This is a future that cannot be avoided if there is immigrant participation in community policing or the cooperative efforts of sanctuary discourses continues.

Martha D. Escobar has shown that captivity continues to move beyond prisons when immigration laws and political organizing maintain carceral paradigms of foreignness and criminality.[14] Angélica Cházaro's work on immigration provisions demonstrates the long history of state efforts to include those without citizenship while also producing categories of punishment that form paradigms of criminality. What Cházaro theorizes as "criminal alien paradigms" reveals the unavoidable nature of carcerality in US immigration law even within existing pathways to legality, as Leisy Abrego has demonstrated. For example, the invention of a socio-legal category of "sanctioned" immigrants requires its opposite—the *unsanctioned* immigrant—to make the concept of "sanctioned" *meaningful as a policing tool.** Indeed, the

---

* Angélica Cházaro and Leisy Abrego have separately shown that the law constructs "criminal alien" categories in both "pro" and "anti" immigrant legislation. These categories then produce a racial logic of punishment within a legal subject position (e.g., criminal alien). Angélica Cházaro, "Challenging the 'Criminal Alien' Paradigm," *UCLA Law Review* 63, no. 3 (March 2016): 594–664; Leisy Abrego et al., "Making Immigrants into Criminals: Legal Processes of Criminalization in the Post-IIRIRA Era," *Journal on Migration and Human Security* 5, no. 3 (2017): 694–715, doi.org/10.1177/233150241700500308.

achievement of what we might call an assimilated figure can only occur when achieved over someone else. In other words, the law's violence is not the racial misrepresentation of individuals per se but rather the creation of racial signifiers that establish a position where some are never quite eligible to even be assimilable if they are too closely aligned with the unsanctioned position of criminality and its racial logic of anti-Blackness.[15] What potentially allows sanctuary to operate like an assimilationist project is the category of immigrant fear as an added value to ongoing policing in service of civil society. The types of immigrant fear, one acceptable and the other correctable, are both oriented toward the incorporation and belonging of immigrants into the civic body, but through the means of policing. As national policing/immigration partnerships continue, in our current moment, to grow through federally funded programs, the racial assemblage of immigrant fear can be understood as an added value to ongoing state-sanctioned efforts to tether immigrants to their own surveillance and the expansion of surveillance over undocumented people and Black and brown communities, as well as to foreclose on broader abolitionist work.[16]

RETHINKING PROTECTION THROUGH ABOLITION FEMINIST THEORY

In my own work, I have struggled to find new ways to talk about the violence of legal protection in statutory law such as the Violence against Women Act—immigration laws that are designed to rescue women from gender and sexual violence but produce protections that normalize the logics of police violence, require survivors to cooperate with policing, and expand prisons without any end to gender-based violence whatsoever. Often, immigration law scholars view such provisions as successful solutions or a mere exception to bigger violence of borders and US immigration. I disagree.

Our conversations on the racial violence of criminalization and immigration cannot afford to avoid abolitionist feminist frameworks, and without such frameworks our analyses, politics, and theorizations struggle to take into account the violence that legal efforts to protect are tied to expectations that someone must always be punished. Feminist of color anti-violence organizing helps us determine how we approach the issue of sanctuary, as it is often viewed as a political solution rather than an emerging condition within existing racial discourses of violence.

Abolitionist feminist of color organizing against gender-based violence has advanced a pivotal contribution to abolitionist thought: a refusal of the contradictory notion that the solution to solve violence against women is to rely on the police. While policing has grown in the name of public safety, we have not seen less violence or less death. Instead, we have witnessed increased community policing of survivors and their communities. Policing in the name of saving the feminized victim *figure* is a policing that imagines, instills, and enforces safety of a "public" devoid of communities of color, migrants, and Indigenous people. Anti-violence organizing strategies and frameworks—such as matrix of violence, transformative justice, carceral creep, and criminalized survival—open this critique for us.[17]

Abolition feminist work and life grace us with language to find ways beyond punishment we have yet to imagine. More specifically, a critical approach to law's protection can be applied to the politics of sanctuary fomented by this racial assemblage of fear, anti-Blackness, and the politics of immigration—sanctuary as a shielding that relies on a presumed and particular kind of racialized safety. Abolitionist anti-violence feminism does not limit its focus on the individualistic protection of a person, and it is not committed in any way to a purity of that protection, in part because of its critique of who is permitted to temporarily benefit from its terms. The focus instead is on the racial and gendered terms upon which public safety is regulated and made accessible through the continual criminalization of Blackness, as well as the denial of Black people any access to that safety yet always subjecting them to its regulation. Indeed, Mimi Kim has argued that the "fetishization of safety" as a policy solution to violence, as well as legislative attempts to build safety without interrogating its underlying racial and gendered terms, are both themselves policing mechanisms over communities of color that impact advocacy and organizing work.[18]

Sanctuary draws parallels to "public safety" when the shield materializes in law and policy to protect some and criminalize others. Anchored in Black feminisms, we might draw from abolition feminist formations to think through what path we might take to not merely reject an existing law or policy for its insufficiency in bringing about justice but rather to produce a politics that refuses the "promises" this purported legislated correction aims to provide.[19] This analytical approach pushes back against legal punishments that the state claims are needed to save women in order to protect a public in which they, and others, are not allowed, forcibly included, or temporarily managed. Thus, when we employ anti-violence feminist of color insights into the politics of protection to reorient the politics of sanctuary, we can see how sanctuary is not an exception within the post-Trump era but rather part of a much larger legacy of legal punishments aimed to protect, rescue, and save as a means of maintaining what Beth Richie has called the "build-up of a prison nation": the ongoing incarceration, policing, and violences enacted to keep the public safe by criminalizing Black women and girls for not fitting the intrinsically racialized victim/perpetrator scheme.[20]

To further connect abolition feminist critiques of public safety with the politics of sanctuary, we can consider how police wielded sexual violence as a specter to justify carceral agendas via sanctuary. For example, in a 2017 *LA Times* article titled "Latinos Are Reporting Fewer Sexual Assaults amid a Climate of Fear in Immigrant Communities, LAPD Says," Police Chief Beck remarked, "Imagine, a young woman, imagine your daughter, your sister, your mother . . . not reporting a sexual assault, because they are afraid that their family will be torn apart."[21] The police chief's quote strategically aims to garner support for sanctuary efforts by invoking sexual violence as he describes a scene in which the figure of a gendered victim becomes a linchpin used for the preservation of local policing institutions against the encroachment of federal immigration agencies in order to keep women safe and, consequently, prevent families from being torn apart. Here, survivors are afforded value primarily through their relational status to others—his concern is *families* being torn apart, rather than the lives of survivors themselves being torn apart. In fact, this latter tearing is not acknowledged at all.

Further, the legal border itself tears families and survivors' lives apart, yet it is the reporting of crime that stands as the solution, not the end of borders and the criminalization of legal status. Sexual violence is not the primary focus; the only reason it is mentioned at all is so it can be paralleled and paired with crime reporting. Echoed across news stories both past and present in sanctuary discourse, LAPD's leveraging of sexual violence as an argument for crime reporting echoes many news stories that suggest immigrants hesitate to approach the police because they are afraid of immigration agencies. Yet, this scenario erases the role that policing has always played in migrant lives and, further, it establishes an assumption that immigrants *should* and *ought to be* the ones to call the cops on each othe. Thus, while legal formations of sanctuary—county ordinances, state legislation, and varying institutional commitments—do not address sexual and gender violence per se, the specter of rape is invoked as a strategy to animate a discourse on safety, sanction, and shielding. Invoking rape to justify these legal formations establishes a paradox in which sanction has nothing to do with gender and sexuality yet has everything to do with it. Because the safety of the public (which includes some and not others) is a central analytical framework used in sanctuary discourse, we need abolition feminisms to disengage its political promises and build conversations on immigration without reproducing the meanings of policing that naturalize crime or reinforce racialized criminalization.

LIBERAL RIGHTS AND RACIAL VIOLENCE

Since the passage of SB 54 in 2018, legal advocacy organizations have documented a decrease in overall ICE arrests, but they have also noted that the majority of law enforcement agencies utilizing policies continue to share information with ICE, provide release date information with certain criminal history of detainees, and exploit loopholes delineated by SB 54 to allow cooperation with federal immigration agencies at police discretion when someone with prior convictions is detained or the individual's name is made available to the public.[22] Such practices have continuously resulted in immigrants being transferred immediately after leaving law enforcement agencies even without a criminal conviction that would typically result in an in-custody transfer directly to ICE.[23] Naomi Paik argues for abolitionist futures for sanctuary and a concern that sanctuary ordinances have cautiously designed categories of criminality in and of themselves and, thus, while law enforcement agencies have failed to comply, an additional concern lies in what law enforcement has already *produced*.[24] With SB 54, legislation constantly changes and advocacy efforts have sought to push for more statewide compliance, but the California Values Act is designed to reduce the inefficient use of local police with federal immigration forces, not to abolish police or border enforcement. Thus, the legal design is to weed out nonviolent offenses while affirming an "acceptable" use of punishment for *more violent* criminality.

The effect of combating deportation of the "good immigrant" while encouraging community policing exemplifies what Treva Ellison invaluably argues is a politics of sanctuary "transcoded into safe space"* and thus reproducing racial "relational differential value" toward premature death.[25] Community policing as an *opportunity* then, constitutes the state's investment in the protection of itself, which reveals the making of the less culpable immigrant along racial lines. Analyzing this new legal subject of "the less" culpable through an abolitionist framework reveals how sanctuary is so easily instantiated through racial punishment endemic in US law. Any effort to establish safety for immigrants through US law must consider the law's ability to make one's legal status criminally culpable in some ways and innocent in others, a duality that is manipulated in the law's writing of "protection" as an expansion of racial punishment.

---

* Ellison traces several formations of this transcoding, including "the move from networks of struggle to resegmented populations, the move from spaces of dependence to racial enclosures, and the move from analogized suffering to protected status." Treva Ellison, "From Sanctuary to Safe Space: Gay and Lesbian Police-Reform Activism in Los Angeles," *Radical History Review* 2019, no. 135 (2019): 95–118.

Chandan Reddy and Jodi Melamed have argued that appealing to liberal rights, such as the right to be safe from a hate crime, can reinforce racial violence rather than end it. They contend that a "liberal rights bearing subject" is a technology of racialization that is endemic to modern racial economies and their forces rather than antagonistic to them.[26] That is, Reddy contends that rights-based frameworks produce racialized legal subjects that bear certain civil rights, but it is through the purported legal *protection* of those subjects' rights that the law's determined right to enact violence trumps any freedom and rights tied to a person or community.[27] Reddy describes this phenomenon as "freedom with violence." Using a queer of color critique, he argues that through racist and racializing violence, as well as a kind of erasure by law, the state wields race as a force that produces two things: oppressive material social conditions for some racialized groups and racialized liberal subjects (such as the less culpable immigrant) who have certain rights to protection. Because the liberal rights–bearing subject has what Reddy calls the "state form as the emancipatory limit," racial violence that can't be reduced to individual experience—such as coloniality, capture, and dispossession, all of which are maintained by sexual violence and the state's regulation of sexuality—is ultimately reinforced by establishing the right to individual protection made possible by the state, such as policing and prisons.[28] Any effort to end violence that *exceeds* the power of the state, such as conceptions of safety and sanctuary *outside of and against* policing, is foreclosed by the state's emancipatory limit. With sanctuary, on one hand we have legislation, ordinances, and immigrant rights politics that reproduce the liberal rights–bearing subject of sanctuary that Reddy and Melamed caution against, while on the other we have abolitionist and decolonial calls to abandon borders and punishment altogether, which expand the range of emancipatory possibilities.

Law's design of sanctuary is one that presents a proposed solution, situated materially far more as what Reddy and Melamed highlight as an "official state anti-racism," or anti-racism that produces police power to differentiate value and valuelessness, than it does a position of fugitivity. Police power to support sanctuary as a refute of federal authority in local jurisdictions, as well as state or county legal promises to establish sanctuary states and cities, categorizes fear through a racial logic. This is what Melamed calls "racialization's trick of displacing and disguising differential value making" both to legitimate new social formations of rights and remain even more committed to violence.[29] It is difficult to raise these critiques amid heightened laws and policies that target undocumented communities in the US, but it is precisely because of this violence that it is equally important to remember that such racist targeting has been ongoing long before this moment, rooted as it is in the historical trajectory of the US nation-state. As Ananya Roy has argued, sanctuary is an "ancient concept" because of the ongoing colonial founding of the nation-state's forms and the imperial expansions in the very technologies of race and rights that produce spaces and places of erasure.[30] What distinguishes this moment, then, is the abolition feminist call to critique the making and promoting of sanctuary as an official "anti-racism" for the benefit of policing as a path through which the violent reach of ICE is purportedly reduced.

ABOLITION FEMINISMS

We must refuse speaking like the law and turn away from the solution-oriented frame of law's sanctuary design toward policing. There is much that can change if we highlight what Andrea J. Ritchie and Monique Morris have argued is the long tradition of those constantly seeking sanctuary from antiblackness in cities and neighborhoods, to find refuge from the already-existing violence of the city, not the city providing refuge away from some other violence.[31] Feminist of color anti-violence movements directly challenge the racialized terms of safety that create, sustain, and institutionalize violence. The reliance on punishment to save women through policing and the expansion of prisons has never resulted in the ending of violence in Black communities and, therefore, in none of our communities. Engaging feminist of color theorizations of gender and sexual violence as state violence can help us map the dangers of sanctuary agendas that protect policing.

In other words, just as we cannot rely on police to solve gender-based violence because gender-based violence is reproduced and reinforced by policing, there can be no actual recipient of protection from police if the policing of immigrant communities continues.

Paula Rojas asks, "Are the cops in our heads and in our hearts?" in her writing on the contradictions of US-based organizing and lessons from Latin America.[32] Her call for organizing work to move beyond the nonprofit-industrial complex and to work through capitalism, racism, and heteropatriarchy contends with the way punishment and policing of ourselves and others can become an entrenched practice within organizing work and must be accounted for. While the constant refrain to call the cops for safety originates from many sources, my focus here is on the production of a kind of discipline that carries punishment beyond institutions of law enforcement, prisons, policing agencies, and into the everyday. Put differently, policing expands beyond its own institution so that the practice of policing becomes so omnipresent that, as Rojas argues, it can require intentional efforts to even *recognize* it. Mimi Kim has examined this problem through her analysis of the "carceral creep," a phenomenon in which the carceral creeps up on anti-violence advocacy efforts more and more until advocates have themselves been folded into the project of policing without realizing it.[33]

Sanctuary's pro-policing agenda is a pathway toward becoming incorporated into racial violence that harnesses immigrant bodies as a form of surveillance of themselves and others. Sanctuary's material form as a promise carries out a *training*: It trains us to be undiscerning of the criminality of Blackness written into punishment, and it trains us to *desire* the law in the form of cooperation, mutual benefit, and public safety.[34] But we do not have to relent to this training; instead of pushing for community policing, we can call for an end to policing and prisons.[35] It is my hope that this discussion provides openings for future analysis that makes clear the need to abolish the law's insatiable desire for a racialized subject to make its legal promise and carceral vision of sanctuary possible. In their policy report, the Bay Area–based political organization Mijente reminds us that we must continue to ask, What would actually constitute a sanctuary city?[36] Used as critical analytical tools, radical feminist of color anti-violence frameworks can help us map abolitionist theorizations of immigrant safety and freedom that show us the worlds we are in or could be.

BIBLIOGRAPHY

Abrego, Leisy, et al. "Making Immigrants into Criminals: Legal Processes of Criminalization in the Post-IIRIRA Era." *Journal on Migration and Human Security* 5, no. 3 (September 2017). https://doi.org/10.1177/233150241700500308.

Asian Americans Advancing Justice–Asian Law Caucus, University of Oxford Centre for Criminology, and Border Criminologies. *Turning the Golden State into a Sanctuary State: A Report on the Impact and Implementation of the California Values Act (SB 54).* (March 2019).

Bierria, Alisa. "Racial Conflation: Agency, Black Action, and Criminal Intent." *Journal of Social Philosophy*, September 5, 2020, josp.12371. https://doi.org/10.1111/josp.12371.

Bierria, Alisa, et al., eds. #SurvivedAndPunished: Survivor Defense as Abolitionist Praxis. Love & Protect and Survived & Punished, 2017. https://survivedandpunished.org/defense-campaign-toolkit/.

"California Values Act." California State Senate, October 5, 2017, CA Govt Code § 7284.12 (2018).

Cházaro, Angélica. "Challenging the 'Criminal Alien' Paradigm." *UCLA Law Review* 63, no. 594 (2016): 596–664.

Deer, Sarah. T*he Beginning and End of Rape: Confronting Sexual Violence in Native America.* Minneapolis: University of Minnesota Press, 2015.

Ellison, Treva. "From Sanctuary to Safe Space." *Radical History Review*, no. 135 (2019).

Escobar, Martha D. *Captivity Beyond Prisons: Criminalization Experiences of Latina (im)migrants.* 1st ed. Austin: University of Texas Press, 2016.

Farley, Anthony. "When the Stars Begin to Fall: Introduction to Critical Race Theory and Marxism," *Columbia Journal of Race and Law*, 1, no. 3 (July 2012).

Gilmore, Ruth Wilson. *Golden Gulag: Prisons, Surplus, Crisis, and Opposition in Globalizing California.* American Crossroads. Berkeley: University of California Press, 2007.

Harris, Heather, et al. *California's Prison Population.* Public Policy Institute of California (San Francisco: 2019). https://www.ppic.org/publication/californias-prison-population/.

Haynes, Dina, et al. "Understanding 'Sanctuary Cities.'" *Boston College Law Review* 59, no. 5 (May 2018): 74.

INCITE!, ed. *Color of Violence: The INCITE! Anthology.* Durham, NC: Duke University Press, 2016.

———. *The Revolution Will Not Be Funded: Beyond the Non-Profit Industrial Complex.* Durham, NC: Duke University Press, 2017.

Kim, Mimi E. "Moving beyond Critique: Creative Interventions and Reconstructions of Community Accountability." *Social Justice* 37, no. 4 (2011): 14–35.

———. "The Carceral Creep: Gender-Based Violence, Race and the Expansion of the Punitive State, 1973–1983." *Social Problems* 67, no. 2 (2020): 251–69. https://doi.org/10.1093/socpro/spz013.

"LAPD Will Not Take on Role of 'Immigration Enforcement' under Trump, Charlie Beck Says." CBS Los Angeles, November 15, 2016. https://losangeles.cbslocal.com/2016/11/15/lapd-will-not-take-on-role-of-immigration-enforcement-under-trump-charlie-beck-says/.

Melamed, Jodi. *Represent and Destroy: Rationalizing Violence in the New Racial Capitalism.* Difference Incorporated. Minneapolis: University of Minnesota Press, 2011. doi:40020234294.

Melamed, Jodi, and Chandan Reddy, "Using Liberal Rights to Enforce Racial Capitalism." *Items: Insight from the Social Sciences.* Social Science Research Council, September 30, 2019. https://items.ssrc.org/race-capitalism/using-liberal-rights-to-enforce-racial-capitalism/.

Morgen, Sam. "Delano Becomes First City in Kern County to Be a Sanctuary City." *Bakersfield Californian*, August 7, 2019. https://www.bakersfield.com/news/delano-becomes-first-city-in-kern-county-to-be-sanctuary/article_08481784-b8b1-11e9-94dd-0701a540d212.html.

Motomura, Hiroshi. "Arguing about Sanctuary." *UC Davis Law Review* 435, no. 52 (2018): 1–35.

Ms. Foundation for Women (2017). https://forwomen.org/wp-content/uploads/2017/09/Centering-Black-women-final-draft6.pdf.

Muhammad, Khalil Gibran. *The Condemnation of Blackness: Race, Crime, and the Making of Modern Urban America.* Cambridge: Harvard University Press, 2011.

Naber, Nadine. "'Look, Mohammed the Terrorist Is Coming!' Cultural Racism, Nation-Based Racism, and the Intersectionality of Oppressions after 9/11." *Scholar and Feminist Online* 6, no. 3 (2008).

Paik, A. Naomi. "Abolitionist Futures and the US Sanctuary Movement." *Race & Class* 59, no. 2 (October 2017): 3–25.

Queally, James. "Latinos Are Reporting Fewer Sexual Assaults amid a Climate of Fear in Immigrant Communities, LAPD Says." *Los Angeles Times*, March 21, 2017.

Reddy, Chandan. *Freedom with Violence: Race, Sexuality, and the US State.* Perverse Modernities. Durham, NC: Duke University Press, 2011.

———. "Race and the Critique of Marriage." *South Atlantic Quarterly* 115, no. 2 (2016): 424–32. https://doi.org/10.1215/00382876-3488524.

Richie, Beth. *Arrested Justice: Black Women, Violence, and America's Prison Nation.* New York: New York University Press, 2012.

Ritchie, Andrea J., and Monique W. Morris. *Centering Black Women, Girls, Gender Nonconforming People and Fem(me)s in Campaigns for Expanded Sanctuary and Freedom Cities.* National Black Women's Justice Institute and Ms.

Foundation for Women, September 2017. https://forwomen.org/resources/sanctuary-city-report/.

Rojas Durazo, A., Alisa Bierria, and Mimi Kim. "Community Accountability: Emerging Movements to Transform Violence." *Social Justice* 37, no. 4 (2011).

Rojas, Paula X. "Are the Cops in Our Heads and Hearts?" In *The Revolution Will Not Be Funded: Beyond the Non-Profit Industrial Complex*, edited by INCITE! Durham, NC: Duke University Press, 2017.

Roy, Ananya. "The City in the Age of Trumpism: From Sanctuary to Abolition." *Environment and Planning D, Society and Space* 37, no. 5 (2019): 761–78.

"San Diego Sheriff Gore Discusses Impact of New 'Sanctuary State' Law." KPBS Midday Edition, accessed June 1 2020. https://www.kpbs.org/audioclips/37963/#transcript.

"SF Police Commission Votes to Adopt Updated Sanctuary City Policies." KTVU Fox, accessed June 1, 2020. https://www.ktvu.com/news/sf-police-commission-votes-to-adopt-updated-sanctuary-city-policies.

Smith, Andrea, and Winona LaDuke. *Conquest: Sexual Violence and American Indian Genocide.* Durham, NC: Duke University Press, 2015.

Transactional Records Access Clearinghouse. "Outcomes of Deportation Proceedings in Immigration Court." May 27, 2020. https://trac.syr.edu/phptools/immigration/court_backlog/deport_outcome_charge.php.

Unzueta, Tania A. *Expanding Sanctuary: What Makes a City a Sanctuary Now?* Mijente (2017).

Volpp, Leti. "The Citizen and the Terrorist." *Critical Race Studies* 49, no. 5 (June 2002): 1575–600.

NOTES

1 Heather Harris et al., *California's Prison Population*, Public Policy Institute of California (San Francisco, 2019), https://www.ppic.org/publication/californias-prison-population/.

2 "LAPD Will Not Take on Role of 'Immigration Enforcement' under Trump, Charlie Beck Says," CBS Los Angeles, November 15, 2016, https://losangeles.cbslocal.com/2016/11/15/lapd-will-not-take-on-role-of-immigration-enforcement-under-trump-charlie-beck-says/.

3 See discussions about the need to critique criminalization in order to adequately understand the reach of sanctuary and to document the range of approaches toward sanctuary—e.g., Haynes et al., "Understanding 'Sanctuary Cities.'"

4 Hiroshi Motomura, "Arguing about Sanctuary," *UC Davis Law Review* 435, no. 52 (2018); Dina Haynes et al., "Understanding 'Sanctuary Cities,'" *Boston College Law Review* 59, no. 5 (May 2018).

5 "San Diego Sheriff Gore Discusses Impact of New 'Sanctuary State' Law," KPBS Midday Edition, accessed June 1 2020, https://www.kpbs.org/audioclips/37963/#transcript.

6 "SF Police Commission Votes to Adopt Updated Sanctuary City Policies," KTVU Fox, accessed June 1, 2020, https://www.ktvu.com/news/sf-police-commission-votes-to-adopt-updated-sanctuary-city-policies.

7 Sam Morgen, "Delano Becomes First City in Kern County to Be a Sanctuary City," *Bakersfield Californian,* August 7, 2019, https://www.bakersfield.com/news/delano-becomes-first-city-in-kern-county-to-be-sanctuary/article_08481784-b8b1-11e9-94dd-0701a540d212.html.

8 See, for example, Muhammad (2011) and Bierria (2020).

9 "California Values Act," California State Senate (October 2017).

10 The United States of America v. The State of California; Edmund Gerald Brown Jr., Governor of California, and Xavier Becerra, Attorney General of California, no. 2:18-cv-00490-JAM-KJN (US District Court for the Eastern District of California, June 2, 2018).

11 Assembly Committee on the Judiciary Hearing, July 5, 2017. Prepared by Merrilees, Alison. California Legislative Information, Bill Analysis, https://leginfo.legislature.ca.gov/faces/billAnalysisClient.xhtml?bill_id=201720180SB54.

12 Alisa Bierria, "Racial Conflation: Agency, Black Action, and Criminal Intent." *Journal of Social Philosophy* (Spring 2020), 1–20, https://doi.org/10.1111/josp.12371.

13 Martha D. Escobar, *Captivity beyond Prisons: Criminalization Experiences of Latina (im)migrants*, 1st ed. (Austin: University of Texas Press, 2016).

14 Angélica Cházaro and Leisy Abrego have separately shown that the law constructs "criminal alien" categories in both "pro" and "anti" immigrant legislation. These categories then produce a racial logic of punishment within a legal subject position (i.e., criminal alien). Angélica Cházaro, "Challenging the 'Criminal Alien' Paradigm," *UCLA Law Review* 63, no. 594 (2016); Leisy Abrego et al., "Making Immigrants into Criminals: Legal Processes of Criminalization in the Post-IIRIRA Era," *Journal on Migration and Human Security* 5, no. 3 (September 2017), https://doi.org/10.1177/233150241700500308.

15 See Alex Weheliye's discussion on the marking of Muslim youth by ICE as *too* Black to be correctable, or perpetually in need of correction, as part of a larger discussion of *Scenes of Subjection*, Saidiya Hartman's "castigated agency" as the blameworthiness of the individual during enslavement and its afterlife, where correctives are bound within any granting of agency to Black life. Yarimar Bonilla Adrienne Davis, Rinaldo Walcott, and Alexander Weheliye, "Panel Discussion on Agency" (paper presented at the Scenes at 20 symposium, Rutgers University, 2017).

16 See Andrea J. Ritchie and Monique W. Morris, *Centering Black Women, Girls, Gender Nonconforming People and Fem(me)s in Campaigns for Expanded Sanctuary and Freedom Cities*, National Black Women's Justice Institute and Ms. Foundation for Women, September 2017, https://forwomen.org/resources/sanctuary-city-report/; Nadine Naber, "'Look, Mohammed the Terrorist Is Coming!' Cultural Racism, Nation-Based Racism, and the Intersectionality of Oppressions after 9/11," *Scholar and Feminist Online* 6, no. 3 (2008); Leti Volpp,

"The Citizen and the Terrorist," *Critical Race Studies* 49, no. 5 (June 2002): 1575–1600.

17 These concepts are just a few examples of rigorous analytical frameworks emerging from abolitionist anti-violence feminist of color theory and practice. For "matrix of violence," see Richie, 2012; for "transformative justice," see Rojas Durazo et al., 2010; for "carceral creep," see Kim, 2020; and for "criminalized survival," see Survived & Punished, 2017.

18 Mimi Kim, "Moving Beyond Critique: Creative Interventions and Reconstructions of Community Accountability," *Social Justice* 37 (January 2011).

19 INCITE!, *Color of Violence: The INCITE! Anthology* (Cambridge, MA.: South End Press, 2006); Andrea Smith and Winona LaDuke, *Conquest: Sexual Violence and American Indian Genocide* (Durham, NC: Duke University Press, 2015); INCITE!, *The Revolution Will Not Be Funded: Beyond the Non-Profit Industrial Complex* (Durham, NC: Duke University Press, 2017); Sarah Deer, *The Beginning and End of Rape: Confronting Sexual Violence in Native America* (Minneapolis: University of Minnesota Press, 2015).

20 Beth E. Richie, *Arrested Justice: Black Women, Violence, and America's Prison Nation* (New York: New York University Press, 2012).

21 James Queally, "Latinos Are Reporting Fewer Sexual Assaults amid a Climate of Fear in Immigrant Communities, LAPD Says," *Los Angeles Times* (Los Angeles), March 21, 2017.

22 Tania A. Unzueta, *Expanding Sanctuary: What Makes a City a Sanctuary Now?* Mijente (2017).

23 See Asian Americans Advancing Justice–Asian Law Caucus, University of Oxford Centre for Criminology, and Border Criminologies, *Turning the Golden State into a Sanctuary State: A Report on the Impact and Implementation of the California Values Act (SB 54).* (March 2019).

24 Naomi Paik has argued that the form of cooperation allows for the constitution of aggregated felony to emerge and grow within sanctuary. A. Naomi Paik, "Abolitionist Futures and the US Sanctuary Movement," *Race & Class* 59, no. 2 (October 2017). See also section 7282.5 of the California Values Act, which illustrates the legal limits of sanctuary by listing reasons why law enforcement officials "have the discretion to cooperate with immigration authorities." These reasons include and are not limited to whether the individual has been convicted of a serious or violent felony or an aggravated felony.

25 Treva Ellison traces several formations of this transcoding, including "the move from networks of struggle to resegmented populations, the move from spaces of dependence to racial enclosures, and the move from analogized suffering to protected status." Ellison, "From Sanctuary to Safe Space," *Radical History Review*, no. 135 (2019): 96.

26 Chandan Reddy, *Freedom with Violence: Race, Sexuality, and the US State,* Perverse Modernities (Durham, NC: Duke University Press, 2011); Jodi Melamed, *Represent and Destroy: Rationalizing Violence in the New Racial Capitalism*, Difference Incorporated (Minneapolis: University of Minnesota Press, 2011); Jodi Melamed and Chandan Reddy, "Using Liberal Rights to Enforce Racial Capitalism," *Items: Insight from the Social Sciences.* Social Science

Research Council, September 30, 2019, https://items.ssrc.org/race-capitalism/using-liberal-rights-to-enforce-racial-capitalism/.

27 Chandan Reddy, *Freedom with Violence* (Durham, NC: Duke University Press, 2011).

28 Chandan Reddy, "Race and the Critique of Marriage," *South Atlantic Quarterly* 115, no. 2 (2016), https://doi.org/10.1215/00382876-3488524.

29 Melamed, *Represent and Destroy,* 12.

30 Ananya Roy, "The City in the Age of Trumpism: From Sanctuary to Abolition," *Environment and Planning D, Society and Space* 37, no. 5 (2019): 761–78.

31 Ritchie and Morris, *Centering Black Women.*

32 Paula X. Rojas, "Are the Cops in Our Heads and Hearts?" in *The Revolution Will Not Be Funded: Beyond the Non-Profit Industrial Complex,* ed. INCITE! (Durham, NC: Duke University Press, 2017).

33 Mimi E. Kim, "The Carceral Creep: Gender-Based Violence, Race and the Expansion of the Punitive State, 1973–1983," *Social Problems* 67, no. 2 (2020): 251–69, https://doi.org/10.1093/socpro/spz013.

34 I am drawing from Anthony Farley's use of "training" as part of a discussion on race and law: Anthony Farley, "When the Stars Begin to Fall: Introduction to Critical Race Theory and Marxism," *Columbia Journal of Race and Law* 1, no. 3 (July 2012).

35 Ritchie and Morris, *Centering Black Women*; Unzueta, *Expanding Sanctuary: What Makes a City a Sanctuary Now?*

36 Unzueta, *Expanding Sanctuary.*

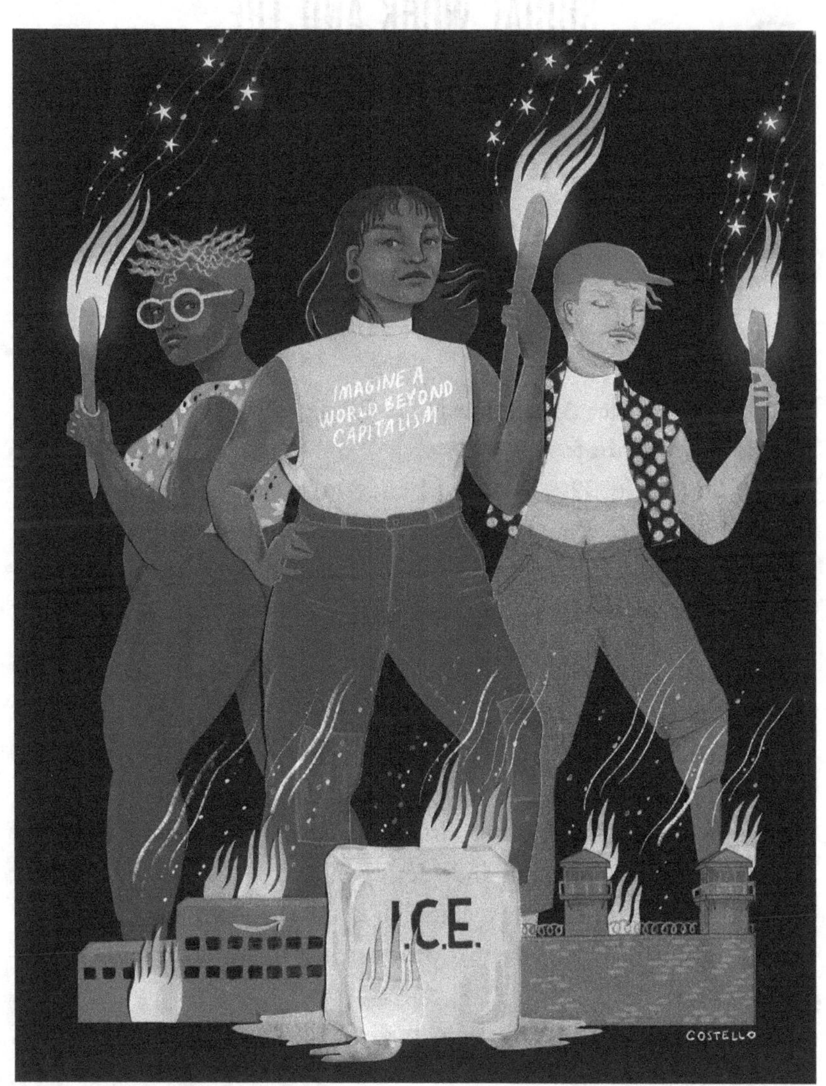

Molly Costello, "Controlled Burns"

SOCIAL WORK AND THE PARTNER ASSAULT RESPONSE PROGRAM

A CRITICAL PATHOLOGY REPORT

Rosalie Donaldson-Kronenbuerger and Mark Mullkoff

Specimen: Partner Assault Response Program (PAR)
Accession Number: 77880029
MRN: 00088976532-0201B **Procedure:** 03/20/2020
DOB: 1980s **Place:** Colonized North America
Gender: Patriarchal object known to circulate, imbed, and (re)produce within colonial practices.[1] Genus europeaus

Lab Report Title: The colonial virus of the of the partner assault response program
Clinic Address: The traditional territory of many nations including the Mississaugas of the Credit, the Anishinabeg, the Chippewa, the Haudenosaunee, and the Wendat peoples that is now home to many diverse First Nations, Inuit, and Métis peoples.
Viral Specimen Type: A colonial state designed, mediated, and funded blueprint interventional program for mandated domestic violence offenders.
Central Strain Properties: Coercive assimilation, homogenization, decontextualization, atomization

Clinical History / Dominant Story:
This specimen emerged within white-dominant, second-wave feminist movements in the 1960s as a product of cis, white, hetero, settler,

male, community-based responses to domestic violence, a social issue that had become newly publicized as such.[2] Central features of this initial grassroots formation of the Partner Assault Response (PAR) program include:

1. Central understanding of the etiology of domestic violence as primarily informed by circulating feminist sensibilities that were critical but also critically limited: Violence enacted by male-identified offenders against female-identified victims at the micro level of intimate relationship mirror broader macro-level social inequity where women's bodies are targets of androcentric and misogynist control. Feminist researchers identified manifestations of patriarchal power that infiltrated and organized medico-legal, education, and other societal institutions. They understood these institutional relations of power as mirroring imbalances of power and violence against women at the micro level of intimate relationships.[3]
2. PAR groups composed of voluntary attendees who joined the self-help circle to share, analyze, and critique experiences within intimate relationships. The goal of this consciousness-raising was to explicitly politicize the personal and foster egalitarian relationships. The intended healing effect of this work within the PAR circle was imagined to change the nature of members' individual intimate partnerships. Working with the circulating feminist rallying call "the personal is political," this foundational circle of PAR groups also imagined that macro-level broader society conditions would shift as a consequence of modeling equitable unions at the micro level.[4]
3. PAR circle formations that were sustained and replicated from the central impulse to reproduce socially equitable relations within individual partnerships and broader communities.

Critical Incident:

Within the context of 1980s neoliberalization, this burgeoning model of feminist practice was soon strategically linked to the growth of the carceral state.[5] The original internal system of the practice became compromised when the whiteness of the form adapted to shifting political conditions and became a host to an additional existing mutation of the colonial virus: the criminal justice system.[6] As a newly developed colonial viral mutation, PAR was redeployed as a mainstream and mandated blueprint intervention into domestic violence. Since then, it has exhibited significant community spread.[7] The specimen currently exhibits deep structural changes; a novel form arising from a pervasive colonial virus.

Microscopic Description of Novel PAR Colonial Virus

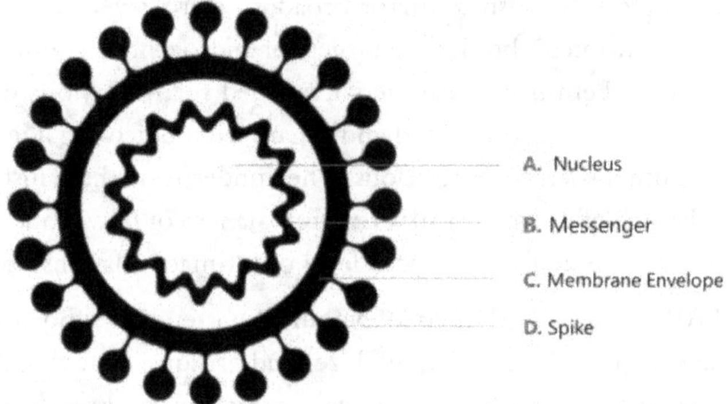

Microscopic view of a coronavirus[8]

A. NUCLEUS

Within the colonial circle of PAR, the State is located at both the nucleus and epicenter of viral spread. The State is positioned as a central authority charged with managing the violence it deploys onto communities and relations through the novel colonial viral form.

A narrow atomizing focus on broader social issues obscures visibility of the role and presence of central macro and mezzo actors in viral deployment. Macro-generated historic and institutional colonial domestic violence and its destruction of culture, community connection, and interdependence are offloaded/shed and concentrated onto detectable distinct micro-level bodies and acts: State-produced "offenders" and discrete individual acts of violence. Pervasive, deep-rooted, systematic and systemic forms of domestic violence become atomized; reduced to a codifiable set of distinct and distinguishable acts and actors. Through this viral vision, domestic violence becomes not a realization of what the State enacts against peoples living on its stolen land, but instead "domestic violence" is reduced and institutionalized into an issue occurring among isolated individuals, dyads, and families. The atomized and disembodied presentation of this colonial weapon supports the leveraging of authority and the State against targeted and abandoned "individuals" who are impacted by domestic violence. The State releases itself from responsibility for its role in the production of and accountability for domestic violence, and repositions itself as a central and benevolent provider of community-based domestic violence service programs such as PAR.

B. MESSENGER

The State acts as parens patriae to dictate rights in a set of commanding relational and behavioral imperatives.[9] As a hemorrhagic colonial form, the virus mutates, replicates, and spreads under the radar, increasing its broad systemic and systematic proliferation.

C. MEMBRANE ENVELOPE

The criminal justice approach severs kinship and breaks community support and response to domestic violence. Community resistance to this viral model can be compromised due to colonial hosts' funding infrastructure: All agencies who offer the PAR program must comply with this viral model's definitions, principles, and objectives in order to receive funding from hosts' funding agency.[10] The viral deployment of accountable humanist subjects moves to produce and replicate distinct detectable bodies: "Victims," "Witnesses," and "Offenders." Pervasive racism and discrimination sheds accountability for historic and institutional violence against marginalized communities.

The State uses homogenization as a strategy for its management of Others[11] and provokes assimilative strategies to re-organize interdependent, fluid, heterogenous groups of people into separate, rigid, individual, homogenized, dehumanized cells. The program structure arranges "offenders" into an inward panopticon to face each other and the State. Through capillary power the State preforms its own invented objects as "deviant and destructive individual actors."[12]

GROSS DESCRIPTION OF NOVEL PAR COLONIAL VIRUS: COLONIZATION AS EPICENTER OF VIRUS

PAR is a broadly distributed institutional-based practice and policy intervention for domestic violence. PAR thrives within neoliberal colonial contexts where systems of community-based support have been systemically and systematically compromised by broader interlocking and interacting structures and processes of domination that promote social division and exclusion. Viral spread is encouraged by structural forms of oppression such as racism, sexism, heteropatriarchy, ableism, ageism, homophobia, and classism.

As PAR is a colonial virus, of particular diagnostic significance to this case is how long-standing processes of colonization operate to obscure the presence of the State as an actor that promotes both domestic violence and the social conditions that sustain it. PAR program definitions actively and intentionally disappear the State as a central organizer of domestic violence and, instead, domestic violence becomes defined as a "crime" for which "individual offenders" are solely responsible.[13] However, despite these program definitions, mandatory program participation becomes apparent as a mere formality or bureaucratic requirement rather than an active construction of any conception of individual accountability.

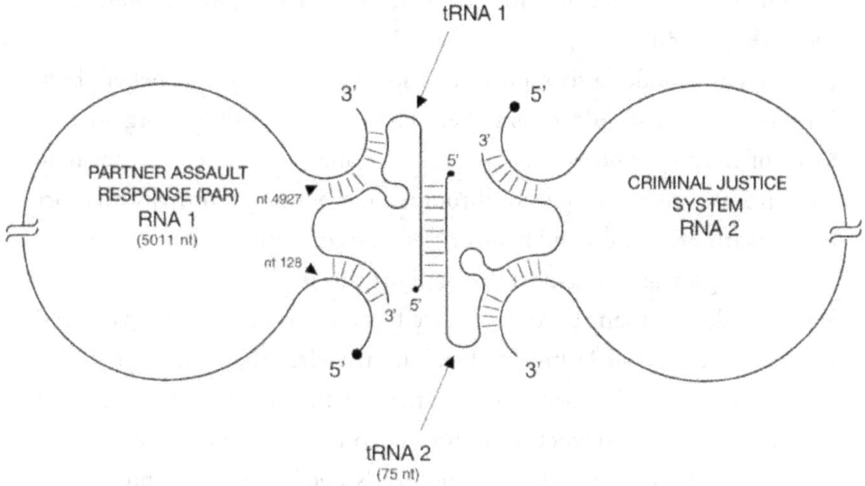

Image altered from original.[14]

Genocidal, extractive, and atomizing forces of colonization move to deplete and divide, attacking systems of thought and orientations toward land, community, self, and others.[15] Within these forces, social issues become disembodied, objective, and sterile clinical presentations that give the appearance of being written by no one from nowhere. PAR as a blueprint interventional program becomes thinkable and actionable through a specific methodological framework organized within Western colonial contexts. Violence is recoded into an "objective" story, discernible through discrete bodies and detectable, individual acts of violence.[16] It disappears complex subjects and instead posits persons as objects to be categorized and systematically processed: "victims" and "offenders."*

Snapshot viral presentations obscure a pervasive colonial system that organizes interlinking systems and processes of domestic violence unleashed at the macro and mezzo levels. Instead, processes of atomization and condensation recode "domestic violence" into an issue of individual pathology arising within isolated families and/or interpersonal dyads.[17] This model serves State interests as it becomes repositioned as a

---

* This process also facilitates the criminalization of survivors, some of whom are categorized as "offenders" and forced into compulsory participation in PAR-like programs. See https://survivedandpunished.org.

benign provider of services for its populace, including its distribution of the PAR program.

This viral model also represents a form of inquiry and belief about how researchers should orient themselves. Post-positivism organizes a form of inquiry whose epistemological ambition is to clearly separate away from a "research object" through a methodological thrust that orients toward prediction and control.[18] Researchers undertake precautions, methodologies, and measures that support this sterile distancing and othering. Violence, then, becomes viewed as a force that can be packaged up and contained in "Others." Held at arm's length, violence is gazed at from a clinical distance within a field of thought/epistemology that works to categorize subjects into distinct containable bodies: "offenders," "victims," and "workers." The broader landscape is organized into violent and sterile spaces. Scientism and its positivist underpinnings—in particular the belief in objectivity in research and its correspondingly sterile methods—constitute colonial viral epicenters.[19]

COMMENT

Cyndy Baskin's analysis of domestic violence teaches us that domestic violence and criminalizing responses to domestic violence share the same colonial root.[20] Julia Chinyere Oparah warned that when attempting to reverse the pandemic of State-affiliated anti-violence responses, "reform-based demands risk absorption into the existing racial-class dynamics of State systems of repression and control."[21] While PAR is imagined as a noncarceral alternative to standard criminal justice responses, it closely genetically resembles the punitive RNA of the prison system, and one's participation can lead to new charges and incarceration. The colonial virus's remarkable ability to replicate itself the same way in vastly diverse contexts is partly why the pandemic has resulted not in the transformation of communities but rather in the strengthening of colonial paradigms. However, akin to the mutual-aid, disaster-relief model, which coordinates efforts to respond to people's needs after the effects of disasters/pandemics are created or exacerbated by insufficient structural responses,[22] the transformative justice movement was initiated by diverse communities who created makeshift anti-carceral interventions to domestic violence that were responsive to community and survivor needs.[23] Transformative justice responses were developed in large part to avoid or resist carceral replications of increased policing and incarceration of communities of color, immigrant communities, and LGBTQ+ communities, including threats to safety and legal status.[24]

While the researchers and authors of this report are motivated by a decolonial and intersectional public health analysis, we likely are carriers of the colonial virus, shedding it over all that we come into contact with in ways that risk destruction through appropriation and extraction.[25] Colonial virus is highly adaptive and adept at masking its presence in those attempting to resist it until it is too late.[26] Leanne Betasamosake Simpson writes that, while "western theory, whether based in post-colonial, critical or even liberatory strains of thought, has been exceptional at diagnosing, revealing, and even interrogating colonialism . . . it fails to resonate with the vast majority of Indigenous Peoples."[27] Therefore, following Simpson's calls for a "resurgence" of Indigenous thought and practices (and in an effort to resist the spread of the colonial virus by the authors of this report given our own exposure), we defer to local knowledges and expertise for determining strategies of resistance.

NOTES

1 Lucas Ballestín et al. "Gender as Colonial Object," *Public Seminar*, July 31, 2018, publicseminar.org/2018/07/gender-as-colonial-object/.

2 Denise Adams, "Certified Batterer Intervention Programs: History, Philosophies, Techniques, Collaborations, Innovations and Challenges," *Clinics in Family Practice*, 5 no. 1 (2003).

3 Parveen Azam Ali and Paul B. Naylor.,"Intimate Partner Violence: A Narrative Review of the Feminist, Social and Ecological Explanations for its Causation," *Aggression and Violent Behavior*, no. 18 (2013): 611–19.

4 Adams, "Certified Batterer Intervention Programs."

5 Mimi E. Kim, "The Coupling and Decoupling of Safety and Crime Control: An Anti-Violence Movement Timeline," in *The Politicization of Safety: Critical Perspectives on Domestic Violence Responses*, ed. Jane K. Stoever (New York: New York University Press, 2019), 15–37.

6 Juergen Dankwort and Juliet Austin, "Standards for Batterer Intervention Programs in Canada: A History and Review," *Canadian Journal of Community Mental Health* 18, no. 1 (1999): 19–38.

7 Dankwort and Austin, "Standards for Batterer Intervention Programs," 19–38; Domestic Violence Action Plan Progress Report Update," Office of Women's Issues, modified May 2012, http://www.women.gov.on.ca/owd/english/ending-violence/dvap_update_2012.html; Patty Hadju, "Setting the Stage for a Federal Strategy against Gender-Based Violence," Status of Women Canada, November 2016, cfc-swc.gc.ca/violence/strategy-strategie/principle-principe-en.html.

8 Microscopic View of a Coronavirus, https://globalhealth.duke.edu/media/news/duke-experts-demand-reporters-stories-about-new-coronavirus.

9 Ministry of the Attorney General, "Partner Assault Response (PAR) Program Standards, 2014/2015," *Victims and Vulnerable Persons Division Ontario Victim Services*, March 25, 2014/2015.

10 Ministry of the Attorney General, "PAR Program Standards."

11 Nicole Penak (scholar, York University) in personal communication with the authors, March 28, 2020.

12 Michel Foucault, *Discipline and Punish: The Birth of the Prison*, 2nd Vintage Books edition (New York: Vintage Books, 1995).

13 Ministry of the Attorney General, "PAR Program Standards."

14 Image credit (image altered from original): Caroline Gabus et al., "The yeast Ty3 retrotransposon contains a 5'–3' bipartite primer-binding site and encodes nucleocapsid protein NCp9 functionally homologous to HIV-1 NCp7," *EMBO Journal* vol. 17, no. 16 (1998): 4878.

15 Ministry of the Attorney General, "PAR Program Standards."

16 Poco Kernsmith & Roger Kernsmith, "Treating Female Perpetrators: State Standards for Batterer Intervention Services," *Social Work* 54, no. 4 (2009): 341–49.

17 Ali and Naylor, "Intimate Partner Violence."

18 Shawn Wilson, *On the Research Journey. Research as Ceremony: Indigenous Research Methods* (Halifax: Fernwood. 2008).

19 Wilson, *On the Research Journey.*

20 Cindy Baskin, "Systemic Oppression, Violence, and Healing in Aboriginal Families and Communities," in *Cruel But Not Unusual: Violence in Canadian Families*, ed. Ramona Alaggia & Cathy Vine (Waterloo: Wilfrid Laurier University Press, 2006), 15–48.

21 Julia Chinyere Oparah, "Rethinking Anti-Violence Strategies, Lesson's from the Black Women's Movement in Britain," in *The Color of Violence: The INCITE! Anthology*, ed. INCITE! Women of Color Against Violence (Durham, NC: Duke University Press, 2006), 13–24.

22 Mutual Aid Disaster Relief, October 15, 2019, retrieved March 28, 2020, from https://mutualaiddisasterrelief.org/about/.

23 Rachel Herzing, "Creatively Intervening in Interpersonal and State Violence," Dulwich Centre Foundation, March 5, 2018, video, retrieved from https://www.youtube.com/watch?v=0G6ugCeszdQ.

24 Ana Clarissa Rojas Durazo, "Medical Violence Against People of Color and the Medicalization of Domestic Violence," in *The Color of Violence: The INCITE! Anthology*, ed. INCITE! Women of Color Against Violence (Durham, NC: Duke University Press, 2006), 179–88.

25 Eve Tuck and K. Wayne Yang, "Decolonization Is Not a Metaphor," *Decolonization: Indigeneity, Education & Society* 1, no. 1 (2012): 1–40.

26 Michael Anthony Hart, "Anti-colonial Indigenous Social Work: Reflections on an Aboriginal Approach," in *Wicihitowin: Aboriginal Social Work in Canada*, ed. Raven Sinclair, Michael Anthony Hart, and Gord Bruyere (Halifax: Fernwood, 2009), 25–41.

27 Leanne Betasamosake Simpson, *Dancing on Our Turtle's Back: Stories of Nishnaabeg Re-Creation, Resurgence and a New Emergence* (Winnipeg: ARP Books, 2011), 31.

PRISON IS NOT FEMINIST, SERVICE IS NOT LIBERATION

PUNISHMENT, SERVICE, AND A WEB OF DETAINMENT

Kayla Marie Martensen

It is the month of June in 2020 and, across the United States, people are rising up in unprecedented numbers against the continued murder of Black people by armed agents of the state during a global pandemic that is devastating the same communities. In Chicago, our city is shut down as the Chicago Police Department attempts to silence insurgents and other protestors while protecting the property of a mostly wealthy, mostly white downtown. In our inner-Chicago communities, there is outrage and pain illustrated by both broken windows and murals painted over the boarded windows proclaiming "Black Lives Matter." The violent state responses to the uprising have popularized a movement to #DefundThePolice, a call to reallocate billions of dollars spent on law enforcement to "the community," a phrase that usually refers to ambiguous notions of social welfare and social services such as medical care, education, and social workers. This essay argues that advocates of defunding the police must critically assess how and to whom police funds are redistributed, for these community sites are *also* often tied to policing and prisons. As an illustration of carceral community services, this essay explores how women and girls of color

"Prison is not feminist" as a proclamation is graciously gifted to us all by the legendary Mariame Kaba.

in communities targeted by policing, surveillance, and control are vulnerable to becoming trapped in a web of carceral institutions in the name of social welfare.

This essay should be read as both a personal testimony and a working introduction to an emerging theoretical framework. Here, I propose the working framework *web of detainment* to explore carceral expansion into youth-based social services, particularly those that function as centers of detention. I argue that social services do not facilitate freedom for young women and girls of color but have, in fact, *reconfigured* the structure of incarceration into their lives through a vast network of social services and punitive institutions.* I explore the relationship between the punishment industry and social welfare, specifically carceral expansion into social services. My reflections are meant to contribute to a broader conversation abolitionist organizers and scholars are having on carceral humanism, including how the social welfare state has perpetrated racialized violence on vulnerable communities.[1] In this era where the call to #DefundThePolice has gained widespread attention and support, I argue that we must be vigilant in avoiding *refunding police* in the guise of social workers and welfare agents. Defunding police is only a *first step* toward realizing a liberated world free of police, policing, surveillance, control, punishment, and violence.

These reflections are inspired by nearly a decade of work with system-involved† and at-risk young women and girls of color, in addition to almost two years of preliminary observations at a juvenile detention center working with young women.‡ This body of experience is coupled with an earlier decade of being an at-risk, system-involved young woman of color myself. Together, observations I accumulated during my unpaid professional work in juvenile detention, courts,

* This is also true for gender-nonconforming youth and young trans men and boys who are misidentified as female by either the juvenile courts or other residential placements they encounter. Cook County, Chicago, juvenile detention claims their LGBTQI Multidisciplinary Team is consulted and makes the "best choice" for the young person regarding gender placement.

† I define "system-involved" as being on official court record.

‡ These observations were collected from 2014 to 2016 as pilot research to design an empirical study.

and probation; unpaid work with community collectives, nonprofits, and grassroots efforts working with system-involved and at-risk youth; and my personal experiences tell a story of young women of color entrapped in a web of detainment, or a system of punitive and service institutions impacting the everyday lives of system-involved young women and girls of color.* I critique wraparound services,† gender-responsive punishment, and carceral reform, emphasizing the extensions of the carceral state that most impact women and girls of color. I contend that police reform movements, including some iterations of #DefundThePolice, must be replaced with frameworks of abolition feminism developed by Black women and other women of color feminist scholars and leaders.

"Web of detainment" describes a set of conditions in which system-involved young women and girls of color get *stuck* in an ongoing cycle of incarceration within various institutions,‡ from youth detention centers to purportedly "nonpunitive" residential placements. The majority of system-involved young women in Chicago come from five zip codes,§ all communities of color, Black or Latinx, that have a history of organized abandonment. My first experience in a residential placement, I was forced into a group therapy session with young people, all people of color, who were detained for smoking weed, being gang-affiliated, having an older boyfriend, and stabbing their sister, and one young man on the spectrum was detained for exposing himself.

---

* These experiences occurred while I was an adolescent through young adulthood in the West and Northwest sides of Chicago, specifically in low-income Latinx communities (Humboldt Park and later Avondale). I share these experiences as someone who was low income and is a first-generation, mixed-race Filipina.

† "Wraparound" service refers to shared information and surveillance by primary youth institutions, such as schools and detention centers, with the goal of providing service at every point of contact with youth.

‡ My empirical research centers the narratives of Latinx/a young women and girls because their experience is marginalized in research and because many of my loved ones are part of Latinx comminutes in the west and northwest sides of Chicago.

§ Demographic data on girls in detention was shared with me accidently during a professional internship in 2016.

Three of the five of them were detained there under court order.* We were placed in our local medical hospital in Humboldt Park, on the top floor, where we were on total lockdown. These residential placements include facilities that work under the guise of group homes, drug rehab centers, mental health facilities, behavioral health hospitals, and other health and housing services. Through the juvenile court, young women and girls are referred to juvenile detention and other residential placements. These referrals may be under direct court order or indirect referrals. State agents like probation officers, school counselors, social workers, and case workers may heavily influence or informally coerce parents and guardians into admitting young women and girls into out-of-home placement. Strengthened and legitimized within the juvenile court system, the growing bond between the social service sector and the carceral state is central to the conceptualization of the web of detainment. Scholars and activists have highlighted pipelines between social welfare institutions and detention for young women of color;[2] however, little attention has been paid to how social services are not merely a pipeline to a youth prison but can be part of a carceral apparatus, transforming social services to *carceral services*, or institutions that *serve* the carceral apparatus. In efforts to identify with and incorporate frameworks of carceral reform—including rehabilitation, restorative justice,† and gender responsiveness—the juvenile courts exhaust local social services and programming, extending those services to system-involved girls as part of their disposition (court orders). These reform efforts can be attributed to a recurring theme dating back to the establishment of the juvenile court system where ideas of social welfare and protection of the child conflate with surveillance, control, and punishment. The web of detainment highlights the ongoing forms

---

* The experience of incarceration at a young age is quite traumatic—my experiences involved close bonds with others experiencing the web, and my observations thus far support this. The level of intimacy of relationships in placements is very high; we shared the details of our lives with each other.

† Further work can explore the ways the state co-opts movements toward juvenile justice reform, like the restorative justice movement, which resulted in restorative practices being implemented in punitive settings, but not actual restorative justice (see Mimi Kim's discussion of the carceral creep as an example of how anti-violence movements can be co-opted by the state (2019)).

of racialized carceral violence that inhabit the policies and practices of social welfare.

Detainment is enacted by a variety of institutions in a haphazard way; girls bounce around between different types of institutions where they are confined, controlled, and surveilled by a range of state and service agencies. On several occasions during my time working inside detention with young women and girls, they would discuss their time in other lockdown facilities. These conversations usually surfaced when girls reminisced about their time together in other facilities and informally inquired about the whereabouts of other young women stuck in the web of detainment. They effortlessly describe being "locked up" in ways that illustrate no distinction between group home, behavioral health hospital, or juvenile detention. For them, there is no distinction between service and punishment. I use "web" as a metaphor to foreground how some young women and girls of color become *stuck* in a carceral network of services, often until they age out of the system. The web functions as one networked entity removing them from their homes, communities, and loved ones. While residential placements have been justified as a response to attend to "girls in crisis," those crises are not defined by the people who are being removed from their homes, but by the carceral state with a history of pathologizing low-income young women and girls of color and punishing their existence.

The web of detainment is also part of a larger web of surveillance, control, and punishment that makes young women and girls vulnerable to systems of confinement. When the juvenile courts collude with local social services, young women and girls are legally responsible to meet the demands of several agencies and institutions, which create a literal or perceived web of surveillance and control. Together, services in the community, inside schools, and sometimes part of churches and even hospitals are co-opted by the juvenile courts in an effort to "treat" young women and girls. These services and residential placements are both private and nonprofit agencies. Young women and girls must report to a variety of agencies while under the watchful eye of formal and informal state agents who are ready to report the smallest infraction, all under the paternalistic guise of care. In essence, young women and girls of color are expected to *prove* they are deserving of remaining physically "free" by successfully maneuvering these services, requiring them to constantly negotiate and navigate in order to avoid escalated punishment and detainment.[3]

Even when young women act in accordance with the expectations of court and service actors and "successfully" avoid disrupting the court order or treatment plan ascribed to them, they can *still* remain under the surveillance and control of the state while living in their community. For example, within hours of a school case worker finding a picture of me throwing up a gang sign, I was publicly humiliated by school officials, the seventeenth-district police, and a gang task force in a "community meeting" in front of my peers and their families. Wraparound services are an approach to social services that unify multiple service providers to create a "coordinated service response."[4] These coordinated, and often *unified*, services are usually meant to be employed as a court diversion strategy for young people, yet to wraparound is to forge alliances between everyday social service institutions and carceral punishment. In this incident I was *wrapped around* by a cooperative carceral service response, ultimately leading to my detainment in residential placement working under the guise of service and care. I was in the seventh grade.

I would later understand this coordinated response as a kind of gender-responsive carceral feminist ideology that stigmatizes "at risk" young women and girls. Gender-responsiveness is best known as a strategy to make women's prisons more "family friendly" and responsive to "women's needs," but it has been analyzed as an excuse to increase prison expansion and normalize an understanding of prisons as institutions capable of providing "care" outside of punishment.[5] However, along with prisons, carceral-service institutions outside of prison also employ gender-responsive strategies. In this context, services seek to provide *treatment* for women and girls based on a stereotype of what they consider to be "gender-specific" needs. This treatment labels young women and girls as "troubled" and severs their primary relationships, including their relationships with their families, who are also put under a carceral microscope. Indeed, instead of supporting girls' self-determined connections to their families, families often see no other alternative but to voluntarily funnel their daughters, granddaughters, and young women in their lives directly into youth detention spaces in an effort to keep the rest of their families and themselves "intact" while avoiding prison. Yet, like gender-responsive policies in prisons, these frameworks fail to critique the gendered structural issues that make young women and girls of color vulnerable to violence and only serve to create what is assumed to be kinder carceral conditions for them.

In the name of service, the carceral surveillance and control of the day-to-day lives of young women and girls of color has orchestrated, in nuanced ways, a complex web of surveillance, control, punishment, exclusion, and incarceration, trapping these young women and girls of color within a system of ongoing detainment. This essay challenges those in solidarity with #DefundThePolice to strategically adopt an abolition politic that carefully critiques the reallocation of funds while allowing communities to have agency to determine their own needs. This will likely mean that some of the folks who raise "defund police" signs over their heads may need to consider the ways they are implicated in a larger *system* of policing. It is ever more important to identify systems of carceral reform that are sure to engulf the momentum of this current moment. With critical engagement through an abolition feminist politic, we can amplify the voices and lived experiences of young women and girls of color who are stuck in the web of detainment to help us reckon with the fact that service is not liberation, it is not transformative, and carceral service is *not* abolition.

BIBLIOGRAPHY

Braz, Rose. "Kinder, Gentler, Gender Responsive Cages: Prison Expansion Is Not Prison Reform." *Women, Girls & Criminal Justice*, November 2006, 87–91.

Carney, Michelle M., and Frederick Buttell. "Reducing Juvenile Recidivism: Evaluating the Wraparound Services Model." *Research on Social Work Practice* 13, no. 5 (September 2003): 551–68. https://doi.org/10.1177/1049731503253364.

Flores, Jerry. *Caught Up: Girls, Surveillance, and Wraparound Incarceration*. Vol. 2. University of California Press, 2016.

Flores, Jerry, Ariana Ochoa Camacho, and Xuan Santos. "Gender on the Run: Wanted Latinas in a Southern California Barrio." *Feminist Criminology* 12, no. 3 (2017): 248–68.

Heiner, Brady T., and Sarah K. Tyson. "Feminism and the Carceral State: Gender-Responsive Justice, Community Accountability, and the Epistemology of Antiviolence." *Feminist Philosophy Quarterly* 3, no. 1 (March 23, 2017). https://doi.org/10.5206/fpq/2016.3.3.

Kilgore, James. "Repackaging Mass Incarceration." *CounterPunch*, June 6, 2014. https://www.counterpunch.org/2014/06/06/repackaging-mass-incarceration/.

Kim, Mimi E. "The Carceral Creep: Gender-Based Violence, Race and the Expansion of the Punitive State, 1973–1983." *Social Problems* 67, no. 2 (2020): 251–69. https://doi.org/10.1093/socpro/spz013.

Morris, Monique. *Pushout: The Criminalization of Black Girls in Schools.* New York: New Press, 2016.

Roberts, Dorothy. "Abolishing Policing Also Means Abolishing Family Regulation." *Imprint*, June 16, 2020. https://imprintnews.org/child-welfare-2/abolishing-policing-also-means-abolishing-family-regulation/44480.

———. *Shattered Bonds: The Color of Child Welfare.* New York: Basic Civitas Books, 2002.

NOTES

1 Dorothy Roberts's critique of child welfare services as an institution integral to the carceral state is a key example of this discussion. Dorothy Roberts, "Abolishing Policing Also Means Abolishing Family Regulation," *Imprint*, June 16, 2020, https://imprintnews.org/child-welfare-2/abolishing-policing-also-means-abolishing-family-regulation/44480; Roberts, *Shattered Bonds: The Color of Child Welfare*, (New York: Basic Civitas Books, 2002).

2 Monique Morris. *Pushout: The Criminalization of Black Girls in Schools* (New York: New Press, 2016); Jerry Flores, Ariana Ochoa Camacho, and Xuan Santos, "Gender on the Run: Wanted Latinas in a Southern California Barrio," *Feminist Criminology* 12, no. 3 (2017): 248–68.

3 Jerry Flores et al. "Gender on the Run."

4 Michelle M. Carney and Frederick Buttell, "Reducing Juvenile Recidivism: Evaluating the Wraparound Services Model." *Research on Social Work Practice* 13, no. 5 (September 2003): 551–68, https://doi.org/10.1177/1049731503253364.

5 Rose Braz, "Kinder, Gentler, Gender Responsive Cages: Prison Expansion Is Not Prison Reform," *Women, Girls & Criminal Justice*, November 2006, 87–91; Brady T. Heiner and Sarah K. Tyson, "Feminism and the Carceral State: Gender-Responsive Justice, Community Accountability, and the Epistemology of Antiviolence," *Feminist Philosophy Quarterly* 3, no. 1 (March 23, 2017), https://doi.org/10.5206/fpq/2016.3.3.

PART THREE

MAKING A CLEARING

Summer-Harmony Twenish, "No Cops on Stolen Land"

A LETTER FOR DARNELLA FRAZIER

A BLACK FEMINIST ABOLITION MAP OF THE FORGOTTEN

Whitney Richards-Calathes

June 2020

Dear Darnella Frazier,

You do not know me but so many people across the world know you already. *Or do they?*

I wanted to write you a letter. I've been doing work—life work, intellectual work, paid work, care work—for a while now around abolition, Black women, around Black feminism. I'm a scholar (I think?), an organizer (I believe), a writer (I'm trying), and a full-time Black woman (I'm proud). And as I've been thinking about what's been going on, I'm realizing I have a lot of questions for myself, for the people out in the streets, for others who write articles about no more jails and no more cops. I have questions about the body in place, about silences, forgotten moments, about unseen acts of punishment and violence experienced by Black women, the tangle between the unspoken analyses of Black calamity at the hands of the state all while we grapple with what it means to *witness.*

See, you were there, at that moment with George Floyd in Minneapolis. You were the one that filmed it—that knee, that neck, those eight minutes, and forty-six seconds, that part when he called out for his mother. Your camera was pointed to that horror. You were there too, on the other side of that moment, which means you're impacted, part of this story. We know that already. *Or do we?*

You saw it all, just a seventeen-year-old Black girl who pressed record on what, maybe, felt like a routine scene: Black body/cop, sidewalk/harassment, the swarming of blue uniforms on a body that could be an uncle, friend, play cousin, neighbor, father. Was it hot that day? I went to college in Minnesota; a young Black girl too, a little bit older than you when I packed my bags for the next life chapter. I grew up in the Bronx, and Minnesota used to feel so different to me, but the lushness of the springtime surprised me when I got there and so did the history of your city's nickname, Murderapolis.

MURDERAPOLIS, 1995

This article in the *New York Times* reported that in 1995, *way before you were even a thought*, as my mama would say, the number of murders in your city was 50 percent higher than in mine. The reporter joked: "Now there are T-shirts that read, 'Murderapolis,' and gallows humor about warning visitors from New York to be careful."[1] People are quick to think that Black death only happens in particular places, places associated with words like "urban," "jungle," "project," "crowded," "immigrant," "majority minority." But don't they know we get killed everywhere? *Or do they?*

The article goes on to say that "the murders have often been linked to drugs, especially crack." Usually that's code for Black and poor and uneven development.[2] Your city grew in those years with refugee communities from Somalia, Laos, Vietnam. Hmong and East African people—some of whom became my closest friends in college—showed a different type of diversity than what I had known back in the concrete mix of New York City. Parts of your city felt recognizable to me, though: segregation and tall buildings filled with Black folks and a big divide between rich and working class all while being seen as "socially progressive" . . . that's familiar. Just like the image of George Floyd is familiar, too. It makes sense why it was dubbed Murderapolis, and it makes sense why this moment, almost twenty-five years in the future, happened in your city. On a lush spring day. I think people understand that. *Or do they?*

MINNEAPOLIS, USA, 2020

You do not know me, young Miss Frazier. But protests across the United States are sparking in response to the video you filmed and bravely shared with us. Hundreds of thousands of people across the nation are taking to the streets declaring #BlackLivesMatter, standing strongly on longtime movements and organizing efforts to address the persistent killing of Black people at the hands of law enforcement. This came at the end of the lockdowns from the COVID-19 pandemic, all of us frustrated, many of us unemployed, too many having freshly buried their own kin. There is this unshakeable weight of collective grief, bodies and voices spilling out, releasing rage, anger, hurt, and a call for something better. One of those calls is to "defund the police." An equally important rally, though, is the cry for justice for Black cis and trans women who have also been murdered at the hands of the state. Campaigns such as #SayHerName work hard to uplift the violence that Black women encounter and challenge the larger movement for police accountability and racial justice to contend with its internalized misogynoir. Breonna Taylor. Dominique "Rem'mie" Fells. Riah Milton. Titi Gulley. At the time of this letter, there fails to be any ongoing accountability for the deaths of these Black women. Black trans actress and activist Indya Moore asks reflectively in her poem "Our Freedom to Be,"

> I know I'm trans but,
> can I come?
> Can I be free too?
> Can I co exist
> in peace
> and
> in love
> With us?
> Can the beginning of
> my liberation
> start at
> the end of white supremacy
> as well?[3]

The death of Black cis and trans women never seems to get the same level of outcry as those of Black men. It's complex and we know it's not either/or. Black feminist thinking creates space and language to illustrate how the lives of all Black people are enmeshed. Anti-Blackness, patriarchy, the gender binary are all forged together in the abduction of Black people, chattel enslavement, the conflation of property and Blackness, sexual terror on the plantation, white supremacy enacted by white women, whiteness flung to maintain systems of heteropatriarchy, prisons that reinscribe gender binaries through modalities of extreme punishment.[4] What if we measured the atrocities of Blackness by rape and gender-based violence rather than by lynching? This is not to put one form of oppression over another. The matrix of domination says we must do otherwise;[5] we are interlocked. But I'm asking the rhetorical question to reflect that our experiences of violence as Black people—men, women, trans, cis, genderqueer—are threaded together and require us to have analyses of depth, to show up for one another, to acknowledge that we are all out here suffering. We need to know this to get free. *Don't we?*

In this midst of all these questions of death, these pictures of Black people buried and gone, I keep thinking about you and what you witnessed. I keep thinking about the backlash you received from white supremacists; the backlash you received from people who asked why you didn't do more; the backlash you felt from Black people who, for no fault of your own, are tired of seeing themselves die over and over and over again throughout the continuum of history.

You bore witness with your camera, reminding us of the thin line we all walk between documenting our anguish because for so long no one else would and what Elizabeth Alexander calls "Black bodies in pain for public consumption."[6] She makes a case that "a practical memory exists and crucially informs African Americans about the lived realities of how violence and its potential informs our understanding of our individual selves as a larger group."[7] We are taught that our lives are undervalued not just through our embodied experiences, but through the replay of our harms; a looped reel that simultaneously hurts and dulls, a tortured repetition that makes it commonplace to feel that we ain't shit.[8] Or at the very least we are one toy gun, hoodie, bag of skittles, iced tea, cell phone, mistake, *wrong place wrong time wrong pronoun wrong skin* away from being ain't shit. Or maybe we become something when we have a hashtag?

Almost thirty years after Rodney King, Alexander keeps writing about these questions and recently penned a reflection about the moment you, Darnella, became a doula and helped all of us see that reel again:

> I call the young people who grew up in the past twenty-five years the Trayvon Generation. They always knew these stories. These stories formed their world view. These stories helped instruct African Americans about their embodiment and their vulnerability. The stories were primers in fear and futility. The stories were the ground soil of their rage. These stories instructed them that anti-black hatred and violence were never far.
>
> They watched these violations up close and on their cell phones, so many times over. They watched them in near-real time. They watched them crisscrossed and concentrated. They watched them on the school bus. They watched them under the covers at night. They watched them often outside of the presence of adults who loved them and were charged with keeping them safe in body and soul.[9]

You belong to the Trayvon Generation, watching, mediated and in real life, always up close. You became the documentarian, projecting the horrors "crisscrossed and concentrated." But what of horrors unseen? Is the documentation of Black death the only avenue toward the veracity of our experiences under punishment, though?[10] When we believe in the abolishment of prisons and white supremacy and settler logics and heteropatriarchy, do we need videos of ourselves getting literally choked out by these systems and the people who protect them? And when the deaths of Black cis and trans women go unrecorded, is the value of our lives put on the backburner of an abolitionist movement? And the question that's really fuzzy in my head, that I'm searching for the answer to is, What version of abolition gets to include you—still alive, unrecorded, but inextricably linked to this movement for Black life?

I know I'm not alone in asking these questions. In fact, I believe it is the responsibility of Black feminist abolitionists to consider these tensions. We commit ourselves to seeing what is right outside the spotlight, what many call the margins, the edges, the wake;[11] I hear other Black women authors contending that this space, what (and who) is just beyond the perimeter of sight, happens to unfortunately and predictably be Black women. Salamishah Tillet writes her fears as she considers her own hesitancy to watch the video you courageously shared with us. "I begin to think about my own reluctance to watch Frazier's video of Floyd's death. But mainly I worried about Frazier and how her fate as an African American girl was forever tethered to those eight minutes and 46 seconds. She not only captured his death, but actively rejected the attempts that sought to cover up the police brutality."[12] Tillet goes on to interview Alexander, and she sounds similarly concerned:

> She was standing at close range not only to a murder in progress, but to four policemen. I can't imagine that proximity, and she keeps filming. A question and a concern that we must ask is, "Who has this child?"
>
> I say that rhetorically because this is not about someone having a family. This is about a larger community saying we must put our arms around this child who did something unbelievably brave, who put herself at risk to do something that would result, we hope, in justice, but that also could save that man's life. And it is so extraordinary how she went back to the scene the next day and had the language to say, "It is so traumatizing."[13]

Who has you after you put down your camera? What about when that feeling of trauma grips your chest or wakes you in the night? Who has you in the moments you are *unwitnessed*, crowds gone, recordings stopped? Black feminist Brittney Cooper echoes Alexander's thoughts on witnessing Black death, the critical consciousness it may require to raise up the current Trayvon Generation. However, Cooper names that these playbacks, which focus on you as integrated spectator (as witness), still keep missing an important ingredient: you, Darnella.

> But at no point in our replaying of the lynching script, what with its accreting Black male victims, overzealous cops, and devious white women, do we ever think about how Black women fit into the story. Femininity is a weapon only if you're white. Black women have no such protections. . . . We keep missing the intersection of race and

> gender when it comes to Black women. But right there at that intersection stands. . . Darnella Frazier.[14]

Cooper goes on to remind us of Rachel Jeantel, who also was a bystander to the unjust murder of a young Black man (is there ever a justified one, though?). She was on the phone as Trayvon Martin was killed on a Florida street, walking home. Positioned as an expert witness in the 2013 trial of George Zimmerman, Martin's killer, think pieces erupted on Jeantel's credibility, articulateness, the veracity of her memory. Or in other words: *Is this trial really supposed to rest on the words of a young Black girl?*

At the very best there is a political reckoning occurring in America right now. And, at the minimum, the uprisings, the growing public dialogues about the abolition of the police and critical conversations on the intersections of race, gender, and state violence—all of these are moments of growth, small victories within a larger movement for abolition and Black life. Either way, in an era where the lens of witnessing Black death is often pointed at Black men, how can we begin to see young Black women like you, Darnella Frazier, and your sister Rachel Jeantel? How can we understand that Black women and girls are victimized by police violence on both sides of the camera, not simply as bystanders or witnesses but also as shadowed figures on the other side of the camera? Why do we keep positioning Black women as negative space, as afterthoughts, as invisible companions on our path to abolition? *Who has these children?*

Cooper goes on to write, "We must begin by recognizing that [Frazier and Jeantel] are worthy of care, love, and outrage too. But to do that, we have to commit to seeing Black women and girls, whether they are sleeping in their beds, chatting with a friend or holding the camera, pleading with the police."[15] We must see you too.

NEW YORK CITY, 1989

Unseen and unnamed are innumerable Black women, whose survival, nuance, complex lives, and bravery become flattened, mere silhouettes relegated to the shadows where we get no names. So much so, that we must meander through time and space to excavate ourselves. Let us go to my city.

A *New York Daily News* article on June 26, 1989, describes a community rally in support of a Black woman who was brutally assaulted, raped, and thrown down an elevator shaft in Brooklyn on May 2 of that year. The article names her injuries in detail: shattered pelvis, broken heels and ankles, the nightmares every night. She has no name, though. Simply, BlackWoman. Almost invisible, an anonymous headline. But she surfaces again, in Kimberlé Crenshaw's landmark 1991 article, "Mapping the Margins: Intersectionality, Identity Politics, and Violence against Women of Color," her Brooklyn BlackWoman identity starkly contrasted with Trisha Meili, the investment banker at the center of the infamous Central Park Five case in New York City. Remember those words that geo-pinpoint Black death? *Urban. Jungle.* Add to that *wildin', wolf pack, monsters.*[16]

The penal system's false narrative of the rape of Mieli in Central Park by several Black youth and BlackWoman's vicious attack happened within the same week. In her canonical article, Crenshaw asks us to consider the racialized and gendered politics behind mass sympathy for Meili and the invisibility of a Jamaica-born Brooklyn BlackWoman moaning in an elevator shaft. So public was Meili's story that Donald Trump bought a full-page advertisement in four New York City newspapers, penning a letter that reflected its bold title: "BRING BACK THE DEATH PENALTY. BRING BACK OUR POLICE!" Brooklyn BlackWoman received only a private hospital visit from Trump a week post–*New York Times* ad and an offer to pay her hospital expenses. No records indicate whether this offer was seen through.

What can be made of this tangle: the now-exonerated Central Park Five, the ways their story has been publicly leveraged to call attention to the cruelties of the injustice system against Black men; Donald Trump's virulent racism and, in effect, calls for lynching at the time; and claims of a white woman harmed at the hands of Black men? All these threads woven together, and still in the backdrop, our BlackWoman, unnamed, silently contribute to themes of intersectionality written by Crenshaw, founder of the #SayHerName campaign. How many of us will remain unnamed? Thirty-one years in the past, like time warping through a prism, dancing around the very issues we face today. The same players, a different era. One would think we wouldn't keep repeating the same stories. *How long will we keep on this ride?*

For these questions I call forth Viviane Saleh-Hanna's concept of "Black Feminist Hauntology," which demands that we remember the repetitive nature of white supremacy not as a legacy of Black unworthiness or Black oppression, but as confirmation of whiteness's abuse, a persistence so haunting that it makes itself the object of study, of disgust, and in need of exorcism. Through Black Feminist Hauntology we have permission to perform seances; our work is to call forth the ghosts that go unnamed, to always see Brooklyn BlackWoman in the story of the Central Park Five, because without her, without the perspective of Black women, whiteness, sexism, heteropatriarchy, anti-Blackness, addictions to punishment cannot fully be undone. Saleh-Hanna writes,

> Black Feminist Hauntology emerges from the intersection where White supremacy (that racializes and genders bodies and institutions) meets the death and un-doing-of-death of its victims. In other words, Black Feminist Hauntology allows us to recognize that that Whiteness cannot be supreme when confronted by its own acts of violence. Black Feminist Hauntology unveils Whiteness in a manner that renders the very term "White Supremacy" an oxymoron.[17]

Hauntology is the reframing of historical violence; the manifests of slave ships are Black bodies, but really we should see them as accountings of white atrocity, of white fear, and of white violence. Ghosts, hauntings, and exorcisms.

Any version of the story of Meili that *ghosts* the unnamed BlackWoman fails to fully undo the mechanisms that switched into gear so seamlessly that night in Central Park. Our focus cannot only be the now-exonerated Black men: Kevin Richardson, Raymond Santana, Antron McCray, Yusef Salaam, and Korey Wise. The work of abolition is also to disassemble the entanglements of structures and systems, not just hold accountability for individual racist behaviors. BlackWoman makes the scaffolding of power clear: Trump's concern is not truly about safety, or he would've been equally as upset about BlackWoman's rape as he was publicly malevolent about Meili; the intersection of whiteness and femininity rang the sirens differently than the moans of a Black immigrant woman in a Brooklyn elevator shaft. Saleh-Hanna writes, "Willed forgetfulness has been foundational to my conceptions of Black Feminist Hauntology as it opens a window to envision and articulate the overbearing silence. . . . Willed forgetfulness is rooted within dominant colonizing cultures and thus impacts all that live within them."[18] Black feminist abolition requires the ghosts be unforgotten. The silences, the shadowed shapes help us know what to exorcise.

All this to say that without you there, Miss Frazier, haunting with your camera, we would've never seen Derek Chauvin's knee killing George Floyd. You cannot be invisible; you are the "oppositional gaze."[19] Black women are the inverse panopticon—gazing back at forces of carceral punishment, exposing them in critically intersectional ways. I just wish that we didn't have our own set of night terrors that accompany this burden. *Or is it a gift?*

CHICAGO, 2007

It is summer in Chicago, and I am in a basement with ten young Black women from the South Side, an area that, like the places we are from, is associated with killings, guns, gangs, drugs, death. We wonder, why do "they" never talk about the racism, the divestment, the white flight? Martin Luther King Jr. marched through Marquette Park in the South Side in August of 1966. The march turned violent, and Dr. King proclaimed that he had rarely encountered mobs so hostile and hate filled as he had in Chicago, not even in the Deep South. Marquette Park is where we are now, young Black girls in the same summer heat that Dr. King felt. Angel is one of us and she sits across from me. We are talking about cops and family and school and arrests. I am here again, back in college, twenty-one at the time, trying to think through my own ideas of Blackness, feminism, police violence, change, and justice. Really, trying to make sense of who I was and how to live in a world that really hurt me. Angel recounts to us a memory of driving in a car with her sister and her sister's boyfriend:

> Now the police. . .they just jumped out of nowhere. Put [the boyfriend] in the back seat. Beat him. BEAT HIM! One of the police beat him! Girl, he just hollerin' and all this! So, the police like, "You bitches got something." . . . It wasn't no drugs. They think that we had the drugs in our vaginas. . . . They [male officers] check, go all in our panties, touching all up on us, girl. All up in the cold. In the snow. Everybody looking out they window while we out there, almost ass naked. That was so embarrassing. They slapped me; said I had a badass mouth. Girl, I'm serious. . . . Like, "Bitch you got a badass mouth, you too pretty to have a mouth like that on you!" But all the time [the officers] calling us all out our names. I'm just talking back. . . telling [them] "We feelin' to go home." [One said], "Bitch you ain't going nowhere." . . . And I just felt real low that night and [they] gave us twenty dollars and said, "Get on the bus."

Black-feminist critical criminologists help to theorize this moment for us. Black girls are consistently "adultified" by law enforcement and institutional structures in their lives,[20] engulfed in tropes of sexual promiscuity,[21] and tightrope walking the dichotomies of being "good" or "ghetto."[22] The robust scholarship built by Black women thinkers and activists gives us language to describe the ways that Black women and girls are entrenched in carceral systems and policing, have long legacies of racialized and gendered state violence, and suffer enormous punishment-oriented consequences from social policy failures and hyperbolized fear toward Blackness (see paragraph on Donald Trump above for a reminder).[23] We now know this. But do we?

What I can't shake, though, every time I recall the moment Angel shares, is that this interaction never got recorded beyond her own memory. Yes, this was before the era of body cameras, but beyond this recollection, not one ticket was written, no violation given. No tally to count our oppression. Simply a story and a twenty-dollar bill thrown degradingly at young Black girls on a Chicago street. A few summers later at a parade in Brooklyn, friends and I were catcalled by police. One in blue pressed up against me and whispered in my ear, "I can't wait to get you in handcuffs, the pink furry kind." Invisible moments, no discernable record except our memories. Darnella, has this ever happened to you? Your friends? Something tells me that you know the lurking anger of policemen and the history behind their badges or else you wouldn't have stopped and pressed record. Trayvon's Generation. *But what about all those silent, unseen moments for us Black girls?*

Tallying us—computing our experience into numbers—has its limits too. Mapping the "the reasons" why women end up in prison or in police custody quickly morphs into a narrative of "gendered pathways" to incarceration, fast becoming the scaffolding onto which we layer reform efforts meant to be *gender-responsive*, rather than interrogate addictions to punishment on Black women's bodies.

Across the United States gender-responsive prison programming has engorged over the last decades, with efforts to paint cells pink, teach women how to knit, and in some extreme instances propose for women to have their young children with them in facilities. In your state of Minnesota, Miss Frazier, the number of women in prison has increased more than ninefold between 1978 and 2017.[24] Granted, we are at a different moment in the conversation now. People now speak of abolishing the police and your city now claims that they will work to defund their police department, even if your state, like all the others, has handcuffed women again and again the last decades.[25] But what about Angel? My twentysomething-year-old self? And maybe you and the memories your flesh holds about close encounters and unwitnessed flashes of fear?

Darnella Frazier, I do not have all the answers. But I know a Black feminist abolition must include us: past, present, and future. Seen and unseen.

MIRA LOMA, ANTELOPE VALLEY, 2017

I want to share one more snapshot with you, Darnella. Bear with me. These are my own recordings of what I've witnessed, and the stories feel just as urgent as the one you captured, mostly because no one was there to press that red record button. This is also one of the roles of Black feminist abolitionists I suppose: archivists, memory holders, storytellers, oral historians, keepers of our own records. For this scene, the spotlight sits on the border of Los Angeles County and the Mojave Desert. It's a carceral nexus—a county jail, a youth detention facility, a state prison, and an empty immigration detention facility called Mira Loma. I visited there once. All empty concrete, bars and barbed wire locking up nothing but workings of the imagination. Ghosts absolutely live there.

Almost a decade ago, Los Angeles County proposed allocating funds to remodel the empty facility, revamping it into a women's correctional facility. The project sat with a bill upwards of $136 million. When I drove through the sandy hills and prefab homes a few years ago, just to bear witness to the haunted monstrosity, the lone security guard who sat in a booth, a Black man who looked like he could be my uncle's best friend, told me simply what we already know: "Prisons are good for the economy, young lady." *But are they?*

A few miles down the road from Mira Loma are the towns of Palmdale and Lancaster. They found a Black man hanging from a tree in Palmdale recently, in front of the town hall, twenty-four-year-old Robert Fuller. They ruled it a suicide, but we all know that broken necks around nooses—and now maybe under the weight of police knees—hold particular places in our collective Black memory that Alexander refers to. These small cities started off as sleepy desert suburbs, though, an influx of Black residents occurring in the last fifteen years or so. Mostly Black women and children are moving in, given vouchers to relocate from the city of Los Angeles to these outermost county edges. Promises of space, yards, and better schools. They've come with their kin to the dusty roads but have been greeted with neighbors who hurl racial slurs and call their kids "voucher moochers."[26] Their emptied Section 8 units back in the city already bulldozed and flattened to make room for "new development." The Black mothers who relocated here experience some of the highest eviction rates from their new desert homes. Midnight raids from law enforcement disrupt sleeping children and startle the silence of night, authorities looking for grounds for expulsion from that promised space and those yards.[27] A woman who moved there once told me that a gang of skinheads came and chased her family out of their home, wielding bats with nails and chains pinned onto them. Black women are apparently not welcome in Palmdale. *But maybe we are in Mira Loma?*

In February of 2019, though, after years of grassroots organizing, the Los Angeles Board of Supervisors voted down the proposed construction of the Mira Loma women's facility. An immense victory. It was an effort of community-based organizations, coalitions, a beautiful network of system-impacted people, many of whom I call friends, colleagues, sisters, allies. So many of these leaders are Black women whose names the public will never know. Black cis and trans women often do the consistent and laboring work of freedom. Harriet Tubman's journeys for freedom are the work of abolition. Slave narratives like that by Harriet Jacobs's *Incidents in the Life of a Slave Girl* are our primary sources, our recordings, of Blackness under enslavement. #BlackLivesMatter was founded by Black queer women. #SayHerName by Crenshaw. There are names you may know, like Dr. Angela Davis, Tamika Mallory, Susan Burton, Marsha P. Johnson, Raquel Willis. And so many more that remain unnamed. It's an invisibility that some may call a superpower or resiliency or, as my mama might tell me, the thankless job of being a Black woman. I want you to know the legacy that you, Darnella, and your sister Rachel, walk in. Black feminist abolition always seeks to acknowledge lineage, our grandmothers, our ancestors. And we want you to remember the victories, especially the ones that are quietly hummed before and after the rallying cries die down. You may be what Julia Chinyere Oparah calls a "Maroon Abolitionist."

> Popular histories tend to focus on formerly enslaved African Americans who sought to win white support through speeches and slave narratives, while less attention is paid to the slave rebellions, mass escapes, and maroon insurgencies that fundamentally challenged the viability and hastened the demise/restriction of chattel slavery. Twenty-first-century maroon abolitionism is . . . rooted in the survival imperative, guided by a sense of urgency, and informed by an understanding of the prison-industrial complex as a war on black communities.[28]

You can pick from many titles now: Rebel. Maroon Abolitionist. Black Feminist Abolitionist. Freedom Archivist. Truth Teller. Black Young Woman. Brave. Righteous Recorder. Or we can just keep saying your name, Darnella Frazier. They are all synonyms.

HERE, NOW, TOMORROW

Take these moments in time and do with them what you will. My hope is that in sharing Black women's experiences that are pushed just outside the frame of vision we can reveal a few important shapes: the structural conditions of racialized gender punishment that zigzag and time travel between decades, cities, from concrete to sand, from footnotes to newspapers, empty cells, and public sidewalks. The interconnectedness of punishment from home to car to online to courtroom. What happens to us, happens everywhere. Our moments exist all throughout time and space because there is a structural, political, historic set of failures and violences. You are not alone, not only in what you just saw, Miss Frazier, but in what you experienced. You are part of our picture; you help us see a more expansive road toward abolition.

Also, these constellations that I've drawn map out the everydayness of Black women's experiences under carceral systems, police violence, mechanisms of displacement, silent episodes of violence, and witnessing of intersectional and interconnected death. The everydayness can ensure that Black women's experiences are part of the tolerated atmosphere of state violence. But spectacle does not always have to be a requirement for fighting back. We should not wait for the obscene in order to feel invigorated for abolition work. The most useful freedom maps are the ones that make relevant everyday objects: rivers that always flow, that tree with a crook in its arm, the mundane door behind which we can find hot food and safety. These are the maps that we fold and keep in our pockets for generations, that we pass down to each other. Abolition work—Black feminist abolition work—does not necessitate searching for only the loud, the atrocious, the dead. Let our tableau be one that we can learn from while it still has the breath of life running through it. Let us learn from you. Let us see you, Darnella, while you are still here with us.

And lastly, I would be remiss if I didn't remind myself, you, and others, that this conversation between us is worthy. Black women have told each other freedom stories for a long time, generations of strategies and wisdom passed down. Did you know that Black women braided roadmaps for liberation in each other's hair? We slipped seeds in between our kinks and curls so that wherever we ended up, we could be fed, safe, and make home. The intimate, informal, familial practices we hold are precious in our liberation work. Do not let anyone tell you otherwise. Thank you for listening, Darnella Frazier. Thank you for teaching me and all of us. I hope we can be better at carrying you, dear child.

In solidarity and with love,

Whitney

NOTES

1 Dirk Johnson, "Nice City's Nasty Distinction: Murders Soar in Minneapolis," *New York Times*, June 30, 1996, https://www.nytimes.com/1996/06/30/us/nice-city-s-nasty-distinction-murders-soar-in-minneapolis.html.

2 Donna Murch, "Crack in Los Angeles: Crisis, Militarization, and Black Response to the Late Twentieth-Century War on Drugs," *Journal of American History* 102, no. 1 (2015): 162–73.

3 Indya Moore, "Can I Come Too?" *Instagram*, June 19, 2020, https://www.instagram.com/p/CBmSMvEH8sV/.

4 Kali Nicole Gross, "Policing Black Women's and Black Girls' Bodies in the Carceral United States," *Souls* 20, no. 1 (2018): 1–13; Sarah Haley, *No Mercy Here: Gender, Punishment, and the Making of Jim Crow Modernity* (Chapel Hill: University Press, 2016); Patricia Hill Collins, *Black Feminist Thought: Knowledge, Consciousness, and the Politics of Empowerment* (New York: Routledge, 2002); Lena Palacios, "Challenging Convictions: Indigenous and Black Race-Radical Reminists Theorizing the Carceral State and Abolitionist Praxis in the United States and Canada," *Meridians* 15, no. 1 (2016): 137–65; Hillary Potter, *Intersectionality and Criminology: Disrupting and Revolutionizing Studies of Crime* (New York: Routledge, 2015); Jason M. Williams, "Race as a Carceral Terrain: Black Lives Matter Meets Reentry," *Prison Journal* 99, no. 4 (2019): 387–95.

5 Collins, *Black Feminist Thought*, 23

6 Elizabeth Alexander, "'Can you be BLACK and Look at This?': Reading the Rodney King Video(s)," *Public Culture* 7, no. 1 (1994): 78.

7 Alexander, "'Can you be BLACK and Look at This?'" 79

8 Amy Louise Wood, "Lynching Photography and the Visual Reproduction of White Supremacy," *American Nineteenth Century History* 6, no. 3 (2005): 373–99. As Wood points out, the composition of lynching photography was designed to demonstrate the civility of the white mob and the monstrosity of the lynching victim. The visual ephemera of the lynching worked, too, as a form of post-hoc evidence for the lynching victim's crime.

9 Elizabeth Alexander, "The Trayvon Generation," *New Yorker*, June 22, 2020, https://www.newyorker.com/magazine/2020/06/22/the-trayvon-generation.

10 Naa Kwate and Shatema Threadcraft, "Dying Fast and Dying Slow in Black Space: Stop and Frisk's Public Health Threat and a Comprehensive Necropolitics," *Du Bois Review: Social Science Research on Race* 14, no. 2 (2017), 535–56.

11 bell hooks, "The Oppositional Gaze: Black Female Spectators." *Black Looks: Race and Representation* 115 (1992): 131. Christina Sharpe, *In the Wake: On Blackness and Being* (Durham, NC: Duke University Press, 2016).

12 Salamishah Tillet, "Elizabeth Alexander on the Spectacle of 'Black Bodies in Pain.'" *New York Times*, June 19, 2020, https://www.nytimes.com/2020/06/19/arts/elizabeth-alexander-george-floyd-video-protests.html.

13 Tillet, "Elizabeth Alexander."

14 Brittney Cooper, "Why Are Black Women and Girls Still an Afterthought in Our Outrage over Police Violence?" *Time*, June 4, 2020, https://time.com/5847970/police-brutality-black-women-girls/.

15 Cooper, "Why Are Black Women and Girls Still an Afterthought?"

16 Stephen J. Mexal, "The Roots of 'Wilding': Black Literary Naturalism, the Language of Wilderness, and Hip Hop in the Central Park Jogger Rape," *African American Review* 46, no. 1 (2013): 101–15; N. Jeremi Duru, "The Central Park Five, the Scottsboro Boys, and the Myth of the Bestial Black Man," *Cardozo Law Review* 25 (2003): 1315.

17 Viviane Saleh-Hanna, "Black Feminist Hauntology," *Champ pénal / Penal Field* 12 (2015).

18 Viviane Saleh-Hanna, "Black Feminist Hauntology," para. 18.

19 bell hooks, "The Oppositional Gaze: Black Female Spectators," *Black Looks: Race and Representation* 115 (1992): 131.

20 Monique Morris, *Pushout: The Criminalization of Black Girls in Schools* (New York: New Press, 2016).

21 Jody Miller, "Getting Played: African American Girls, Urban Inequality, and Gendered Violence," *Journal of African American History* 94, no. 3 (2009): 448–51.

22 Nikki Jones, *Between Good and Ghetto: African American Girls and Inner-City Violence* (New Brunswick: Rutgers University Press, 2009).

23 Beth E. Richie, *Compelled to Crime: The Gender Entrapment of Battered Black Women* (New York: Psychology Press, 1996); Angela Y. Davis, "Public Imprisonment and Private Violence: Reflections on the Hidden Punishment of Women," *New England Journal on Criminal & Civil Confinement* 24 (1998): 339; Julia Subury, "Celling Black Bodies: Black Women in the Global Prison Industrial Complex," *Feminist Review* 70, no. 1 (2002): 57–74; Hillary Potter, *Intersectionality and Criminology: Disrupting and Revolutionizing Studies of Crime* (New York: Routledge, 2015); Jodie M. Lawston and Erica R. Meiners, "Ending Our Expertise: Feminists, Scholarship, and Prison Abolition," *Feminist Formations* (2014): 1–25.

24 Vera Institute of Justice, "Incarceration Trends in Minnesota," 2019, https://www.vera.org/downloads/pdfdownloads/state-incarceration-trends-minnesota.pdf.

25 Dakin Andone, Christina Maxouris, and Josh Campbell, "Minneapolis City Council Members Intended to Defund and Dismantle the City's Police Department," June 8, 2020, CNN, https://edition.cnn.com/2020/06/07/us/george-floyd-protests-sunday/index.html.

26 Whitney Richards-Calathes, "Inheritances of Injustice / Transference of Freedom: An Intimate Project on Black Women's Intergenerational Relationships and the Consequences of the Punishment System," dissertation, Graduate Center, City University of New York, 2019.

27 Rahim Kurwa, "Deconcentration without Integration: Examining the Social Outcomes of Housing Choice Voucher Movement in Los Angeles County," *City & Community* 14, no. 4 (2015): 364–91.

28 Julia Chinyere Oparah (formerly Julia Sudbury), "Maroon Abolitionists: Black Gender-Oppressed Activists in the Anti-Prison Movement in the US and Canada," *Meridians* 9, no. 1 (2009): 11–12.

RADICAL MOTHERING FOR THE PURPOSES OF ABOLITION

Nadine Naber, Johnaé Strong, and Souzan Naser

At the time of this writing, we are only halfway into 2020 and it has been a tumultuous six months. The initial effects of COVID-19 coupled with the current uprisings against police violence have torn us from our common sense of normalcy. We began the year with a deadly virus outbreak that still threatens the world. Declared a global emergency by the World Health Organization (WHO) on January 30, the novel coronavirus continues to claim the lives of the most vulnerable among us in the United States, revealing all too quickly that racial capitalism, not simply COVID-19, is the disaster. We witness racial capitalism in the "denigration of the work of care"[1]—as evidenced in the failure to provide personal protective equipment for care workers or large-scale testing across society. It flares up, too, in the generalized idea that the poor people of color and Indigenous people who disproportionately make up the vulnerable labor population of "essential" workers should die to save an economy that already exploits and devalues them.

The new year also started with the familiar and disturbing history of Black people being murdered at the hands of law enforcement officers. In addition to the February 23 murder of Ahmaud Arbery by a white father and his son and the March 13 murder of Breonna Taylor, an EMT and aspiring nurse, by Louisville police officers, George Floyd, a forty-six-year-old Black man, son, father, and brother, was killed by Minneapolis police on May 25. With his face pinned down on the cold concrete ground and the weight of officer Derek Chauvin's body pressed against his neck for over eight minutes, the final cries from George Floyd calling, calling, calling for his mother reverberated in the minds and hearts of mothers across the nation. As national protests erupted and filled the streets in the aftermath of his horrific murder, mothers, biological or not, responded politically to his murder and to all victims of state violence.

This sudden shift in the already toxic state of living brought about by the global pandemic and the violence of US empire building and racial capitalism across the globe affords us the opportunity to uplift centuries of communal wisdom that abounds all around us. In this moment of mass anxiety at the loss of work and economic security, the uprisings in the US have expressed righteous anger stemming from five hundred years of US settler and imperial state violence built into this country's laws and ingrained in its culture. They also express outright refusal of continued abuse by a country built on the mass genocide of Black and Indigenous peoples. Indeed, the condition for the existence of US empire is genocide, including ongoing systems of slavery and settler colonialism and expansion, including US support for Israeli settler colonialism. In the pages to come, we will see how these conjoined histories brought us together as activists and writers committed to a decolonial feminist abolitionist vision. While brought about by tragedy, this moment offers a profound opportunity to restructure not only such things as how we work, shop, and travel but also how we fight for an abolitionist future and care for one another.

In this essay, we focus on what social movements committed to prison abolition can learn from one group of people in particular: mothers and caretakers trapped within the prison-industrial complex. First, we argue that the context of the COVID-19 pandemic, coupled with the mass mobilizations led by the movement for Black lives, affirm how racial capitalism and settler colonialism extend globally while reverberating back onto BIPOC lives and bodies in the US with distinct implications for people who mother. Second, we contend that mothering, defined broadly as the people conducting the labor of care, can light the way for our path forward, one that simultaneously dismantles the world of policing while building a world where policing and prisons are no longer necessary. Third, we uplift what we call "identification on behalf of the collective," where we map a liberated methodology that positions the authors' struggles as mothers in solidarity with system-impacted people who mother, people who are themselves advancing a relational model of care that disrupts neoliberal individuated modes of relating. Fourth, the work of those system-impacted people who mother gives us a blueprint of how to realize a revolutionary movement.

Indeed, the invisible histories of state violence, particularly US state violence against Black mothers, are long and deep. They reach back centuries from the rape and sexual assault of enslaved African women as a means for reproducing enslaved people in service to white capital to the killing of black mothers like Korryn Gaines, whom police killed in her own apartment in front of her two children. Bearing witness to their mother's murder through injustice and police violence, Korryn's children will no longer know their mother's loving embrace or have her to tuck them into bed at night.

The stories of these lives bring to stark light a chilling fact: people who do the labor of mothering are expected to accelerate the progress of capital and serve as nurturers for their family and community systems, all while enduring systematic targeting, including murder, by the same state apparatus from which they are fighting to protect their loved ones. As a result, mothers trapped within the prison-industrial complex in one way or another have been modeling what it looks like to integrate care work (often conceived of as "service") and political organizing as part of a collective, revolutionary project.[2] Yet all along, the labor, visions, and strategies of these very individuals tend to remain invisible within many social movements in ways we now have an opportunity to uplift and reconsider.

There has long existed in many of our organizing spaces a silent devaluing of the realm of reproduction,[3] including mothering and caretaking, whether biological or nonbiological. While those who are mothering attend, lead, and assume the responsibility of caretaker in organizing spaces, it is often true that our positions as anchors of our movements' micro-communities are overlooked and not actively engaged as assets. The increased neoliberal professionalization of organizing puts pressure on movements to focus on and respond to questions about the metrics of productivity, such as, How many actions can be executed, how many members are joining, and how many dollars can be raised in grant funding? Core principles of relationship-building and collaborative thinking suffer due to the need for more campaigns, more rallies, and more wins—understandable priorities. On the ground, social movement resistance to the neoliberal professionalization of activism reinstates the discrepancy in value between "political organizing" and "service" and has the effect of intentionally or unintentionally reinforcing the devaluing of mothering and caretaking forms of labor.

Yet, we are now at a time when protesters facing white supremacy, brutal militarized policing, and heightened economic devastation require strategies of collective care more than ever before—including "feeding, clothing, and housing each other and those in need in their community based on the principles of reciprocity and solidarity."[4] We are reminded that the strength of our movements is tied with the strengths of our relationships, the depth of our connectedness, and the necessity of mothering at home, in the streets, and beyond.

Here, we deploy what we call liberated research methodologies that connect our own life histories to the work we do with our organization Mamas Activating Movement for Abolition and Solidarity (MAMAS) and with people who have been incarcerated themselves or who have children currently or previously incarcerated. We define mothering as caring activities that have historically been specifically gendered as female/feminine, while we recognize that such caring work is not performed exclusively by those recognized as women or by those biologically related to those receiving care. *Ultimately, our goal is to affirm that the labor of mothering in the context of state violence operates as an inherently radical act, and that political organizing and care work (especially reproductive labor) involve a permeable, interconnected relationality necessary to the labor of abolishing the prison-industrial complex and creating the alternative society abolitionists have been calling for.*

LIBERATED RESEARCH METHODOLOGIES

We cofounded MAMAS in order to integrate the perspectives of people who mother into social movements, scholarly debates, media discussions, and policy processes about the systems that sustain US empire and white supremacy, including policing and prisons, immigration bans, and colonization and war. All along, we have integrated the scholarly component of MAMAS with the public-facing activist, media, and policy components through a set of liberated research methodologies. We operationalize liberated research methodologies to develop research through relationships of mutual trust, respect, and accountability with social movements and their needs and visions; produce research and analysis for the purposes of social change and abolition; and disrupt the power relationship between researchers and research participants.[5]

This essay is based on ideas that emerged within our working group on policing and prisons and interviews with working group members. The working group meets weekly (virtually during the global pandemic) as a space for healing and political strategizing. Our work intensified after COVID-19 began, when mother-survivors of police torture realized their loved ones were facing death in COVID-19-infested jails and prisons. Together, we integrate the voices of mother-survivors of police and prisons with social movements and protests, press conferences, and media debates about the impact of COVID-19 on prisoners and the violence of policing in Chicago. We have also been sharing stories and interviewing each other to consolidate collective wisdom about radical mothering into a framework that can contribute to theories and practices of abolition.

To affirm a process of (collective-relational-dialectical) knowledge production, we map and analyze both how the authors' life conditions contributed to the kinds of questions our research asks about mothering and abolition and the stories of mother-survivors of police torture. We recognize that nothing can fully dismantle the hierarchy between those of us authoring this essay and the people whose stories we write about. Yet we affirm that the authors' life stories and those of the mother-survivors we represent below amplify one another, and dialectically and relationally foster our collective theorization of radical mothering for the purposes of abolition. There is voluminous feminist literature on precisely this point. As in any research (although often denied by the violence of the academic-industrial complex / scientific objectivity), the historical and political conditions shaping the lives of the authors contribute as much to the production of knowledge as do the stories of the people the research represents.[6] By positioning our life stories (as authors) into our analysis, we also seek to challenge the often sensationalized and objectified realities of Black and brown mothers trapped in the prison-industrial complex. As authors and analysts, the conditions shaping our own lives have helped us enter this project through a politics of solidarity, as we will see below, and to affirm the often unrecognized but necessary movement labor conducted by mother-survivors of police torture. All of us are part of this story.

INSPIRATIONS

We draw upon key themes emerging out of the intersection of feminist abolition and Black feminist thought. Abolition studies has established that the problem of prisons extends within and far beyond prison walls. As Ruth Wilson Gilmore explains, the expulsion of individuals from their communities creates "greater instability in a community of people," especially since "households stretch from neighborhood to visiting room to courtroom, with a consequent thinning of financial and emotional resources."[7] In this sense, what takes place behind prison walls trickles down into neighborhoods and local families and communities. Therefore we refer to people who are mothering incarcerated people as survivors of prisons and police in their own right. As Mary L. Johnson, mother of Chicago police torture–survivor Michael Johnson stated, "As long as my son is doing life, I'm a lifer."[8] As survivors of police torture, the mental and physical health and economic realities of mother-survivors have been devasted by the police torture followed by the incarceration of their loved ones.

Abolitionist theories, specifically feminist abolition, have importantly insisted not only on the necessity of dismantling prisons but also on the necessity of building the alternative future society we want through everyday practices in our lives now. Feminist abolitionist activists and community organizers—like Alisa Bierria, Andrea J. Ritchie, Beth E. Richie, Mariame Kaba, Shana M. griffin, Lee Ann S. Wang, Shira Hassan, Kelly Hayes, and many more—established the significance of a politic that would both transform and care, dismantle and heal, based upon a collective commitment to guaranteeing the survival and care of all peoples.[9]

Their visions had everything to do with supporting people of color survivors of sexualized violence for whom relying on policing and prisons for justice only produced more harm. From this standpoint, Bierria explains, they worked toward "community-based strategies for safety, support, and accountability that [do] not rely upon police and prisons."[10] Bierria, referring to the work of Communities against Rape and Abuse (CARA), says they "collaborated with survivors and their communities to develop ideas for meeting those survival needs collectively, an effort that became known as community accountability or transformative justice."[11] Long before the term "abolition" became a common framework for working to end the prison-industrial complex, these scholar-activists committed not only to ending state and interpersonal violence but also to creating "a society based on radical freedom, mutual accountability, and passionate reciprocity."* Essential to our analysis is the idea that abolition is not only a political vision about ending prisons and police but also a practice committed to creating a new way of life that begins now. Alexis Pauline Gumbs, teaching us that abolishing the prison-industrial complex requires sustaining our

---

* See INCITE!'s "Statement on Gender Violence and the Prison Industrial Complex":

> We seek to build movements that not only end violence, but that create a society based on radical freedom, mutual accountability, and passionate reciprocity. In this society, safety and security will not be premised on violence or the threat of violence; it will be based on a collective commitment to guaranteeing the survival and care of all peoples.

INCITE! Women of Color against Violence, "The Critical Resistance–INCITE! Statement on Gender Violence and the Prison Industrial Complex," in *Abolition Now! Ten Years of Strategy and Struggle against the Prison Industrial Complex*, ed. CR10 Publications Collective (Oakland, CA: AK Press, 2008), 25.

communities, says, "If we can feed and sustain each other, we have less need to call on or depend on the state or the status quo. The knowledge that we have communities of support can awaken our bravery and ignite our imaginations for a transformed world." Gumbs adds, abolition "means freedom now and day by day. It means accountability and love growing everywhere."[12]

Writing in 2020, we take up how abolitionists have been uplifting the concepts of care work and mutual aid to capture the kinds of practices necessary for the alternative society we are striving for. Mariame Kaba, organizer, abolitionist, and founder of Project NIA, teaches us that "everything worthwhile is done with other people."[13] Dean Spade describes mutual aid as "when people band together to meet immediate survival needs usually because of a shared understanding that the systems in place are not coming to meet them, or not fast enough—if at all." Spade adds that individuals are most familiar with mutual aid efforts after a natural disaster like earthquakes or storms when people rescue each other or distribute food and water. However, other types of mutual aid efforts like childcare collectives, free food programs, community bail funds, and housing needs for formerly incarcerated individuals are essential to effect true change when the larger structures and systems we live under fail the most vulnerable among us.*

---

* Spade provides a clear distinction between solidarity and charity, explaining that solidarity / mutual aid is "when people get together to meet each other's basic survival needs and we can do it together RIGHT NOW!" Unlike charity, solidarity / mutual aid is a highly participatory process that builds people's ability to mobilize. Charity, on the other hand, is a passive nonparticipatory process in which rich people or social service organizations give resources to individuals in need, and typically that support is conditional or comes with stipulations. The major difference between solidarity and charity is that with solidarity the focus is on the issues with the systems/structures in place, not the individuals. Another idea we might integrate is the Black feminist tradition that understands violence multi-dimensionally—intimate and imperial, economic and emotional, around the world and around the corner. Engaging political work on multiple registers like this is central to the heart of mutual aid because it helps us reimagine our scope of responsibility to one another. Dean Spade, "Solidarity Not Charity: Mutual Aid and How to Organize in the Age of Coronavirus," interview (with Mariame Kaba) by Amy Goodman, *Democracy Now*, March 20, 2020, https://www.democracynow.org/2020/3/20/coronavirus_community_response_mutual_aid.

Black feminist thought inspires our theorization of politicized mothering. A widespread feminist idea is that mothering is an inherently oppressive practice mired in the patriarchal nuclear family and lacking in possibilities for resistance and agency. This widely held convention frames mothering and activism as inherently conflictual, as though mothering is merely an unfairly gendered burden that confines women to a depoliticized heteropatriarchal private sphere. In this analysis, mothers are merely extensions of their biological children.[14] Yet histories of slavery and the brutality of racial capitalism, including police violence, have intentionally targeted Black women's reproductive capacities and politicized Black motherhood. Many Black feminists have affirmed that mothering has never been a sentimentalized identity confined to the domestic heteropatriarchal space of the nuclear family. In the face of white supremacy and state violence, Black feminists like Patricia Hill Collins have asserted the significance of mothering beyond biology, or "other-mothering." Collins argues that mothering becomes a collective responsibility out of both the remaking of extended, multigenerational, African kinship structures among enslaved Africans *and* striving to protect and care for children targeted within collective struggles against racism.[15] Gumbs disaggregates motherhood from biology through her definition of revolutionary mothering as less of a gendered identity and more of "a possible action, a technology of transformation that those people doing the most mothering are teaching us right now."[16] Since Black women's reproductive labor has consistently been defined by the struggle to uplift Black people collectively in the face of racial domination, mothering entails both healing, caring, and loving while resisting oppression. As Audre Lorde explains, raising Black children "in the mouth of a racist, sexist, suicidal dragon" requires teaching love, resistance, and survival if one's children are going to survive.[17]

We are specifically inspired by the idea that Black mothering is not only politicized but also essential to the liberation of Black people. Angela Davis writes that without Black women, the movement against slavery would have been delayed, or not reached the result it did. They were a necessity to fight back because they had the ability to accomplish things men couldn't. Black women could raise the master's children, come to know the family, and fight back from inside the home. They thought of everyone—even once their freedom was gained, the next goal was to buy back the freedom of their family. After that, they had the same strength to fight the same battles as the men.[18] Lorde reminds us of the significance to both connect Black women across the world and commit to unbounding bio/cis/hetero/Eurocentric family formations. We too have witnessed what Lorde refers to as a global "history of the use and sharing of power." She explains this "sharing of power from the Amazon legions of Dahomey . . . to the economically powerful market-women guilds of present West Africa . . . [a] tradition of closeness and mutual care and support."[19] We believe, as Lorde teaches us, that the courage of all of those who mother to bring the fullness of our warrior spirits is embodied in dispossessed women all over the world who strategize clever and sustaining ways to resist and care for their loved ones with babies on their backs, both biological and nonbiological. Lorde described the pervasive language of governments as "calculated to reduce a Black nation's aspirations in the eyes and ears of white Americans."[20] We, as radical people who mother in solidarity with dispossessed mothers in other nations name the ways in which this language has reared its ugly head in the transnational spaces of Chicago. It relates to our mothering specifically as we have felt the subconscious subscription to heteropatriarchal politicization of mothering as a burden to the more urgent "work" of our organizing spaces and we have felt the cries of children as a delay to meeting progress and over time. Yet we have persisted to transform spaces so that they involve sharing food and childcare, having breaks at meetings, and placing children at the center. We hold these as values of care, all expanded by those who are mothering. Indeed, we have witnessed tactics of "care bears" at direct actions, jail support, cop watching, and the like as deeply interwoven with a politics of care passed down through our cultural sensibilities and our shared global histories as BIPOC armed with the necessity to always think of the collective.

This intervention is necessary at a juncture in history where distance and capitalist competition and individualism are increasingly pervasive.

Here, we demand that care be increasingly understood, as we've always understood it, as critical to our survival. Bringing the idea of politicized mothering and the necessity of mothering to resistance, Gumbs refers to revolutionary mothering as the "lifeforce toward the world we can only transform together." In this sense, our work uplifts the idea of activating mothering as a mechanism (or tool) of resistance.[21]

By bringing together abolitionist feminism and Black feminism, we propose the framework of radical mothering for abolition in order to recognize the conditions of state violence that inspire radical mothering and the kinds of care work that take the form of reproductive labor (such as raising and caring for children) that are necessary for both dismantling systems of prisons and policing and building alternative societies through our everyday life practices, rooted in connectedness, relationality, and love.

MOTHERING IS A RADICAL ACT

The authors of this text were activists before we were mothers. Our relationship to our biological children was not the impetus for our activism. Mothers can be politicized in many ways, not only in the heteropatriarchal ways mother-activists tend to be recognized—only in terms of their reproductive capacities, for instance, as mothers of martyrs or as faces/symbols/emblems of the land/nation. Our entry into mothering expanded the scope of our activism, inspiring relationships to mothering that were rooted in, while transcending, our relationship to our children. We map and analyze the conditions that led us to perceive radical mothering as an abolitionist strategy precisely because our own experiences and analyses are intertwined with those of our comrades, the mother-survivors of police torture we address above. Long before we began mothering our own children, each of us witnessed radical mothering across multiple global contexts.

Our commitment to mapping and analyzing radical mothering was born out of witnessing how mothering and activism enhance, rather than constrain, each other. Our commitment was born in the contradiction we recognized in the devaluing of reproductive labor in our organizing spaces despite its necessity to sustaining and expanding movement activities—from protests to sit-ins to mass mobilizations. This recognition inspired each of us to approach political organizing differently and to ultimately form our collective together. Here, we name and highlight the conditions that activated us into seizing the possibilities of radical mothering, many of which extend far beyond our own biological motherhood and are essential to imagining abolitionist futures. In this sense, we seek to disrupt the normative gendered concepts that attempt to define social movements—from "the radical man-hero" to the "woman as symbol of the nation" (whether mother of martyrs or emblems of the land or the people) and to affirm mothering itself as a radical act.

Johnaé Strong: As a Black woman, I was raised to see the connection between my family and the families around me, in each city I lived from Detroit, Michigan, to Shelby, North Carolina. Whether I was in Honduras or Ghana, Togo or France, the oppression of people of African descent across the globe resulting from global white supremacy and anti-Blackness was always clear and palpable. Living in the US for most of my life, I am always inspired by comrades who led the #FeesMustFall movement in South Africa when they said, "If you want to help Africa, dismantle the beast of Imperialism and White Supremacy in America."[22] I found hope in the collectives of Mamas and Babas and young people on the African continent who take care of one another as second nature. I realized the powerful notion of collectivism has not been lost. Now that I must consider my two young children and husband as I fight for a free society, whether subconsciously or consciously, this practice of interconnectedness has deepened my approach to organizing. Mainly, my children have awakened my first vocation in collective education and teaching.

One morning my daughter, Jari, woke up muttering, "I tried to broke the jail and I couldn't broke it." She is three years old. Sitting in the backyard in Chicago one afternoon, we saw the blue lights flashing down the street and my son, Akeim, became visibly upset and pushed himself under my arm for me to hold him. Akeim has been to almost every protest I participated in between 2013 and 2018 and knows the chants and songs by heart and has his own critical analysis of the police. More than that, he is seven years old and clings to his mother when he is afraid. It is with this lived experience, inspired by histories of collectivism across the African continent, that I come to the work in earnest for responses that span beyond a moment and solutions that can sustain a movement for liberation for my family, for your family, for all families.

Organizing for Black lives in Chicago reinforced my interest in alternative organizing strategies. On the anniversary of the death of Rekia Boyd, as a leader of Black Youth Project 100 Chicago chapter, I brought several members to support another organization in a noise action in front of the house of Dante Servin, the officer who murdered Rekia. In a matter of a half hour, my comrades and I were surrounded by three police cars full of cops, and a drunk Servin and his girlfriend came outside with a video camera. As several of our folks were triggered and yelled at Servin and the officers that "Rekia should be here," I heard officers demand we stop "being aggressive." Everything in my body clenched tight as I realized we could potentially not make it out of this situation alive; I could possibly not make it to my son Akeim. At 5'3" and 125 pounds, I shouted with every ounce of strength I could for all my folks to get into our cars and leave while we could. The ride home was silent and without words. I swore I would never risk myself or my children for anything I was not sure would lead to tangible and sustained liberation for my people. I came to believe that work is much less loud and positions healing justice, caretaking, and collectivist strategies to build up a community capacity beyond protest.

Souzan Naser: This work is deeply personal to me. I was born in Palestine and raised on the southwest side of Chicago, in the heart of one of the largest, concentrated Arab American communities in the US. I am a second-generation community activist who grew up in the ranks of the Arab Community Center. As a young girl I observed my parents' and their comrades' commitment to this center. Reproductive forms of labor, such as feeding each other, opening our homes to the movement, and caring for the sick and elderly were integrated into our strategies for building a base. I watched with a keen eye as these fierce fighters for justice dedicated their time and energy to advance both the social and political work of my community. As children, we learned our passion for Palestinian liberation from our elders who passed on sensibilities of hope and resistance to children. Our mothers and aunts especially enveloped young people into our community organizations through dance and other art-based programming.

They prepared me for my trips back home to Palestine and where I witnessed firsthand the violent and oppressive conditions that my people are living under—from Israel's use of mass incarceration to its systematic attacks on Palestinian women's bodies as an attack on Palestinian reproduction to caging my people behind walls and borders, all to further the US-backed, Zionist project of settler colonialism. Throughout my life, I saw Black struggle in the US as a mirror of what I witnessed back home. In Chicago, I have been involved in actively integrating the work of the US Palestinian Community Network with the struggle for Black lives. This connection has been decades in the making as Black and Palestinian movements have grown hand in hand.

Once I became a mother, my political commitment grew. I further cemented my determination to contribute to raising politically conscientious youth who will stand firm, rooted, and grounded in the liberation of Palestine and of oppressed people across the globe.

As people revolted against the depths of racial inequality in the US on June 5, 2020, thousands of miles away in Palestine, my people were revolting. US police violence against Black people and protesters continues to resemble Israeli state violence against Palestinians protesting the colonization of their land.

When I first met the mother-survivors of police torture through my work with MAMAS, I immediately understood the brutality of state-sanctioned violence that has been trickling down from the incarceration of their sons into their own everyday lives. Only five days after the murder of George Floyd, a thirty-two-year-old autistic Palestinian man, Eyad al-Hallaq, was shot and killed by Israeli police forces while walking to his special-needs school. Despite his caregivers' pleas—"He's disabled!" and "I'm with him!"—the Israeli forces shot him three times in close range with a rifle. Like US police who kill Black people, Israeli officers who murder Palestinians are rarely held accountable. From Palestine to Minneapolis, the demands to abolish overfunded, hypermilitarized racist forces—from the army to the police—are flooding the streets.

According to B'Tselem, a human rights organization in occupied Palestine, in the last ten years Israeli occupation forces have killed more than 3,400 Palestinians. Only five have been convicted.[23] In the face of one of the strongest militaries in the world, Palestinians have had enough—from land theft to restriction of movement, home demolitions, torture and brutal force, settler violence, and the impeding annexation of larger and larger swathes of their land, Palestinians are filling the streets in protest as I write. As I join protests for Floyd in Chicago, I catch a glimpse of their signs on my computer screen that read "I can't breathe since 1948" covered in photos of Floyd and Hallaq. I came into MAMAS haunted by the thought of Palestinian caretakers like Eyad's, holding up families and communities after state-sanctioned murder all the while empowered by the mothers and aunties who welcomed youth into political spaces and provided us with the hope and sense of community we needed to sustain our strength and our resistance.

Nadine Naber: Growing up in the Bay Area of California, on trips to my homeland, Jordan, a nation-state created out of the legacy of British colonization, I met my father's cousins, whose mothers had led leftist feminist movements, who were active in the Arab Women's Organization in Baqa Palestinian Refugee Camp, and had integrated women-led humanitarian and charitable work into the Palestinian struggle for liberation.[24] From these and other elders, I learned that one of the very purposes of militarized Jordanian authoritarian rule was to sustain the interests of US empire in the Arab region and North Africa, including the colonization of Palestine. I also learned that the labor of mothers and caregivers was essential to the first Palestinian Intifada, or uprising, beginning in 1987, not only as symbols of the nation but also on the front lines of resistance. At the time, I heard stories about mothers playing a central role in cooperatives, whereby the movement produced their own products while boycotting Israeli ones. Mothering forms of labor, such as baking goods or running schools and childcare centers, contributed to growing the collective consciousness that was essential to the continuation of the Intifada.

In California, among my large extended immigrant family, I witnessed mothers and aunties holding the community together while striving to protect us from the struggles that Arab immigrant communities faced. These included anti-Arab racism, and the real and imagined surveillance of our community in service of Israeli colonization and, later, the war on terror. My mother and the aunties who raised me modeled what it means to define one's individual needs and desires through those of the collective. In my twenties, I became active in a leftist Arab movement focusing on Palestinian liberation and ending the war on Iraq in coalition with BIPOC movements of the 1990s. There, with members of a small feminist collective, I developed a shared consciousness about how women and gender nonconforming people were conducting the reproductive labor necessary to sustain our movement's work. Yet this labor was only valued when we enacted masculinist forms of activism—giving speeches, leading marches, and writing statements. In retrospect, we realized that while we formed feminist collectives to uplift all forms of movement labor, we did not do enough to sustain the participation of women whose possibilities for activism were quelled by the experience of becoming a mother.

And yet caring and care work, made manifest through accountability to our communities, was foundational to the success of our activism. In my thirties, I spent many years coworking on INCITE!'s anti-militarism campaign in coalition with women of color organizing against the prison-industrial complex.* My anti-militarist comrades and I knew that the US bombing of Afghanistan would not liberate but further harm Afghan women. Similarly, those of us fighting to end policing and prisons understood that the criminal justice system provides no justice for survivors of gender violence, only disempowers, and alienates them.[25] INCITE!'s insistence on community accountability as an alternative to calling the police inspired my realization of the power that lies within all oppressed people to resist and reimagine

---

* Julia Chinyere Oparah, Alisa Bierria, Andrea J. Ritchie, Beth Richie, Shana M. griffin, and Mimi Kim, among others.

the society we want to live in. This became clearer to me than ever before when the Ford Foundation denied a $100,000 grant to INCITE! because of our anti-Zionist stance. Rather than compromising our solidarity with Palestinian liberation, we relied upon each other, building the resources our movement needed to thrive.

Yet my activism diminished after I entered the struggle called fertility. I eventually gave birth to two children while managing the pressures of state violence—from post-9/11 imperialist immigration bans impacting my life partner, an Egyptian immigrant and father of my children, to US-funded authoritarianism in Egypt that has been increasingly and violently targeting many members of our chosen family through torture, virginity testing, incarceration, and more in efforts to quell the Egyptian revolution. In 2011 my partner returned to Egypt for the revolution he and his Egyptian comrades had been fighting for. While I became "the mother who stayed behind with the kids" while he went to fight on the front lines, my mothering was never confined to domestic space. My politicized Arab identity necessitated politicized mothering. In one incident, I removed my African Arab toddler son from a daycare that blamed his typical toddler tendencies such as expressing frustration through biting or challenging disciplinary structures disproportionately targeting Black and Brown boys on our commitment to raise him bilingually. I also joined other mothers in a struggle to end celebrations of 9/11 "heroes" in schools that reinforce militarized patriotism and racism against Arab and Muslim schoolkids. All along, with feminist mothers from the Arab region and North Africa, we have been protecting our children from the virulent Zionist attacks that consistently physically, verbally, and virtually target us for speaking out against Israeli settler colonialism.

Becoming a mother, I found myself increasingly disconnected from the women of color and Arab leftist spaces that I had for so long considered to be my home. Reflecting on my life in Egypt in the early 2000s, I remembered how the children there were granted more attention and love within activist spaces and how family members and neighbors tended to share more childcare responsibilities. I started noticing how, back then, even some of the most self-identified radical feminist of color organizing spaces excluded people who mother from a central seat at the table. As the Hosni Mubarak regime used gender violence like virginity testing and mother-shaming of protesters (for example, as "bad mothers" who deserve to be punished), I realized that activist mothering can powerfully disrupt heteropatriarchal concepts. Activist mothering upends the trope of "the respectable woman who stays home to care for the nation's children"—a concept essential to sustaining militarized patriarchy. When the George Floyd protests broke out and Chicago mayor Lori Lightfoot raised the bridges to lock protesters downtown to arrest them for breaking curfew, I remembered the counterprotest strategy Egyptian authoritarians used to quell the revolution. I also recalled the many stories of my comrades of all genders who relied upon reproductive forms of labor to sustain the Tahrir Square sit-in. Biological mothering was not the impetus for their involvement (for example becoming a mother of a martyr). Yet I was inspired to rethink who "counts" as an agent of revolution, what kinds of movement labor matter, and what spaces are necessary for sustaining a revolution. After the fall of Mubarak, when a violent counterrevolution crushed the aspirations of millions for an alternative future, one lesson became clear: If we are going to launch a revolution here in the US, we are going to need a plan for the kind of society we want after we win.

Our work with MAMAS was born out of these histories and our interest in reframing whose work our movements will value and the relations of not just protest but care needed to sustain the spirit of revolution for longer than we ever did before.

THE POWER OF MUTUAL AID AND IDENTIFICATION ON BEHALF OF THE COLLECTIVE

Here, we focus on the stories of approximately ten people. Most participate in MAMAS's police and prisons working group and are caring for their sons who were physically or psychologically tortured by police into making false confessions. These individuals, Bertha, Denice, Rosemary, Regina, Armanda, Esther, Kathy, and Frank include biological mothers as well as fathers and friends and family members who participate in reproductive labor supporting police torture survivors. Most are Black and Latinx and two, who are responsible for mothering Matthew Echevarria, an incarcerated Puerto Rican man, are white. We also interviewed folks with incarcerated female family members (Bella). All these individuals identify as survivors of police and prison violence in their own right. We met these individuals while participating in activism related to prison abolition and ending police violence led by organizations like the Black Youth Project, the Campaign to Free Incarcerated Survivors of Police Torture, and the Chicago Torture Justice Center, and our work is indebted to the long-standing movements against police torture in Chicago and, especially, feminist and queer abolitionist organizing.*

For decades, the courts in Illinois, particularly the Circuit Court of Cook County, routinely disbelieved and dismissed survivors' allegations of torture. Yet after decades of organizing, a powerful movement won reparations for police violence and continues to demand justice around police violence and prison abolition.[26] Now Chicago is the only city in the US with a Torture Inquiry and Relief Commission (TIRC), an administrative agency put in place to provide torture survivors with an avenue to have their claims heard in court. At the same time, the purpose of TIRC remains largely unfulfilled due to the lack of investment in the necessary financial resources and human power to meet its mission and mandate. As a result, many torture survivors remain behind bars.[27]

Through our work together in MAMAS, we learned how mother-survivors of police violence in Chicago have been practicing collective care and mutual aid to survive and resist injustice for decades. While not everyone in our working group identifies as an abolitionist (partly due to the disconnect between movement leadership and survivors), their

---

* No list could ever capture this invaluable work over the years. We acknowledge all of the folks we have worked with and learned from, including, but not limited to: Andrea J. Ritchie, Joey Mogul, Alice Kim, Monica Cosby, Rachel Caidor, Beth Richie, Deana Lewis, Maya Schenwar, Kelly Hayes, Sangi Ravichandran, Aislinn Pulley, and organizations like Moms United against Violence, Love and Protect, and many more.

stories and strategies align with abolitionist conversations about the significance of care work to the struggle to end the systems of policing and prisons. We believe the reproductive labor of mother-survivors can light the path forward.

Regina Russell, mother of torture-survivor Tamon Russell, says when she first met Armanda, mother of torture-survivor Gerald Reed, she turned to her union brother, Joe, and whispered to him, "She's telling my story." Like Gumbs, who says, "Our survival and our healing is linked to yours,"[28] Regina describes feeling helpless and suffering in silence until she connected with Armanda's strength, which gave her permission to break her own silence and, for the first time, publicly share the story of what happened to her own son. Armanda says she is going to stay in the fight to release her son until the bitter end because there are so many others going through the same struggle.

While folks like Regina and Armanda call on their courage and use their voices to advocate and care for themselves, their children, the children of the other mothers, and all incarcerated people, they insist on the interconnectedness of care work and political organizing. This dual strategy has the effect of breaking down capitalist forms of isolation and individualism that take a disproportionate toll on their lives as they take on the state in a demand for justice.

JeNae Taylor, while working as the fellowship coordinator for the National Bailout Collective, talked with us about the power of connection between mothers impacted by incarceration:

> For them to embrace each other and be like "Yo! What's up?" and say "Hello" and introduce themselves because cages isolate us intentionally and for folks to have one experience [of] cages and be a part of the mass bailout and do a deep dive of political education to get answers to the questions they have answers to and to meet each other and anticipate the glow up it fulfilled at that moment—I will never forget. I think that is the coolest thing because we get to tear down isolation and be a part of fellowship together.

Connecting with each other provides nourishment and breaking the isolation that comes with living with the ripple effects of incarceration. Bella, founder of Sister Survivor Network and daughter to parents who were incarcerated, tells us she learns collective ways of being from her mother's incarceration: "What my mother and other folks she knows [who] have been incarcerated do is give themselves permission to see themselves in a different way, as valuable and not disposable. I want to follow in my mother's footsteps. She has never left any of her friends behind. I have had my mother's examples to show me that in real life and real time."

Indeed, building such a collective sense of self constitutes a challenge to neoliberalism's prioritization of the individual—and profit—over all else. Folks who work with MAMAS can model collective ways of being for each other and for anyone willing to look at incarceration through a critical lens. At the mercy of courts, and often excluded from access to adequate legal aid and information and excluded from professional networks connected to the criminal justice system, activists with MAMAS combine sharing knowledge as a practice of collective care and as political resistance.

Bertha Escamilla's son, torture-survivor Nick Escamilla, was released in 2008, but Bertha continues to collect data on the cases of all Chicago's torture survivors, including many who were tortured by cops whose violence is not yet publicly known and those who have yet to qualify for reparations. Mothers, loved ones, lawyers, researchers, and activists have all relied on the data she shares—including information on ninety-two cases of police violence—to seek justice. She investigates police reports, locates information about each case, contacts family members by phone or meets them at the courthouse, and explains to them what to do and what to look for. Reflecting on the need for collective information sharing and relationship building, Bertha explains, "We are put into this situation where we don't have any knowledge of what we're supposed to do. We're not educated to know about the law. We are factory workers or just driving a bus. We [mothers] encourage other mothers to look for things pertaining to their case, so they know what to ask the lawyers. We do this with a lot of the families." Forced to learn the law and figure it out collectively, Bertha and other activists with MAMAS replace a corporate, individualist system that depends on control over people and knowledge for the purposes of exploitation with a horizontal system of knowledge sharing for the purposes of resistance. In community, they are caring for each other and those behind bars through both emotional support and fighting for justice on the premise that organizing, and care, are simultaneously revolutionary. Here, collective care work is a way of life, born out of the realities of mothering while being targeted by prisons and police. Bella remembers how her mother, who served years in prison, continued to write letters to her still-incarcerated friends and their children after she was released. "I see a whole lot of women in my family who take on those roles. It's not really amplified in a way that a lot of other work is because it is not work for them. It is life."

Caring for incarcerated people extends far beyond the individual and far beyond biology to include extended relatives, friends, and neighbors as central actors in collective mothering and caretaking. Armanda describes how her work against state violence will continue long after her son, Gerald, is released from prison:

> I have had some people tell me when Gerald gets out your fight is over, but *no*, my fight is just beginning. Thinking about what I have been through and the people [who] were there to support me and thinking there are other men locked up in prison, some whose families are gone and, some of them, their mothers are no longer around. I talk to some of those young men out there in those facilities. Gerald puts me on the phone to talk to them because they have nobody else. That is what I am fighting for. He is not there by himself.

Esther Hernandez, whose sons are Juan and Rosendo, says she is fighting for everyone, not only her own child: "Every year in November we hold a potluck and fill out Christmas cards for all of them [people incarcerated with her sons]. The ones who are out tell me we are giving them hope. We are all here to fight for our loved ones. Together we have something to offer. All around Chicago, there is corruption with the police, and we want to let people know it is going on."

Indeed, folks connected to MAMAS care for many individuals to whom they are not biologically related. Kathy Wanek Levettman's best friend's son, Matthew Echevarria, is an incarcerated torture survivor. As Kathy puts it, "The thing is, I love him too now. I have my own personal relationship with him, that's why I don't drop out." Likewise, Bertha regularly visits and speaks to prisoners on the phone over a decade after her biological son's release: "I am involved with anyone who has loved ones incarcerated."

They work tirelessly not only to support those they love but also to send a message to the criminal justice system and to society more broadly. They reject narrowly conceived definitions of family and take collective responsibility for each other's children, caring and demanding justice all at once. When they show up in the courtroom for each other, they are deliberate about the message it sends, as Esther explains:

> The judges look at that. When judges see an empty courtroom, it could harm your case. I always tell people, "Let's go." Our community was a target by the corrupted cops, so our thing is to bring awareness. We like to support whenever there is a court hearing for the guys. We do rallies in front of the courthouse, and we want to expose these detectives for the corruption they have done. We want to bring our loved ones home and to expose these detectives for the corruption they have done. There are many of them.

This collective care work thus serves very practical purposes such as the sharing of information and resources, but it also has symbolic power. Being present to witness and support each other's struggles disrupts the 1950s heteropatriarchal-capitalist ideal of the "nuclear family"—and rejects the negative stigmatization of those who are incarcerated as well as those who love them. Caring for one another unleashes collective organizing power—whether it is by mobilizing people to show up in court or raising the political consciousness of people unaware of the racist and corrupt police and prison systems.

MAMAS LEADING THE WAY FORWARD

Nationalist, colonialist, and capitalist forces seek to devalue and exploit individuals, families, and communities; people who mother have long been targets of these systems because the caring work they do stand as obstacles to this process. In Chicago, mother-survivors share a fierce determination to collectively challenge repressive systems and corporate vultures who profit from incarceration. They nurture one another, declare their love for each other, and seek not only to bring their own children home but also to expose and protest the inhumanity of the entire prison system. As they integrate care and collective unity with resistance, they are a force to be reckoned with. While they stand on the front lines of the fight for future generations, social movements of all types would do well to let them lead by example.

Left-leaning social movement rhetoric often insists that "we are not a direct service organization," as if to imply that providing services and support is somehow disconnected from the loftier political goals of justice and liberation. Collective practices of mothering show that dismantling harmful structures like the prison-industrial complex must be an ongoing collective endeavor that recognizes the power and well-being of all sectors of our communities as essential resources. They show that mothering labor is movement work that must be nourished, uplifted, and contended with.

If the aim of abolition is to build another, better society and if the current surge of support for Black Lives Matter and for defunding and abolishing police make the violent injustices of capitalist control ever more visible, then we need a renewed commitment to horizontal politics, collective labor, and to recognizing the often invisible and highly gendered forms of work that enable social movements to survive and thrive.

The ultimate outcome of this current pandemic and today's mass uprisings remains unknown. One thing we have learned again and again, from contexts like #NoDAPL, Tahrir Square, and far beyond, is that protests against militarized state violence require care work if the movement—or the revolution—is going to survive. Today, masses of protestors wear masks and use distance when possible, and care for one another in an unprecedented situation of protesting during a pandemic, enacting the many ways of fighting for life while protecting life.

This time, we need to insist that no one takes for granted any longer the care work that has always been exceptionally urgent to our movements. Whether faced with extraordinary events such as natural disasters, political revolutions, virulent new diseases, or the mundane operations of violent institutions, the movement strategies of those who mother—centered on the integration of care work and political organizing—constitute some of the most urgently collective ways of being in the world. Indeed, the labor of mothering in the face of state violence is an inherently radical act.*

NOTES

1 Naomi Klein, "Movement Building in the Time of the Coronavirus Crisis: A Left Feminist Perspective on 21st Century Racial Capitalism in This Moment, with Rising Majority and Angela Y. Davis," recorded April 2, 2020, https://www.facebook.com/watch/live/?v=1001191156942525&ref=watch_permalink.

2 See Leyla Savloff, "Deviant Motherhood: House Arrest and Social Belonging in Argentina," *Social Text* 38, no. 1 (March 2020), 67–88. Savloff's study of an Argentinian arts-based collective for formerly and currently incarcerated women offers one recent example of the ways in which mothers impacted by incarceration mobilize radical forms of collective care as resistance to state violence. For additional work on radical care that resists neoliberal co-optation, see the full "Radical Care" issue of *Social Text* in which Savloff's article appears.

3 See Silvia Federici, "Social Reproduction Theory: History, Issues, and Present Challenges," *Radical Philosophy* 2, no. 4 (Spring 2019), https://www.radicalphilosophy.com/article/social-reproduction-theory-2.

4 "People's Strike and the Uprising: An Open Letter to All Forces Fighting for Our Lives," People's Strike, accessed June 22, 2020, https://peoplesstrike.org/peoples-strike-and-the-uprising-an-open-letter/.

5 Here, we draw upon Nadine Naber's "Liberate Your Research" workshops: Nadine Naber, "Liberated Workshops," accessed September 9, 2020, https://nadinenaber.com/liberate-your-research/.

6 For further feminist critiques of the academic-industrial complex, see Maria E. Cotera, "Women of Color, Tenure, and the Neoliberal University," in *Academic Repression: Reflections from the Academic Industrial Complex*, eds. Anthony J. Nocella II, Steven Best, and Peter McLaren (Chico, CA: AK Press, 2010), 328–36; Gabriella Gutiérrez y Muhs et al., eds., *Presumed Incompetent: The Intersections of Race and Class for Women in Academia* (Boulder, CO:

---

* We work from a number of important assumptions: That people who mother incarcerated individuals are survivors of gender violence, specifically reproductive injustice, given that the state violently denies them the ability to mother and to care for and protect their children; the criminal justice system blatantly covers up state violence by calling their mothering into question, assuming that unfit parenting is to blame for their child's "criminality"; the purpose of the criminal justice system is to serve and protect white supremacy and racial capitalism; and we have to care for ourselves and each other on the long road to justice.

University of Colorado Press, 2012); Sekile M. Nzinga, *Lean Semesters: How Higher Education Reproduces Inequity* (Baltimore: Johns Hopkins University Press, 2020); Andrea Smith, "Native Studies and Critical Pedagogy: Beyond the Academic-Industrial Complex," in *Activist Scholarship: Antiracism, Feminism, and Social Change*, eds. Julia Chinyere Oparah (formerly Julia Sudbury) and Margo Okazawa-Rey (New York: Routledge, 2009), 37–54.

Foundational feminist theorization on the influence of researcher positionality on knowledge production includes Patricia Hill Collins, "Learning from the Outsider Within: The Significance of Black Feminist Thought," *Social Problems* 33, no. 6 (1986): S14–S32; Donna Haraway, "Situated Knowledges: The Science Question in Feminism and the Privilege of Partial Perspective," *Feminist Studies* 14, no. 3 (Autumn 1988): 575–99; Sandra Harding, "Rethinking Standpoint Epistemology: What Is 'Strong Objectivity'?" in *Feminist Epistemologies*, eds. Linda Alcoff and Elizabeth Potter (New York: Routledge, 1993), 49–82; Nancy C. Hartsock, "The Feminist Standpoint: Developing the Ground for a Specifically Feminist Historical Materialism," in *Discovering Reality*, eds. Sandra Harding and Merrill B. Hintikka (Dordrecht, Netherlands: D. Reidel, 1983), 283–310; and Uma Narayan, "The Project of Feminist Epistemology: Perspectives from a Nonwestern Feminist," in *Gender/Body/Knowledge*, eds. Alison M. Jaggar and Susan Bordo (New Brunswick, NJ: Rutgers University Press, 1989), 256–72.

7 Ruth Wilson Gilmore, *Golden Gulag: Prisons, Surplus, Crisis, and Opposition in Globalizing California* (Berkeley, CA: University of California Press, 2007), 16.

8 Mary L. Johnson, "A Mother Confronts Police Torture in Chicago," PraxisCenter: Arcus Center for Social Justice Leadership, Kalamazoo College, November 30, 2015, http://www.kzoo.edu/praxis/a-mother-confronts-police-torture-in-chicago/.

9 INCITE! Women of Color against Violence, "The Critical Resistance–INCITE! Statement on Gender Violence and the Prison Industrial Complex," in *Abolition Now! Ten Years of Strategy and Struggle against the Prison Industrial Complex*, ed., CR10 Publications Collective (Oakland, CA: AK Press, 2008), 22, 25; Setsu Shigematsu, Gwen D'Arcangelis, and Melissa Burch, "Prison Abolition in Practice: The LEAD Project, the Politics of Healing, and 'A New Way of Life,'" in *Abolition Now*, 137.

10 Alisa Bierria, "BAR Abolition and Mutual Aid Spotlight," interview by Dean Spade and Roberto Sirvent, *Black Agenda Report*, May 13, 2020, https://www.blackagendareport.com/bar-abolition-mutual-aid-spotlight-alisa-bierria.

11 Alisa Bierria et al., "Taking Risks: Implementing Grassroots Community Accountability Strategies," accessed September 10, 2020, https://solidarity-us.org/files/Implementing%20Grassroots%20Accountability%20Strategies.pdf.

12 Liz Samuels and David Stein, eds., "Perspectives on Critical Resistance," in *Abolition Now*, 11.

13 Mariame Kaba, "Everything Worthwhile Is Done with Other People," interview by Eve Ewing, *Adi Magazine*, Fall 2019, https://adimagazine.com/articles/mariame-kaba-everything-worthwhile-is-done-with-other-people/.

14 Nadine Naber, "The Radical Potential of Mothering during the Egyptian Revolution of 2011," *Feminist Studies*, forthcoming, 2021.

15 Patricia Hill Collins, "Black Women and Motherhood," in *Black Feminist Thought: Knowledge, Consciousness, and the Politics of Empowerment* (New York: Routledge, 2000): 187–215; Audre Lorde, "Name of Essay," in *Sister Outsider* (New York: Crown Publishing, 2007), loc. 7783, Kindle edition.

16 Alexis Pauline Gumbs, "M/Other Ourselves: A Black Queer Feminist Genealogy for Radical Mothering," in *Revolutionary Mothering: Love on the Front Lines*, eds. Alexis Pauline Gumbs, China Martens, and Mai'a Williams (Oakland, CA: PM Press, 2016), 23.

17 Audre Lorde, "Man Child: A Black Lesbian Feminist's Response," in *Sister Outsider* (New York: Crown Publishing, 2007), loc. 4278, Kindle edition.

18 Angela Y. Davis, "Reflections on the Black Woman's Role in the Community of Slaves," *Massachusetts Review* 13, nos. 1/2 (Winter–Spring 1972), 81–100.

19 Audre Lorde, "Eye to Eye: Black Women, Hatred, and Anger," in *Sister Outsider: Essays and Speeches* (Berkeley, CA: Crossing Press, 2007), 151.

20 Audre Lorde, "Grenada Revisited: An Interim Report," in *Sister Outsider: Essays and Speeches* (Berkeley, CA: Crossing Press, 2007), 184.

21 Alexis Pauline Gumbs, "M/other Ourselves," 26.

22 Staff writer, "#FeesMustFall Leaders Explain What Decolonised Education Means," *Business Tech*, 2016, https://businesstech.co.za/news/trending/141333/feesmustfall-leaders-explain-what-decolonised-education-means/amp/.

23 Linah Alsaafin, "Family of Slain Autistic Palestinian Not Optomistic over Inquiry," Al Jazeera, June 3, 2020, https://www.aljazeera.com/news/2020/6/3/family-of-slain-autistic-palestinian-not-optimistic-over-inquiry.

24 See Nicola Pratt, "A History of Women's Activism in Jordan: 1946–1989," *7iber*, May 26, 2015, https://www.7iber.com/society/a-history-of-womens-activism-in-jordan-1946-1989/.

25 INCITE!, "The INCITE!–Critical Resistance Statement on Gender Violence and the Prison Industrial Complex," 2001, https://incite-national.org/incite-critical-resistance-statement/.

26 See "The Reparations Ordinance," Chicago Torture Justice Memorials, accessed June 22, 2020, https://chicagotorture.org/reparations/ordinance/. See also Joey Mogul, "Chicago Activists Obtain Reparations for Chicago Police Torture Survivors," *Guild Notes*, accessed June 22, 2020, https://www.nlg.org/guild-notes/article/chicago-activists-obtain-reparations-for-chicago-police-torture-survivors/.

27 See Alice Kim et al., *The Long Term: Resisting Life Sentences Working Toward Freedom* (Chicago: Haymarket Books, 2018) and Joey L. Mogul, Andrea J. Ritchie, and Kay Whitlock, eds., *Queer (In)justice: The Criminalization of LGBT People in the United States* (Boston, MA: Beacon Press, 2011).

28 Alexis Pauline Gumbs, "Freedom Seeds: Growing Abolition in Durham, North Carolina," in *Abolition Now*, 154. "I am because we are."

all incarceration
is family separation

Mon M, "All Incarceration Is Family Separation"

TEACHING ABOLITIONIST PRAXIS IN THE EVERYDAY

Qui Alexander

When I was twenty-four, I was invited to be a part of a transformative justice collective in my West Philadelphia neighborhood. At the time, I had no idea what transformative justice was or what a collective of folks "doing" transformative justice actually looked like. I learned that I was being invited to join a group of folks trying to figure out how to respond to sexual violence in our local community. Specifically, they worked with people who caused harm, to hold them accountable and help them change their behaviors.

I had so many questions. *So, you work with people who hurt people? Why not just call the police?* There was a part of me that knew why they didn't call the police. The same part of me that froze when I questioned if I should call the police while I watched domestic violence happen in my home. The part of me that understood that the police wouldn't make this situation better—they would only bring chaos to my family. I knew deep down the police were not safe, but I didn't know there was something we could do about it, or that the police could be the target of a community-centered critique. Through these community organizers, I began to learn about prison abolition, non-punitive community accountability, and strategies for responding to harm and violence without causing more harm and violence.

This collective, Philly Stands Up, invited me to *study*[1] with other queer folks who were working to embody an abolitionist praxis. This praxis is what Dylan Rodríguez refers to as a "fundamental critique of existing systems of oppression while *attempting to actively imagine as it practices forms of collective power that are liberated from hegemonic paradigms.*"[2] As both an analysis and practice, Rodríguez argues that this praxis is inherently pedagogical, teaching us how to create ways of being that transform our reliance on carceral state power and the logics that perpetuate it.[3] Being a part of Philly Stands Up taught me ways of enacting an abolitionist praxis in my everyday life. This embodiment of everyday practices of abolition—or abolitionist praxis—meant unlearning the ways we participate in a culture of punishment, exploitation, and individualism, in our own lives, in our relationships, and in our larger communities.

Praxis was particularly impactful to me as an educator. Abolitionist praxis challenged not only what I thought education was, but also what it meant to be an educator. Schools are rooted in the same carceral logics as prisons, so much so that many argue that schools are part of the larger nexus of the prison-industrial complex.[4] To enact an abolitionist praxis within the context of education is to challenge the very conception of what we understand education to be and who an educator is. The people, places, and experiences that taught me were never recognized in my formal education.

My formal education was extremely punitive while simultaneously teaching me that my education was the only thing that would prevent me, as a Black gender-variant person, from being incarcerated. Savannah Shange refers to this experience as carceral progressivism, defined as the "paradoxical dynamic in which multiracial social reforms succeed not despite, but through their collusion with antiblack logics of captivity and disposability."[5] It is through a carceral progressivist paradox that education is positioned as a solution to incarceration while simultaneously using police officers to enforce discipline and surveillance within school buildings as a measure of "safety."[6] Carceral progressivism posits education as a solution to societal oppression through "emancipating" students from enclosures, or what Shange calls "brick walls of disposability, punishment, and control,"[7] rather than abolishing the conditions that create those enclosures. In fact, as Damien Sojoyner argues, both schools and prisons function as enclosures of

Black life.[8] My own formal education enforced the carceral logics I seek to resist in my work.

I learned abolitionist praxis from folks committed to the liberation of queer and trans Black people; I learned from independently published community literature, like zines scattered in public and private spaces; or through passing conversations with comrades, outside of the bodegas lining the streets most often impacted by policing and prison. Because I was politicized outside of formal education spaces, my desire for understanding how people gain critical consciousness toward liberation is rooted in community organizing. Organizers have longstanding traditions of community education that foster critical consciousness—effectively addressing oppressive omissions in formal education that normalize power differentials within their own communities—through practicing radical forms of pedagogy in their homes, in community centers, and on street corners.[9] My pedagogy, and the pedagogies for which I advocate, are committed to abolitionist praxis. Such pedagogies perform a liberatory politic applied to theory, teaching, and other educative practices, both on and, especially, off campus.

In this essay I explore various practices of teaching an abolitionist praxis. This essay is composed of three sections. First, I theorize pedagogies of abolition, using a queer Black feminist approach to critical pedagogies outside of schools. Second, I perform pedagogies of abolition through narrative. Informed by everyday abolitionist praxes developed by the abolitionist organization Critical Resistance (CR), I tease out three praxeological drives through which to realize pedagogies of abolition in everyday life. And third, I close my essay, reflecting on the broader implications of pedagogies of abolition for Black trans educators like myself.

THEORIZING PEDAGOGIES OF ABOLITION

Abolitionist praxis is not limited to a onetime event; it is something that is embodied in the everydayness of life; enacted through our relationships to self and others.[10] Abolitionist praxis is a place where abolitionist commitments and practices come into conversation.[11] As CR members argue, abolition is both a vision and a strategy for liberation, something we are working toward (the abolition of interlocking systems of oppression) as well as a method we enact to get there (the creation of anti-oppressive cultures).[12] It is both a political orientation as well as an everyday practice that works to transform ourselves, our relationships, and our communities.

My abolitionist commitments are rooted in the Black radical tradition, and more specifically a queer Black feminist lens.[13] Queer Black feminism as defined by the Combahee River Collective in their 1977 statement is a framework that works toward the liberation of all oppressed people, rooted in the experiences of Black women, understanding that the systems of oppression that oppress Black women—including but not limited to racism, sexism, heterosexism, and classism—are interlocking. Queer Black feminism seeks to develop an analytic that understands how the synthesis of those oppressions impact the everyday lives of Black women and gender nonconforming folks. M. Jacqui Alexander names what a queer Black feminist praxis enacts: an understanding of how our sociopolitical contexts impact our everyday lives. Alexander writes, "One of the earliest lessons we have all learned from feminism is that the personal is political: the insight that some of the most infinitesimal details of our lives are shaped by ideological and political forces much larger than our individual selves."[14] In short, queer Black feminisms have sought to abolish the interlocking sociopolitical systems of oppression and domination (particularly, racial capitalism, imperialism, and patriarchy) that shape the material experience of Black women and gender nonconforming folks. These abolitionist commitments inform my intellectual positionality within an abolitionist praxis.

Black feminist educator bell hooks has argued that education as a practice of freedom "connects the will to know with the will to become."[15] Building on Paulo Freire's conceptualization of liberatory education, hooks asserts that education is most useful when it connects ideas being taught with student's actual life experiences, aiding them in their own "struggle for self-actualization."[16] For hooks, engaged pedagogy requires educators to commit to self-actualization and to participate in the shared labor of knowledge production within the spaces they facilitate.

hooks's approach challenges the carceral logics of the teacher as the all-knowing overseer, writing, "I do not expect students to take any risks that I would not take, to share in any way that I would not share."[17] Her argument demonstrates that education as a practice of freedom requires a practice of vulnerability from both student and teachers, something that a culture of punishment is not conducive to. This engaged pedagogical approach works to create new ways of being that actively resist the reliance of carceral logics embedded within systems of schooling. Engaged pedagogy is not limited to formal educational settings; it can be applied to any setting that holds space for collective transformation. Abolitionist praxis teaches us that spaces for collective transformation can manifest anywhere there is a commitment to resist and transform the (carceral) logics of state power.

What are the practices that teach us to create these new ways of being? What pedagogies help us embody an abolitionist praxis? What are the pedagogies of abolition that (already) exist in our communities? These questions lead me to explore the notion of pedagogies of abolition or the practice(s) of teaching an embodied abolitionist praxis, to better understand Black trans people's lived experiences of surviving and resisting the carceral state. Our Black trans embodied experiences exist within the matrix of the interlocking systems of oppression that abolition seeks to transform. As folks who sit at the intersections of race, class, and gender oppression, our subjugated knowledges offer unique insights in recognizing not only how pedagogies of abolition manifest, but also what they produce for our lives.* I seek to center the embodied wisdom that comes from living in the everydayness of these oppressive structures that are very specific to the bodies that experience them.

As a queer Black trans person studying education, I struggle to integrate the lessons of abolitionist struggles in my communities into the

---

* I use the term "subjugated knowledges" in the tradition of Patricia Hill Collins, who wrote in her pathbreaking book, *Black Feminist Thought: Knowledge, Consciousness, and the Politics of Empowerment*, "Subjugated knowledges, such as Black women's culture of resisitance, develop in cultural contexts controlled by oppressed groups (2000).

rigid bounds of academic inquiry. By examining pedagogical practices only in formal education spaces, I am left frustrated by the neoliberal approaches to teaching that continue to reform inherently flawed structures to maintain the status quo. Formal systems of schooling were not liberatory places for me, so I began to look for liberatory praxis outside of those spaces. For guidance, I look to feminist thinkers like Angela Davis, who has grounded her intellectual work within a larger anti-prison political struggle, including her work with CR.

CR articulates three praxeological drives toward transformative action that work in service of abolition across pedagogical contexts—both in and out of the classroom. These drives are crafted to dismantle systems of oppression, to change cultural practices/logics that perpetuate those systems, and to build the resources and alternative structures to support the type of world in which we want to live. I pick up these drives, devised outside of the academy, to consider the ways everyday practices of resilience and resistance against the state teach us how to embody an abolitionist praxis. To accomplish this, I will explore three pedagogical practices I have engaged outside of formal education spaces, that have taught me how to embody commitments to dismantle, change, and build. Those pedagogical practices are: politicization, healing justice, and speculative fiction—all of which have taught me how to better embody an abolitionist praxis.

PERFORMING PEDAGOGIES OF ABOLITION

Politicize

Politicization is a process of developing a critical analysis of systematic oppression and learning how it impacts the lives of people living within those systems. Understanding the ways in which systems of power and oppression impact one's everyday life creates an analysis of those systems that can only be developed by interrogating where one sits within them. Paulo Freire's liberatory praxis is a practice through which one begins to understand being oppressed, not as a pejorative descriptor but as a positionality within a larger structure of power. Freire writes,

> To surmount the situation of oppression, people must first critically recognize its causes, so that through transforming action they can create a new situation, one which makes possible the pursuit of a fuller humanity. But the struggle to be more fully human has already begun in the authentic struggle to transform the situation.[18]

Understanding how one is situated within systems of power is the beginning of dismantling one's own assumptions and beliefs about how power operates in the world. Neoliberal schooling does not teach about the ways systematic oppression defines our sociopolitical lives, but community organizers have used politicization as a tool to build critical consciousness and address the gaps of formal education within their communities.[19]

As a Black Puerto Rican, I draw my own understanding of politicization from the lineage of the Young Lords Party (YLP). The YLP was a youth-led, Black Puerto Rican organization largely modeled after the Black Panthers, based primarily in New York with smaller local chapters in other major cities around the country. The YLP spoke out against the government for ignoring the needs of their communities and actively worked to address those needs themselves. These initiatives included free breakfast programs, health screenings, and political education. The main purpose of political education was to help community members understand what it meant to be an oppressed person within a global system of injustice.

The YLP politicized their community members largely through their newspaper, *Palante*. An excerpt from the newspaper reads,

> Bullets and bombs aren't the only ways to kill people. Bad hospitals kill our people. Rotten forgotten buildings kill our people. Garbage and disease kill our people. And the schools kill our people. Inefficient administrators + racist uncaring teachers + overcrowded classrooms + irrelevant curriculums + old, lying textbooks + an attitude of "don't ask too many questions" + a prison atmosphere = genocide (the mass killing [of] people). But students and parents everywhere are rising up against these conditions. We understand that by herding us into these brainwashing centers, our enemy is trying to kill our desire to learn, to destroy our ability to get the

> skills and knowledge we need to fight a society that needs us only for cheap labor and manpower for its racist wars against other Third World people.[20]

The YLP recognized that the public school system did not teach young people to think about their own identities, let alone teach them about systems of oppression that their schools normalized through exclusionary curricula. The YLP used politicization to teach their communities that the Puerto Rican identity is political and that their everyday lives were directly impacted by the effects of racial capitalism and imperialism. They used this to mobilize community members toward liberatory action that often looked like serving their community in ways the government neglected. By meeting the basic needs of their communities (food, shelter, healthcare, and more), their action/service was rooted in self-determination for Puerto Rican people and liberation from their dependence on the US government.

Politicization for the YPL was part of a radical practice of *dismantling.* By politicizing their community members, they worked to dismantle their community's need to depend on institutions that oppress them. Their collective action worked to dismantle these institutions' power within their community, ultimately working to transform their conditions. Politicization, as a pedagogical practice, teaches us that dismantling the systems of power creates the conditions in which oppressed people can begin to work toward liberation.

Freire argues that, for the oppressed, understanding oppression as something that is possible to transform must become "the motivating force for liberating action."[21] One must understand their positionality to transform their conditions. This recognition shifts how the experience of being oppressed is understood. Carceral logics perpetuate the individualistic idea that our circumstances are a consequence of being "bad people." An abolitionist praxis can help us realize ourselves as part of a community that is collectively targeted by systems of subjugation. This shift toward understanding the experience of "being oppressed" as a positionality in which one is targeted as a member of a collective by virtue of their identity, rather than a consequence of one's own individual inadequacy, opens the possibility to transform that positionality. My own politicization as a Black Puerto Rican trans person taught me how to recognize carceral logics at play by helping me understand the sociopolitical power structures that shape our cultural practices. A practice of learning to dismantle larger systems of oppression and domination in my everyday life is crucial to learning to embody an abolitionist praxis.

Healing Justice

Changing cultural practices and beliefs that are rooted in and perpetuate the systems of oppression we are working to dismantle requires healing and transformation of the impacts of trauma in our lives, on both an individual and collective level. Healing and transforming this trauma can happen through a practice of healing justice. Cara Page and Susan Raffo, two foundational healing justice practitioners, assert, "Healing justice refers to an evolving political framework shaped by economic and racial justice that re-centers the role of healing inside of liberation that seeks to transform, intervene and respond to generational trauma and violence in our movements, communities and lives and to regenerate our traditions of liberatory and resiliency practices that have been lost or stolen."[22] Healing justice is an explicitly political framework that prioritizes healing within our liberatory movements for justice. Page and Raffo contend that if we seek to respond to harm and violence in our communities without causing more harm, we must intentionally and deliberately tend to the impacts of trauma.

Healing justice has existed in the homes and communities of Black and brown, queer and trans folks, long before it became a politicized framework. Healing exists not only on a physical level but simultaneously on emotional, mental, and spiritual levels. Non-Western ways of knowing incorporate a resonance between the body and the mind, and that mental, emotional, and spiritual distress can manifest as physical ailments. Therefore, healing is never just a practice of treating the body but also treating one's mind and spirit.[23] Therefore, transforming our conditions requires healing from the hurt and the trauma of being oppressed so that our transformation is not from oppressed to oppressor, as Freire teaches us, but to a liberated subject.

Healing justice gives us an opportunity to think about the healing in justice and the justice in healing.[24] This framework is the foundation for systems of mutual aid that are not dependent on the medical-industrial complex or other larger institutions that prioritize profit over people. The medical-industrial complex only makes room for healing in ways that are predetermined by Western colonial constructs based on addressing illness, rather than focusing on wellness.[25] Healing justice offers a framework to understand how systems of oppression impact both our thinking and our bodies. Our bodies hold the memory and trauma of violence done to not just us but also to our ancestors and lineages. As Raffo argues,

> Our bodies, our communities, our memories carry all the times when we experienced or witnessed violence, systemic disrespect, or marginalization. When we are working together to change systems and beliefs, we are also carrying the fallout from those systems and beliefs inside ourselves. . . . Ending oppression means ending how it exists in our communities and in the systems around us—and it means ending how it lives within our bodies.[26]

The impact of trauma and violence on our lives, both individually and collectively, influence how we can integrate the work of change into our lives. Living in a punitively driven society leads us to internalize carceral logics to some extent. Healing justice teaches us how to address our internalized and collective trauma to transform the logics we use to shape our relationships and communities.

Healing in this regard can happen in numerous ways, but healing justice considers the somatic work needed to change the cultural practices we seek to transform. When our bodies are given opportunity to rest and restore, something oppressed people are not often afforded, we begin to understand our experiences as more than just our material conditions. Our bodies offer us information about how we are processing what is happening in our world. When we shift what is happening in our bodies, it allows us to change our perceptions and actions. Rather than continue enacting the logics of punishment and shame, we can move from a place of care and understanding.

Healing justice teaches us that we must also tend to our bodies and spirits if we want to unlearn carceral logics embedded within our everyday lives. Raffo explains that what we are holding in our bodies "affects how deeply we can dream and how far we can vision."[27] Trauma that lives in our bodies can impact our own capacity to vision a life outside of the trauma we've experienced. Healing justice works as a pedagogical practice that teaches us how to embody this change.

Speculative Visioning

In order to build new possibilities for addressing harm without relying on the state, we must actively practice visioning. Arguing that our ability to build a new world grounded in justice and liberation requires us imagining it into existence, Walidah Imarisha writes, "When we talk about a world without prisons . . . we are talking about a world that doesn't currently exist."[28] Imarisha's view challenges us to build the capacity of our imaginations, or what Mia Mingus refers to as "flexing" our imagination muscles.[29] With adrienne maree brown, Imarisha asserts that any organizing we do in order to create a world that abolishes systems of dominance and oppression is a project of speculative or visionary fiction. They write, "Visionary fiction encompasses all of the fantastic with the arc always bending towards justice. We believe this space is vital for any process of decolonization because the decolonization of the imagination is the most dangerous and subversive form there is: for it is where all other forms of decolonization are born. Once the imagination is unshackled liberation is limitless."[30] These thinkers teach us that imagination is essential to an abolitionist praxis and visionary fiction gives us, in their words, "permission to move beyond that edge" of what we think is possible. This speculative practice allows people to reject the prison-industrial complex as a solution to societal problems and imagine ways to genuinely address harm in our communities.

What would it look like if we had a world that didn't spin on the existence of / require poverty, exploitation, or violence? What would it feel, smell, taste like if the folks who were most impacted by systems of oppression got to live their lives outside of those confines? What would liberation look like if we all had access to it? Speculative fiction gives us a set of tools to imagine our lives beyond the prison and the logics that legitimize it. While imagination is not something that is often encouraged in current school systems that emphasize "rationality" and "objectivity," it is precisely the skill we need to challenge ideas of conformity and control. If one cannot imagine themselves existing in a different set of circumstances, how can they ever make it a reality? Building alternatives and resources for the world we want to live in requires tangible change that can only come to life if we imagine those alternatives and resources first. Our visions of the future can only be as strong as our practice of imagination. By growing our capacity to vision, we create the space needed to bring us closer to understanding what liberation looks like.

CONCLUSION

These three practices have been instrumental in my own work to embody an abolitionist praxis. As a queer Black trans person, my embodied experiences exist within the matrix of the interlocking systems of oppression that abolition seeks to transform. Black trans folks' subjugated knowledges, as folks sitting at the intersections of race, class, and gender oppression, offer unique insights in embodying an abolitionist praxis. Thinking of politicizing, healing justice, and speculative fiction as *pedagogies of abolition* recognizes the embodied wisdom that comes from living in the everydayness of the oppressive structures we hope to abolish. These methods created by Black, queer, and trans communities to survive and resist the carceral state continue to teach us how to *dismantle* systems of oppression, to *change* cultural practices/logics that perpetuate those systems, and to *build* the resources and alternative structures to create the world in which we want to live.

hooks defines being a feminist as having an active practice of anti-sexism by working to eradicate sexist ideas and actions, emphasizing that feminism, as a political position informed by both ideology and practice, must transform our own internalized sexism and misogyny.[31] I believe an abolitionist praxis requires a similar commitment. While this call to action can (and should) be taken up by any (and every) one, I argue this praxis has specific implications for folks whose bodies and lives sit at the intersection of gender, race, and class oppression. Queer Black trans experiences offer a way of reading race, class, and gender at work; a method of recognizing the contradictions and complexities of living in a white supremacist, capitalist, (cis)heteropatriarchal world, a world built in ways structurally that oppress Black trans folks. Black trans people are not only disproportionately victims of violence but are also disproportionately policed and incarcerated.[32] Therefore, our investment in abolition is essential to our liberation.

In a Sunday school session hosted by the organization Dream Defenders, Angela Davis asserted,

> If we want an intersectional perspective, the trans community is showing us the way. . . . The trans community taught us that it is possible to effectively challenge that which is considered the very foundation of our sense of normalcy. If it is possible to challenge the gender binary, then we can certainly effectively resist prisons, jails, and police.[33]

The embodied experience of queer Black trans folks works a pedagogy for liberation by teaching us how to radically transform our world. While I encourage my accomplices to take up these practices to work in service of Black liberation, I urge you to let queer Black trans folks steward this work. Abolition is a call to usher in a new world, and Black trans people are not afraid of that world. We have been craving it, we have been praying for it, we been dreaming about it.* We share the dreams of our ancestors, aching and yearning for a new world order, and we are ready to bring it to fruition.

BIBLIOGRAPHY

Agid, S., et al. *The CR Abolition Organizing Toolkit*. Oakland, CA: Critical Resistance, 2004.

---

* See, for example, the prayers and testimonials from the powerful collection *The Black Trans Prayer Book*, edited by J Mase III and Dane Figueroa Edidi.

Alexander, M. J. *Pedagogies of Crossing: Meditations on Feminism, Sexual Politics, Memory, and the Sacred*. Durham, NC: Duke University Press, 2006.

Aviles, A. M., E. R. Dávila, and R. D. Benson. "City of Wind, City of Fire: Education and Activism in Chicago, 1966–1975." *International Journal of Critical Pedagogy* 10, no. 2 (2019): 35.

Bassichis, M., A. Lee, and D. Spade. "Building an Abolitionist Trans and Queer Movement with Everything We've Got." In *Captive Genders: Trans Embodiment and the Prison Industrial Complex*, 2nd ed., edited by E. A. Stanley and N. Smith, 21–46. Chico, CA: AK Press, 2015.

Carruthers, C. *Unapologetic: A Black, Queer, and Feminist Mandate for Radical Movements*. Boston: Beacon Press, 2018.

Collins, P. H. *Black Feminist Thought: Knowledge, Consciousness, and the Politics of Empowerment*. New York: Routledge, 2000.

Combahee River Collective. "A Black Feminist Statement." *Women's Studies Quarterly* 42, no. 3/4 (Fall/Winter 2014): 271–80.

Davis, A. Y. *Are Prisons Obsolete?* New York: Seven Stories Press, 2003.

Dream Defenders. *Sunday School: Abolition in Our Lifetime*, 2020, https://www.youtube.com/watch?v=RtpRiAoIoy4.

Dumas, M. J. "'Waiting for Superman' to Save Black People: Racial Representation and the Official Antiracism of Neoliberal School Reform." *Discourse: Studies in the Cultural Politics of Education* 34, no. 4 (2013): 531–47. https://doi.org/10.1080/01596306.2013.822621.

Edidi, D. F., and J. Mase III. *The Black Trans Prayer Book*. Lulu Press, 2020.

Enck-Wanzer, D. *The Young Lords: A Reader*. New York: NYU Press, 2010.

Freire, P. *Pedagogy of the Oppressed*. New York: Seabury Press, 1970.

Gumbs, A. P. "Freedom Seeds: Growing Abolition in Durham, North Carolina." In *Abolition Now! Ten Years of Strategy and Struggle against the Prison Industrial Complex*, edited by CR10 Publications Collective. Chico, CA: AK Press, 2008.

Harney, S., and F. Moten. *The Undercommons: Fugitive Planning and Black Study*. New York: Minor Compositions, 2013.

hooks, bell. *Teaching to Transgress: Education as the Practice of Freedom*. New York: Routledge, 2004.

———. *Feminism Is for Everybody: Passionate Politics*. 2nd ed. New York: Routledge, 2014. https://doi.org/10.4324/9781315743189.

Imarisha, W. "Rewriting the Future: Using Science Fiction to Re-envision Justice." Bitch Media, no. 66 (Spring 2015). https://www.bitchmedia.org/article/rewriting-the-future-prison-abolition-science-fiction.

Imarisha, W., and adrienne maree brown. *Octavia's Brood: Science Fiction Stories from Social Justice Movements*. Chico, CA: AK Press, 2015.

Imarisha, W., et al. "The Fictions and Futures of Transformative Justice: A Conversation with the Authors of *Octavia's Brood*." *New Inquiry*, April 20, 2017. https://thenewinquiry.com/the-fictions-and-futures-of-transformative-justice/.

Kelly, E., et al. "Philly Stands Up!: A Portrait of Praxis, an Anatomy of Accountability." In *Beyond Survival: Strategies and Stories from the Transformative*

Justice Movement, edited by L. L. Piepzna-Samarasinha and E. Dixon. Chico, CA: AK Press.

Love, B. L. *We Want to Do More Than Survive: Abolitionist Teaching and the Pursuit of Educational Freedom*. Boston: Beacon Press, 2019.

Meiners, E. R. "Ending the School-to-Prison Pipeline / Building Abolition Futures." *Urban Review*, 43, no. 4 (2011): 547–65. https://doi.org/10.1007/s11256-011-0187-9.

Morales, A. L. *Medicine Stories: Essays for Radicals*. Durham, NC: Duke University Press, 2019.

Page, C., and S. Raffo. *Healing Justice at the US Social Forum: A Report from Atlanta, Detroit and Beyond*, 2011. Available at https://www.susanraffo.com/blog/healing-justice-at-the-us-social-forum-a-report-from-atlanta-detroit-and-beyond.

Piepzna-Samarasinha, L. L., and E. Dixon, eds. *Beyond Survival: Strategies and Stories from the Transformative Justice Movement*. Chico, CA: AK Press, 2020.

Raffo, S. "What Is Healing Justice and How Would It Affect This Gathering?" Susan Raffo blog, December 2017. http://susanraffo.blogspot.com/2017/12/what-is-healing-justice-and-how-would.html.

Raffo, S., C. Page, and A. Taneja. "Healing Histories: Disrupting the Medical Industrial Complex." Susan Raffo blog, September 2019. https://www.susanraffo.com/blog/healing-histories-disrupting-the-medical-industrial-complex-1.

Robinson, C. J. *Black Marxism: The Making of the Black Radical Tradition*. Zed Books, 1983.

Rodríguez, D. "Abolition as Praxis of Human Being: A Foreword." *Harvard Law Review* 132, no. 6 (2019): 1575–1613.

———. "The Disorientation of the Teaching Act: Abolition as Pedagogical Position." *Radical Teacher* 88, no. 1 (Summer 2010): 7–19. https://doi.org/10.1353/rdt.2010.0006.

Shange, S. *Progressive Dystopia: Abolition, Antiblackness, and Schooling in San Francisco*. Durham, NC: Duke University Press, 2019.

Sojoyner, D. M. "Black Radicals Make for Bad Citizens: Undoing the Myth of the School to Prison Pipeline." *Berkeley Review of Education* 4, no. 2 (2013): 241–63. https://doi.org/10.5070/B84110021.

———. *First Strike: Educational Enclosures in Black Los Angeles*. Minneapolis: University of Minnesota Press, 2016.

NOTES

1 S. Harney and F. Moten, *The Undercommons: Fugitive Planning and Black Study* (New York: Minor Compositions, 2013).

2 D. Rodríguez, "Abolition as Praxis of Human Being: A Foreword," *Harvard Law Review* 132, no. 6 (2019): 1612.

3 D. Rodríguez, "Disorientation of the Teaching Act: Abolition as Pedagogical Position," *Radical Teacher* 88, no. 1 (Summer 2010): 7–19, https://doi.org/10.1353/rdt.2010.0006.

4 E. R. Meiners, "Ending the School-to-Prison Pipeline / Building Abolition Futures," *Urban Review*, 43, no. 4 (2011): 547–65, https://doi.org/10.1007/s11256-011-0187-9; S. Shange, *Progressive Dystopia: Abolition, Antiblackness, and Schooling in San Francisco* (Durham, NC: Duke University Press, 2019); D. M. Sojoyner, "Black Radicals Make for Bad Citizens: Undoing the Myth of the School to Prison Pipeline," *Berkeley Review of Education* 4, no. 2 (2013): 241–63, https://doi.org/10.5070/B84110021.

5 Shange, *Progressive Dystopia*, 157.

6 Meiners, "Ending the School-to-Prison Pipeline."

7 Shange, *Progressive Dystopia*, 55.

8 Sojoyner, "Black Radicals."

9 A. M. Aviles, E. R. Dávila, and R. D. Benson, "City of Wind, City of Fire: Education and Activism in Chicago, 1966–1975," *International Journal of Critical Pedagogy* 10, no. 2 (2019): 35.

10 L. L. Piepzna-Samarasinha and E. Dixon, eds., *Beyond Survival: Strategies and Stories from the Transformative Justice Movement* (Chico, CA: AK Press, 2020).

11 P. Freire, *Pedagogy of the Oppressed* (New York: Seabury Press, 1970).

12 S. Agid et al. *The CR Abolition Organizing Toolkit* (Oakland, CA: Critical Resistance, 2004).

13 C. Carruthers, *Unapologetic: A Black, Queer, and Feminist Mandate for Radical Movements* (Boston: Beacon Press, 2018); Combahee River Collective, "A Black Feminist Statement," *Women's Studies Quarterly* 42, no. 3/4 (Fall/Winter 2014): 271–280; A. Y. Davis, *Are Prisons Obsolete?* (New York: Seven Stories Press, 2003); A. P. Gumbs, "Freedom Seeds: Growing Abolition in Durham, North Carolina," in *Abolition Now! Ten Years of Strategy and Struggle against the Prison Industrial Complex*, ed. CR10 Publications Collective (Chico, CA: AK Press, 2008); bell hooks, *Teaching to Transgress: Education as the Practice of Freedom* (New York: Routledge, 2004); B. L. Love, *We Want to Do More Than Survive: Abolitionist Teaching and the Pursuit of Educational Freedom* (Boston: Beacon Press, 2019).

14 M. J. Alexander, *Pedagogies of Crossing: Meditations on Feminism, Sexual Politics, Memory, and the Sacred* (Durham, NC: Duke University Press, 2006), 283.

15 hooks, *Teaching to Transgress*, 19.

16 hooks, *Teaching to Transgress*, 17.

17 hooks, *Teaching to Transgress*, 21.

18 Freire, *Pedagogy of the Oppressed*, 47.

19 M. J. Dumas, "'Waiting for Superman' to Save Black People: Racial Representation and the Official Antiracism of Neoliberal School Reform," *Discourse: Studies in the Cultural Politics of Education* 34, no. 4 (2013): 531–47, https://doi.org/10.1080/01596306.2013.822621; A. M. Aviles, E. R. Dávila, and R. D. Benson, "City of Wind, City of Fire."

20 D. Enck-Wanzer, *The Young Lords: A Reader* (New York: NYU Press, 2010), 127.

21 Freire, *Pedagogy of the Oppressed*, 49.

22 C. Page and S. Raffo, *Healing Justice at the US Social Forum: A Report from Atlanta, Detroit and Beyond*, 2011, 3, available at https://www.susanraffo.com/blog/healing-justice-at-the-us-social-forum-a-report-from-atlanta-detroit-and-beyond.

23 Alexander, *Pedagogies of Crossing*; A. L. Morales, *Medicine Stories: Essays for Radicals* (Durham, NC: Duke University Press, 2019).

24 People's Movement Center, n.d.

25 S. Raffo, C. Page, and A. Taneja, "Healing Histories: Disrupting the Medical Industrial Complex," Susan Raffo blog, September 2019, https://www.susanraffo.com/blog/healing-histories-disrupting-the-medical-industrial-complex-1.

26 S. Raffo, "What Is Healing Justice and How Would It Affect This Gathering?" Susan Raffo blog, December 2017, http://susanraffo.blogspot.com/2017/12/what-is-healing-justice-and-how-would.html.

27 S. Raffo, "What Is Healing Justice?"

28 W. Imarisha, "Rewriting the Future: Using Science Fiction to Re-envision Justice." Bitch Media, no. 66 (Spring 2015), https://www.bitchmedia.org/article/rewriting-the-future-prison-abolition-science-fiction.

29 W. Imarisha et al., "The Fictions and Futures of Transformative Justice: A Conversation with the Authors of Octavia's Brood," New Inquiry, April 20, 2017, https://thenewinquiry.com/the-fictions-and-futures-of-transformative-justice/.

30 W. Imarisha and adrienne maree brown, *Octavia's Brood: Science Fiction Stories from Social Justice Movements* (Chico, CA: AK Press, 2015), 4.

31 bell hooks, *Teaching to Transgress: Education as the Practice of Freedom* (New York: Routledge, 2004).

32 M. Bassichis, A. Lee, and D. Spade, "Building an Abolitionist Trans and Queer Movement with Everything We've Got," in *Captive Genders: Trans Embodiment and the Prison Industrial Complex*, 2nd ed., eds. E. A. Stanley and N. Smith, 21–46 (Chico, CA: AK Press, 2015).

33 Dream Defenders, *Sunday School: Abolition in Our Lifetime*, 2020, https://www.youtube.com/watch?v=RtpRiAoIoy4.

TOOLS FOR BUILDING DREAM WORLDS THAT SERVE US

A REVIEW OF *FUMBLING TOWARDS REPAIR* BY MARIAME KABA AND SHIRA HASSAN

Xhercis Méndez

In 2020 the national and transnational Movement for Black Lives (M4BL) coupled with a global pandemic laid bare the antiblackness, white supremacy, and structural racism that have been constitutive of capitalism and its militaristic arm of policing since their inception. The pandemic, which brought the settler-colonial economy of the United States to a grinding halt, and then a reluctant "reopening" has made the ever-growing degrees of economic disparity painstakingly visible. Moreover, it has underscored the fragility of capitalism and its inability to sustain us through crises as millions continue to lose their jobs and get evicted from homes as the weight of racialized capitalism continues to endanger and take its toll on our essential workers and most vulnerable communities and families.

However, in the midst of all this devastation, the M4BL has functioned as a beacon of hope illustrating to the world the power and abolitionist visions of Black feminist and queer, trans, and nonbinary organizing. The movement has reached a tipping point with coordinated calls to defund the police and the "people's budget" demanding that those resources be reinvested in areas that contribute to Black life and well-being.* The call to abolition is a battle that has long been fought, one that has its roots in enslaved Africans' resistances to slave catchers, and one that continues to include a confrontation with current modes of policing as well as the prison-industrial complex and its imbrication with global armed forces and increasing militarization. As more people find themselves compelled to consider a world without policing, in a context of produced instability, there seems to be a growing sense that we have been taught to over-rely on violent state systems to resolve social problems and have become deskilled in the process. This is where Mariame Kaba and Shira Hassan's workbook, *Fumbling Towards Repair: A Workbook for Community Accountability Facilitators* (AK Press, 2020), offers an incredibly grounded and praxical intervention focused on building up facilitators' skills, relationships, and capacities to address harm within our communities so that we become less reliant on violent state systems while simultaneously imagining and cocreating a world without prisons.

The authors of this workbook, Kaba and Hassan, are two longtime organizers, practitioners, and facilitators of community accountability and transformative justice processes. While Kaba and Hassan arrive to this work via different routes, both as survivors and facilitators, they each have witnessed firsthand the ways in which policing has either escalated the harm to or further endangered already systematically marginalized communities seeking assistance thus leading to what Ruth Wilson Gilmore has described as state-sanctioned premature death.[1] Given the ways in which accessing police has not been a viable option for either of them, Kaba and Hassan instead have contributed their energies to facilitating community accountability processes with the vision of minimizing the violence and addressing the conditions that enable it in their communities for the next generation to come. Their more than fifteen years of experience as facilitators coordinating complex community accountability (CA) processes and navigating all their nuanced challenges form the foundation of this workbook.

---

* To learn more about the Movement for Black Lives see https://m4bl.org/policy-platforms, and the People's Budget Campaign, https://m4bl.org/week-of-action/tuesday/.

Kaba and Hassan inform readers early on that the workbook is primarily intended for current and future facilitators already familiar with community accountability and transformative justice. It is an incredibly rich offering to facilitators invested in organizing responses to harm, beyond the state, particularly focused on survivors of sexual assault, intimate-partner violence, and gender-based violence. This is significant because these are some of the most pervasive and persistent forms of harm in communities and some of the most oft-used justifications for maintaining the system of policing and the prison-industrial complex in the name of "public safety."

Particularly notable is the humility with which Kaba and Hassan share their experiences, suggestions, strategies, and tools, the tenor of which is captured by the very title of the workbook, *Fumbling Towards Repair.*[*] The workbook opens with framing thoughts by both authors as well as disability justice and transformative justice organizer Mia Mingus,[†] who reminds readers that transformative justice and community accountability are full of "complicated stories" and that we must redefine what success looks like by tuning into what others might dismiss as "small victories." In her opening statement, Hassan shares that "the workbook is hard-won knowledge, and it comes from my own experiences and the experiences of those I love—some of whom did not survive violence. It's the workbook I wish I'd had 15 years ago, and it represents the culmination of many mistakes. It's intended to be pushed back on, improved, and re-written by the next group of people who figure out how to adapt the work for their times." Kaba echoes Hassan's invitation to this work by reminding readers that the workbook is a product of "hard lessons" learned through "trial and error" and that what she is offering is "not a dictate or THE LAW" but rather "a way to give back some of what [she has] been gifted by

* I want to extend my gratitude to friend and fellow transformative justice practitioner Donna Harati for sharing her experiences utilizing the workbook, and for her particular attentiveness to the humility and grace with which it was offered.

† To learn more about Mia Mingus's work and the Bay Area Transformative Justice Collective see https://leavingevidence.wordpress.com. There you will find more resources, such as pod mapping and apology templates, that also contribute to transformative justice and community accountability.

experience and the generosity of others." Their opening statements reflect their larger collective philosophy about the work of abolition, which includes being committed to generosity in the face of human error and an invitation to continue to try new things and be creative about intervening in harm because we have no ready-made models for how best to proceed. It is this philosophy that guides not only their work but also the construction of their workbook and the incredible lessons offered throughout.

The workbook is organized into three key areas that include color-coded banners to visually assist in identifying activities, resources, and examples and thought-provoking quotes that are beautifully illustrated by Molly Costello and Rachel Hoffman. The first area, "Key Frameworks That Inform This Work," lays the foundation by offering readers working definitions and concrete examples of core debates and concepts such as the differences between victim and survivor, as well as the distinctions that need to be considered in relation to trauma-informed practice, harm reduction, healing justice, prison-industrial complex abolition, transformative justice, and CA. Not only are many of the definitions crowdsourced from other facilitators and community organizers, but each subsection ends with an activity geared to provide facilitators an opportunity to clarify and refine their own definitions of these core frameworks in response to what they have just read. As a result, the workbook activates a form of call-and-response, thus inviting readers to cocreate with its authors. One highlight in this section is the Q&A resource on common questions raised about police and prison abolition drafted by Dean Spade, which briefly stages reframing responses to those concerned with what we do about "the murderers, rapists, and sociopaths."[2] In addition, this section of the workbook is replete with values that empower facilitators to be patient, ask for help when needed, and embrace the "messiness" of this work.[3]

However, this is not to suggest that community accountability and transformative justice processes have no structure. On the contrary, one of the exciting resources concluding the first section is the "Ten Guiding Questions for Any Community Accountability Process," which serves to emphasize Kaba's opening statement that a key ingredient for an effective process is "*assessment* of the overall situation and assessing our own capacity and skills."[4] This resource sets readers up for the second key area, titled "Food for Thought in Facilitating CA Processes." Section A in this area of the workbook provides facilitators an opportunity to assess themselves, their capacities, and skills through a series of activities designed to, for example, gauge levels of empathy and listening abilities. Section B continues this exploration by presenting readers with a series of vexing issues that are part and parcel of CA processes. For example, how can a facilitator discern between the more carceral logic of punishment and consequences that result from a harmful action? This question matters because, as the authors suggest, transformative justice processes ideally would not seek to reproduce a punishment model of justice if abolition is the goal. However, recognizing that these lines are often blurred during a CA process, Kaba and Hassan present readers with a range of gray areas that are not meant to be resolved but rather to be kept as open and ongoing questions that allow facilitators to hone their skills and instincts. Throughout this section, Kaba and Hassan share useful tools such as the disposability versus the boundaries or natural consequences chart, the interpersonal conflict analysis form, and the public apology template. In Section C, the authors turn to some of the more technical aspects of holding a CA process, where they share their recommendations for how to organize key roles and create support teams. Throughout this section they provide samples of everything from meeting preparation checklists and agenda templates to sample contracts for people who have been harmed and social media tips.

The final area of the workbook is filled with a series of activities for facilitators to do on their own or with others with whom they seek to build teams or community. Significantly, this section implicitly reminds facilitators that they are not outside of these processes but must also practice transformation and accountability daily. The activities in this area focus on self-reflection and building emotional intelligence through journaling, art, and circle practice. The section culminates with a case study, "When Everybody Is a Survivor," that affords facilitators an opportunity to sit with the complexity and ambiguity that characterize many of these cases.[5] It is a particularly powerful note to end on because it challenges readers to consider the role of mental health, such as post-traumatic stress disorder, and to resist the impulse to place people into the neat binary categories of "survivor" and "perpetrator" within these processes. More importantly, it serves as a moving example of how facilitators or support teams can reflect on, learn, and recover from missteps as we all fumble toward repair.

Altogether, the workbook underscores the intentionality, commitment, and love with which Kaba and Hassan approach the work of abolition and community accountability. Throughout the text they weave in the insights of abolitionist thinkers and community organizers and point us to the contributions of many of those whom they have learned from along the way, thus modeling their belief that we do not do this work alone and we cannot change things by ourselves. Kaba and Hassan conclude the workbook by rallying us to "get magical!" so that even if we do not have the resources we need in this moment, we remember that it is up to us to "dream the world we want to create."[6]

NOTES

1 Ruth Wilson Gilmore, "Race and Globalization," in *Geographies of Global Change*, 2nd edition, ed. P. J. Taylor, R. L. Johnstone, and M. J. Watts (Oxford: Blackwell, 2002), 261.

2 Mariame Kaba and Shira Hassan, *Fumbling Towards Repair: A Workbook for Community Accountability Facilitators* (Chico, CA: AK Press, 2020), 17–20.

3 Kaba and Hassan, *Fumbling Towards Repair*, 39.

4 Kaba and Hassan, *Fumbling Towards Repair*, emphasis added.

5 Kaba and Hassan, *Fumbling Towards Repair*, 150–54.

6 Kaba and Hassan, *Fumbling Towards Repair*, 153.

Tabitha Arnold, "seachange," 2020

CONTRIBUTORS

Qui Alexander is a queer, trans, Black Puerto Rican scholar, educator, and organizer. They are currently an assistant professor of gender, sexuality, and trans studies in curriculum and pedagogy at OISE, University of Toronto. Their work and scholarship centers queer Black feminist praxis, Black trans studies, political education, transformative justice, and abolition. Grounded in their experiences as a community organizer, Qui views their scholarship as a place to articulate the cultural work they do in relation to their communities. Believing education is a practice of freedom, Qui strives to center personal and collective transformation in every educational space they hold and cocreate.

Alisa Bierria is a Black feminist philosopher and an assistant professor in the Department of Gender Studies at UCLA. Her writing can be found in numerous scholarly journals and public anthologies, including her coedited volume, *Community Accountability: Emerging Movements to Transform Violence*, a special issue of *Social Justice*. She has been an advocate within the feminist anti-violence movement for over twenty-five years, including cofounding Survived & Punished, a national abolitionist organization that advocates for the decriminalization of survivors of domestic and sexual violence.

Jakeya Caruthers is an assistant professor of English and Africana studies at Drexel University. Her research attends to Black political aesthetics within twentieth- and twenty-first-century cultural production as well as race, gender, sexuality, and state discipline. Jakeya is a principal investigator of an inside-outside research initiative with Survived & Punished California that maps pathways between surviving gender violence, incarceration, and radical possibilities for survivor release. She is also collaborating on a digital archive of feminist decriminalization campaigns waged over the last fifty years.

Rosalie Donaldson-Kronenbuerger is a trauma therapist and parent of two. The author resides as a settler in Tkaronto.

Romina Garcia is a doctoral candidate in the Department of Ethnic Studies at the University of California, Riverside. As a doctoral student, Romina's research focuses on examining the structural and administrative anti-Black violence that encompasses women of color, in particular Black women within anti-violence work. She is a founding member of CARA (Critical Anti-Violence Research and Action), which is a UC-based collective that converges thought and action to end racialized gendered violence through an abolitionist and decolonial feminist approach.

Ren-yo Hwang (they/them)'s community-based scholarship examines late-twentieth-century carceral technologies, abolition, transformative justice, and QTBIPoC anti-violence activism. Hwang's first book, *Trans of Color Entrapments: Carceral Coalitions and Identitarian Violence,* follows the emergence of hate crimes, community policing, and gay/trans jailing in 1980s Los Angeles. Their scholarship is published or forthcoming in *QED: Journal of GLBTQ Worldmaking, Foucault Studies, Transgender Studies Quarterly,* and *Critical Ethnic Studies Journal.* They are an assistant professor of gender studies at Mount Holyoke College.

Jessica Issacharoff is a mitigation specialist with the Louisiana Capital Assistance Center. She holds a BA in history and English from Grinnell College and a PhD in literature from Duke University. Jessica has also organized with local and national labor and civil rights organizations in Durham, North Carolina, and New Orleans, Louisiana. Before starting at LCAC she was a postdoctoral fellow in law and society at the Newcomb Institute at Tulane University, completing research on women's incarceration.

Colby Lenz is a long-term advocate with the California Coalition for Women Prisoners and the Transgender Advocacy Group, and a cofounder of Survived & Punished, a national organizing project to end the criminalization of survivors of sexual and domestic violence. Colby has twenty years of experience in grassroots organizing, community-engaged research, and policy advocacy addressing the intersections of criminalization, incarceration, and gender-based violence. Colby is deputy director of policy and community research at the UCLA Center for the Study of Women.

Brooke Lober is a social movement scholar, researching legacies of anti-racist and anti-Zionist feminisms in the Bay Area and teaching courses in gender and women's studies at UC Berkeley. Brooke is the coeditor of a special issue of the journal *Sinister Wisdom* (Fall 2022), which gathers stories and interviews from Out of Control: Lesbian Committee to Support Women Political Prisoners, a group whose activities spanned twenty-five years. Brooke's writing is published in the scholarly journals *Feminist Formations*, *Women's Studies*, the *Journal of Lesbian Studies*, *Meridians*, and *Abolition* and on numerous websites of radical culture.

Kayla Marie Martensen (she/her) is a doctoral candidate at the University of Illinois, Chicago, in the Criminology, Law, and Justice Department and an instructor at Loyola University, Chicago, where she teaches classes related to punishment, race, gender, and social justice. Her areas of interest include critical carceral studies, feminist abolition, prison abolition, gender violence, and youth studies. Currently, Kayla's research focuses on the intersection of punishment and service, where she critiques expansion of carceral logic and practice into community agencies and "nonpunitive" residential placements.

Dayjha McMillan (they/she) is a dreamer and schemer, committed to the lifelong practice of playing as a healing endeavor. A Leo sun, Aquarius moon, they are always striving to understand "balance" and how it appears in their daily passions. They self-created an interdisciplinary focused BA titled Law, Diversity and Justice: Critiquing the American Dream using Critical Race Theory, Counternarratives, and Feminist Theory, with a minor in education and social justice. Dayjha is currently in the Community Impact Fellowship in Seattle, Washington, working with WA-BLOC (Washington Building Leaders of Change), an all-woman, majority-Black-led grassroots organization, and finishing up an internship with KEXP, a local radio station.

Xhercis (Sir-sis) Méndez is an associate professor and vice chair of women and gender studies and queer studies and a founding member of the Collective for Justice, Equity and Transformation at Cal State University, Fullerton. She works with faculty, staff, students, and administrators to identify the root causes of harms such as microaggressions, relationship violence, and campus sexual assault, creating actionable pathways toward accountability and healing. Her writings include titles such as "Beyond Nassar: A Transformative Justice and Decolonial Feminist Approach to Campus Sexual Assault" and "Notes Toward a Decolonial Feminist Methodology: Revisiting the Race/Gender Matrix." Beyond the academy, she works with various community organizations and serves as a consultant, facilitator, and strategist to organizations seeking to address systemic harm, racism, and anti-Blackness.

Mark Mullkoff is a narrative therapist, DJ/producer, and a father. The author resides as a settler in Tkaronto.

Nadine Naber is an award-winning author, public speaker, and activist. She is a professor at the University of Illinois and directs the project Liberate Your Research. She has authored or coedited five books. She cofounded Arab and Muslim American studies at the University of Michigan; the Arab American Cultural Center at the University of Illinois; and the organizations the Arab Women's Solidarity Association North America and Mamas Activating Movements for Abolition and Solidarity.

Souzan Naser was born in Palestine and raised on the Southwest Side of Chicago, in the heart of one of the largest Arab American communities in the US. She is a second-generation community activist who dedicates her time to the board of the Arab American Action Network and the US Palestinian Community Network, and she cofounded Mamas Activating Movements for Abolition and Solidarity. Souzan works as a counselor and associate professor at Moraine Valley Community College, where she has won awards for her work increasing diversity on campus.

Whitney Richards-Calathes is an artist, writer, researcher, organizer, and transformative justice practitioner. Receiving her PhD from the Graduate Center at the City University of New York, Whitney has focused her work on intergenerational relationships between Black women and girls and how they make home while navigating punishment systems. In addition to academic work, Whitney is a community researcher, collaborating with organizers in participatory, creative, and justice-oriented projects. Whitney is from the Bronx and loves the ocean.

Andrea J. Ritchie is a Black, lesbian, immigrant survivor who has been documenting, organizing, advocating, litigating, and agitating around policing and criminalization of Black women, girls, trans and gender nonconforming people for the past three decades. She is the author of *Invisible No More: Police Violence against Black Women and Women of Color* and coauthor of *Say Her Name: Resisting Police Brutality against Black Women*, *Queer (In)Justice: The Criminalization of LGBT People in the United States*, and *No More Police: A Case for Abolition*. She cofounded the Interrupting Criminalization initiative with Mariame Kaba, as well as the In Our Names Network, a network of over twenty organizations working to end police violence against Black women, girls, and trans and gender nonconforming people. She currently hosts the Invest/Divest Learning Communities at the Community Resource Hub and supports dozens of organizations across the US working to divest from policing and invest in community safety.

Red Schulte (they/them) is a community organizer and zine maker. They helped organize the Justice for Alisha Walker Defense Campaign, are a collective member of Hacking//Hustling, and are a founding member of the Support Ho(s)e collective and of Bluestockings Cooperative. They formerly organized with cherished comrades of Survivors against SESTA (which sunset active organizing in July 2018), Survived & Punished NY, and Red Canary Song.

Hyejin Shim has over a decade's experience in supporting survivors of domestic and sexual violence, particularly immigrant, refugee, queer/trans, and criminalized survivors of abuse. Her work includes grassroots community organizing as well as formal direct service work in domestic violence and sexual assault agencies. She is a cofounder of Survived & Punished, a national organization dedicated to supporting criminalized and incarcerated survivors of gender-based violence.

Tamara Lea Spira (she/her) is an associate professor of queer studies with a joint appointment in American cultural studies and Fairhaven College of Interdisciplinary Studies at Western Washington University, and she is a former University of California President's Postdoctoral Fellow. Her writings can be found or are forthcoming in venues including *Radical History Review*, *Boundary2*, *Identities*, *Feminist Theory*, *Feminist Formations*, *NACLA Journal of the Americas*, the *Feminist Wire*, *Feminist Studies*, *Signs*, and *E-misférica*. Dr. Spira's first book, *Movements of Feeling: Feminist Radical Imaginations in Neoliberal Times*, is under contract with University of Washington Press. Her second book, on queering reproductive justice and family abolition, is under contract with the University of California Press.

Madi Stapleton (she/her) is an independent scholar based in Kansas City, Missouri. She holds an interdisciplinary BA in critical race feminist and queer studies from Fairhaven College. Her areas of interest include biopolitics, reproductive justice, and feminist/queer literature. She is currently working on two projects: one analyzing Lorraine Hansberry and Pat Parker's literary critiques of the medical-industrial complex, and another tracing the politics of land, queer masculinity, and attachment through the film *Brokeback Mountain*.

Johnaé Strong is a writer, healer, and creative based in Chicago, Illinois. She has a background in education and international studies and has spent the past ten years in social movement organizing. Her work integrates political education, healing, and organizing with a focus on Black girls. Her greatest work is her children: Akeim and Jari. Johnaé is on all social media @strong_visions.

Verónica N. Vélez is an associate professor in secondary education and education and social justice. Her research focuses on Latinx im/migrant mother activism, community-based participatory action research in grassroots contexts, popular education, and (re)imagining cartographic tools for movement building and critical inquiry. Alongside Dr. Daniel Solorzano, she codeveloped Critical Race Spatial Analysis, a framework and methodological approach that seeks to deepen a spatial consciousness and expand the use of geographic information systems (GIS) in critical race research in education. Her work has been published or featured in *Women and GIS: Mapping Their Stories*, *Educational Forum*, *Harvard Educational Review*, the *High School Journal*,

Association of Mexican American Educators Journal, Educational Foundations, Seattle University Journal for Social Justice, Contemporary Justice Review, and *Race, Ethnicity, and Education.*

Alisha Walker (she/her) is an artist, advocate for criminalized survivors and sex workers, and a current member of the Support Ho(s)e Collective. As a formerly incarcerated person, she has also organized alongside formations such as Love & Protect, Survived & Punished, and Moms United Against Violence & Incarceration.

Lee Ann S. Wang is an assistant professor of Asian American studies and social welfare at UCLA. Her writing and collective practices center feminist thought and relational ways of being and knowing, with critical inquiry into the racial assemblages of gender violence, policing, and immigration law.

ARTIST BIOS

Tabitha Arnold is a visual artist and political organizer. Born in Chattanooga, Tennessee, she now lives and works in Philadelphia. Her meticulous, tactile images speak to the radical past and ongoing struggle that threads all working people together. Arnold's textiles have traveled to exhibits in Baltimore, Pittsburgh, and Philadelphia, including the Woodmere Museum and the Pennsylvania Academy of Fine Art. In 2020, her touch-interactive tapestry, "Our Sutured City," was highlighted in the international ALT. CTRL showcase at Game Developers Conference, San Francisco. Her work was recently profiled in *Hyperallergic* and *Lux Magazine* and featured on the cover of *Dissent* magazine. She was the 2021 artist in residence at Glen Foerd, where her work is now on view.

kai lumumba barrow (born in 1959, Chicago) lives and works in New Orleans. Interested in the praxis of Black radical imagination, she works at the intersection of art and activism. Experimenting with an abolitionist vernacular, barrow's paintings, installations, and sculptures transgress ideological and carceral borders. For more information see, www.kailbarrow.com.

Yola Gómez is a first-generation, queer, xicanx, nonbinary femme activist and writer. Growing up on the US-México border, their activism and writing grew out of personal experiences with racism and violence. Yola is a felon with assault on an officer charges and former sex worker who has sought to use their experiences as a means to agitate, educate, and organize others. In 2019, Yola graduated with an MFA in creative writing from Oregon State University. Soon after, in 2020, they won Flying Ketchup's Hybrid

Manuscript Award for their unpublished book *We've Always Been Weeping* and *Searching for the Dead*. Their work has been featured in *Puro Chicanx Writers of the 21st Century* and the forthcoming anthology *Weeping Women: The Haunting Presence of La Llorona in Mexican and Chicanx Lore*. Their work appears in literary journals including *Entropy*, *Nat.Brut*, *Utterance*, and *Cutthroat*. Despite their publication record, Yola defines themself as an academic outsider and literary saboteur, keeping their sights set on abolition.

Shana M. griffin is a Black feminist activist, researcher, sociologist, artist, abolitionist, and mother. Her practice is interdisciplinary, research-based, activist-centered, and decolonial, centering the experiences of Black women most vulnerable to the violence of poverty, incarceration, polluted environments, reproductive regulation, economic exploitation, housing discrimination, and climate change. Shana is the founder of PUNCTUATE, a feminist research, art, and activist initiative, and creator of DISPLACED, a multimedia public history project tracing the geographies of Black displacement in New Orleans. Her latest projects are SOIL, which interrogates the carceral spaces of what is left behind in and on the grounds of sugarcane plantations through archival research, soil collection, and photography and the initiative, "Theirs Was a Movement without Marches," which documents the narratives of low-income Black women organizing in public housing and the abolitionist strategies they employed in their work.

Inés Ixierda is a queer Mestizx interdisciplinary artist, cultural worker, and community organizer in Oakland, California, unceded Ohlone Land.

Mon M is an Indian illustrator, writer, and abolitionist feminist organizer based in Lenapehoking, now so-called Brooklyn. Their work focuses on supporting organizers with art for promotions, fundraisers, and posters, and features comics, landscapes, and animations. They are a coauthor of "8 to Abolition" and now organize for an end to the borough-based jails plan in NYC and support the National No New Jails Network, as well as the Sick of It Disability Inside/Outside Pen Pal Project. The defense of survivorship, and the intimate relationship between carceral systems and bodies, particularly those belonging to queer and trans people, have been an integral part of shaping their politics.

Shellyne Rodriguez is an artist, educator, writer, and community organizer based in the Bronx. Her practice utilizes text, drawing, painting, collage, and sculpture to depict spaces and subjects engaged in strategies of survival against erasure and subjugation.

Jasmine Tabor (they/them) is a Black, queer writer from the Deep South, an Undergraduate Mellon Mays Fellow at Spelman College class of 2021 and receiving their MFA at Syracuse University class of 2024. They write about healing, mourning, and the praxis of transformation; they juxtapose Black childhood and elderhood through photography and writing. Jasmine is a dreamer and, in being so, they spend a lot of time reconnecting with their childhood self through daydreams. Their ruminations consist of writing when it's inconvenient, quiet mornings spent with the stereo turned down low, and solemn art. Works appear (or are forthcoming) in the *Agnes Scott Literary Journal*, Columbia University's *Undergraduate Literary Criticism Journal*, and *Stellium Literary Magazine*. They currently work as a Carolina Youth Action Project Fellow and a Saga Education Fellow, facilitating popular education, prison abolition, and algebra.

Summer-Harmony Twenish is a queer Algonquin Anishinabekwe from Kitigan Zibi (in so-called quebec, canada). They are an emerging, self-taught, multidisciplinary artist working primarily in digital art, painting, and textiles. Their work is inspired by their own Anishinabe worldviews and queer/Indigenous feminist ideas and aims to be unapologetically vulnerable, anti-colonial, and confrontational. They have had artwork featured in places like *Briarpatch Magazine*'s *Land Back* issue and *Together Apart*, a zine project focusing on queer and trans Indigenous identities and relationships. They have also had artwork displayed in *biskaabiiyang: returning to ourselves*, a group exhibition at the All My Relations Arts gallery in Minneapolis, Minnesota, in 2021. They are currently part of the N'we Jinan Emerging Artist Program, and they hope to eventually be able to blend their creative practice with their passion for community organizing, education, and youth-centered arts programming.

INDEX

V

W

Y

Z

ABOUT HAYMARKET BOOKS

Haymarket Books is a radical, independent, nonprofit book publisher based in Chicago. Our mission is to publish books that contribute to struggles for social and economic justice. We strive to make our books a vibrant and organic part of social movements and the education and development of a critical, engaged, and internationalist Left.

We take inspiration and courage from our namesakes, the Haymarket Martyrs, who gave their lives fighting for a better world. Their 1886 struggle for the eight-hour day—which gave us May Day, the international workers' holiday—reminds workers around the world that ordinary people can organize and struggle for their own liberation. These struggles—against oppression, exploitation, environmental devastation, and war—continue today across the globe.

Since our founding in 2001, Haymarket has published more than nine hundred titles. Radically independent, we seek to drive a wedge into the risk-averse world of corporate book publishing. Our authors include Angela Y. Davis, Arundhati Roy, Keeanga-Yamahtta Taylor, Eve Ewing, Aja Monet, Mariame Kaba, Naomi Klein, Rebecca Solnit, Olúfẹ́mi O. Táíwò, Mohammed El-Kurd, José Olivarez, Noam Chomsky, Winona LaDuke, Robyn Maynard, Leanne Betasamosake Simpson, Howard Zinn, Mike Davis, Marc Lamont Hill, Dave Zirin, Astra Taylor, and Amy Goodman, among many other leading writers of our time. We are also the trade publishers of the acclaimed Historical Materialism Book Series.

Haymarket also manages a vibrant community organizing and event space in Chicago, Haymarket House, the popular Haymarket Books Live event series and podcast, and the annual Socialism Conference.

ALSO AVAILABLE FROM HAYMARKET BOOKS

Abolishing State Violence: A World Beyond Bombs, Borders, and Cages
Ray Acheson

Abolition. Feminism. Now.
Angela Y. Davis, Gina Dent, Erica R. Meiners, and Beth E. Richie

Assata Taught Me
State Violence, Racial Capitalism, and the Movement for Black Lives
by Donna Murch

Community as Rebellion
A Syllabus for Surviving Academia as a Woman of Color
Lorgia García Peña

How We Get Free: Black Feminism and the Combahee River Collective
Edited by Keeanga-Yamahtta Taylor

Freedom Is a Constant Struggle
Ferguson, Palestine, and the Foundations of a Movement
Angela Y. Davis, edited by Frank Barat, preface by Cornel West

Rehearsals for Living
Robyn Maynard and Leanne Betasamosake Simpson

#SayHerName
Black Women's Stories of State Violence and Public Silence
African American Policy Forum, edited by Kimberlé Crenshaw
Foreword by Janelle Monáe

We Do This 'Til We Free Us
Abolitionist Organizing and Transforming Justice
Mariame Kaba, edited by Tamara K. Nopper
Foreword by Naomi Murakawa

CPSIA information can be obtained
at www.ICGtesting.com
Printed in the USA
JSHW021125290922
31138JS00007B/7